DEEP IN MY HEART

DEEP IN MY HEART

by *William M. Kunstler*

FOREWORDS BY JAMES FORMAN
AND DR. MARTIN LUTHER KING, JR.

William Morrow & Company, New York, 1966

Second Printing January 1971

Copyright © 1966 by William M. Kunstler

Published simultaneously in Canada
by George J. McLeod Limited, Toronto.

Printed in the United States of America.

Library of Congress Catalog Card Number 66–12742

To those Americans, young
and old, black and white—who
risked all they hold dear
in defense of the Constitution
of the United States

". . . oh, deep in my heart,

I do believe,

We shall overcome some day."

Last three lines of the modern adaptation of the old Negro church song, "I'll Overcome Someday," which has become the anthem of the civil rights movement.

Contents

Acknowledgments

Although this book is dedicated to the thousands of civil rights workers whose devotion to democratic principles made it possible, it would be unforgivable not to mention the many lawyers who worked alongside them. They may represent only an infinitesimal fraction of the American Bar but they have left an indelible mark on the history of their times. While I have not worked closely with each one, they have all, in one way or another, contributed their skills, their energies and their sensibilities to the causes in which I found myself involved.

With sincere apologies for any omissions, I list them here:

MORRIS B. ABRAM
ROBERT ABRAMS
OSCAR W. ADAMS, JR.
L. A. ADRIAN
THOMAS ADRIAN
WILLIAM LEE AKERS
THOMAS ADLER
SADIE T. M. ALEXANDER
NORMAN AMAKER
ANTHONY G. AMSTERDAM
FRANK A. ANGLIN
HARRY ANSORGE
CHESTER ANTIEAU
EDWARD ARDZROONI, JR.
SELMA ARNOLD
HENRY ARONSON
I. M. AUGUSTINE
BEVERLY AXELROD

EDWIN BALDWIN
BARBARA BELCHER
WILLIAM T. BELCHER
DERRICK BELL
MURPHY BELL
BENJAMIN BENDIT
JOSEPH S. BERGER
MARTIN M. BERGER
ARTHUR BERGGREN
GERALD BERLIN
JACK BERMAN
MILTON BERNER
ORZELL BILLINGSLEY
ROBERT BOEHM
LEONARD BOUDIN
SHELLIE BOWERS
MARTIN R. BRADLEY, JR.
RICHARD H. BREINER

MILTON E. BRENER
JACK A. BRIAN
ALVIN BRONSTEIN
ARNOLD BROWN
R. JESS BROWN
SEYMOUR BUCHOLZ
HARRIET BUHAI
PHIL BURLESON
MOSES C. BURT
SIMON L. CAIN
HAROLD CAMMER
ROBERT CARROW
ROBERT L. CARTER
KIM CLARK
LEROY CLARK
SAM HOUSTON CLINTON, JR.
DAVID COHEN
JULIUS COHEN
STEVEN J. COHN
ROBERT F. COLLINS
GENE CONDON
CHARLES S. CONLEY
JOHN CONYERS, JR.
NATHAN CONYERS
ANNE COOPER
EUGENE COTTON
EUGENE CRANE
ISAIAH W. CRIPPINS
GEORGE CROCKETT
EPHRAIM CROSS
SOL A. DANN
EMERSON L. DARNELL
SAMUEL DASHIELL
E. A. DAWLEY
DICKINSON R. DEBEVOISE
HUBERT T. DELANY
ROBERT B. DELANY
ROBERT DELLA VALLE
NANETTE DEMBITZ
WALTER E. DILLON, JR.

HENRY DI SUVERO
HOWARD DIXON
JAMES DONALD
NILS DOUGLAS
JOHN H. DOYLE III
THOMAS DOYLE
BENJAMIN DREYFUS
JOHN DUE
JOHN J. DUFFY
CLIFFORD R. DURR
LOLIS ELIE
WILLIAM E. ELSTON
THOMAS I. EMERSON
MORRIS L. ERNST
CHAUNCEY ESKRIDGE
FRANK A. EVANS, JR.
STANLEY FAULKNER
DOUGLAS FERGUSON
BERNARD J. FIEGER
THOMAS L. FIKE
SHIRLEY FINGERHOOD
DAVID B. FINKEL
JOHN E. FITCH
SUSAN G. FONER
ROBERT L. FONER
HERBERT FORER
JOSEPH FORER
JOSEPH A. FORREST
OSMOND K. FRAENKEL
TERRY FRANCOIS
JAY FRANK
ESTHER STRUM FRANKEL
REGINALD FRAZIER
DAVID M. FREEDMAN
BERNARD FISHMAN
OSCAR N. GASKINS
HERMAN B. GERRINGER
ELMER GERTZ
ROBERT GNAIZDA
ELEANOR F. GOLDMAN

NEAL GOLDMAN
ALVIN H. GOLDSTEIN
ERNEST GOODMAN
RICHARD GOODMAN
ROBERT GOODMAN
FRED GRAY
JACK GREENBERG
GEORGE R. GREENE
JACK GREENE
STUART GREENE
THELMA GREGORY
JOSEPH R. GRODIN
SAMUEL GRUBER
JEREMIAH S. GUTMAN
WALTER HAFNER
CARSIE A. HALL
PETER HALL
PATRICK HALLINAN
VINCENT HALLINAN
EDWIN C. HAMADA
WILLIAM HARRELL
RUTH L. HARVEY
WILLIAM L. HIGGS
PHILIP HIRSCHKOP
DONALD HOLLOWELL
ELEANOR HOLMES
LEN W. HOLT
JOHN O. HONNOLD
EMANUEL H. HORN
NORMAN C. HOWARD
LEON HUBERT
E. A. HUNTER, JR.
STEPHEN J. HYMAN
ADOLPH IMMERMAN
ROY JACKSON
MARTIN JACOBS
EARL M. JOHNSON
CLARENCE B. JONES
THOMAS JONES
J. A. JORDAN

LEONARD KARLIN
HASKELL KASSLER
SANFORD M. KATZ
MARY KAUFMAN
ALLAN KEMPLER
THEODORE W. KHEEL
C. B. KING
ARTHUR KINOY
PAUL L. KLEIN
WILLIAM KOPIT
MILTON KOSS
RICHARD KRANDLE
MICHAEL J. KUNSTLER
JAMES LAFFERTY
JAMES W. LAMBERTON
MARK LANE
ANNA R. LANGFORD
MORRIS LASKER
FRANKLIN T. LASKIN
REUBEN LAWSON (deceased)
ROBERT W. LENTZ
ANTHONY LESTER
JOSEPH LEVIN
ALAN H. LEVINE
JACK G. LEVINE
HARRY LEVITAN
ROBERT Z. LEWIS
HARRY LOHSTROH
JOE R. LOODINE
HARRY LORE
DAVID LUBELL
JONATHAN LUBELL
LOUIS LUSKY
EDWARD LYNCH
CONRAD LYNN
MALCOLM MACKILLOP
C. C. MALONE
HUGH MANES
MARIA L. MARCUS
PETER MARCUSE

xiv   ACKNOWLEDGMENTS

BEN MARGOLIS
EMANUEL MARGOLIS
CHARLES R. MARKELS
JOHN E. MARQUSEE
GEORGE MARTINEZ
GEORGE MASCONE
LEWIS MAYERS
ALISTER McALISTER
THOMAS D. McBRIDE
CARL McCORMICK
JAMES E. McCREADY
JAMES T. McDONALD
CHARLES McKINNEY
FLOYD McKISSICK
JOHN McLAUGHLIN
MICHAEL MELTZNER
WILLIAM MESSING
IRVING MEYERS
JOY MEYERS
ERWIN MILLER
HARRY S. MILLER
HUGH B. MILLER
MAX R. MILLMAN
SAMUEL B. MITCHELL
HOWARD MOORE, JR.
VERNON A. MOORE
CHARLES MORGAN, JR.
BARBARA A. MORRIS
STEPHEN R. MORSE
EDWARD MOSK
RUTH MOSKOVITZ
CONSTANCE BAKER
  MOTLEY
ANDREW C. MUSE
JAMES NABRITT III
ISADORE NEEDLEMAN
ALLEN NEIMAN
SAMUEL NEWBERGER
STANLEY NEWMAN
WALTER B. NIVENS

PAUL O'DWYER
CHARLES OLDHAM
MAYNARD J. OMERBERG
WILLIAM T. PATRICK, JR.
JACK PEEBLES
JOHN DeJ. PEMBERTON
MARSHALL PERLIN
FRANK S. PESTANA
LEO PFEFFER
FRANK E. PHILLIPS
WILLIAM G. PHOENIX
ELEANOR JACKSON PIEL
ROBERT PLATH
ROBERT G. PLATOFF
SHAD POLIER
ALEXANDER POLIKOFF
MARTIN POPPER
JOHN M. PRATT
EVE PREMINGER
JAMES P. PREOVOLES
DIXON PYLES
VICTOR RABINOWITZ
CARL RACHLIN
GEORGE NIMS RAYBIN
JOSEPH A. RAUH, JR.
LELAND H. RAYSON
LOUIS REDDING
DAVID REIN
FRED REINHEIMER
RONALD REOSTI
PHILIP ROACHE
DEAN ROBB
CATHERINE G. RORABACK
ERNST H. ROSENBERGER
IRVING ROSENFELD
BARNEY ROSENSTEIN
LEONARD H. ROSENTHAL
EDGAR ROSS
WILLIAM ROSSMOORE
WILLIAM FITTS RYAN

WARREN SALTZMAN

HENRY WILLIAM SANDS

HENRY W. SAWYER III

GEORGE SCHIFFER

THOMAS SCHNEIDER

MAX SCHOENGOLD

FERDINAND P. SCHOETTLE

MORRIS SCHUSTER

DAVID SCRIBNER

RICHARD SCUPI

FAITH SEIDENBERG

HERBERT SEMMEL

RALPH SHAPIRO

ARTHUR SHORES

CLAUDIA H. SHROPSHIRE

ROBERT H. SHUTAN

JOHN SILVERBERG

TOBIAS SIMON

LOIS R. SIVIN

GEORGE SLAFF

BENJAMIN E. SMITH

HIRAM E. SMITH

NATHAN S. SMITH

WILLIAM G. SMITH

LAURENCE SPEISER

MARTIN SPIEGEL

SAMUEL P. SPORN

PETER SPRUANCE

MICHAEL B. STANDARD

MORTON STAVIS

ELLIOT G. STEINBERG

RALPH J. STEINBERG

EDWARD STERN

LEWIS A. STERN

CHARLES B. STEWART

OLIVER C. SUTTON

PERCY SUTTON

HENRY J. SZYMANSKI

MOE L. TANDLER

HERBERT H. TATE

ROBERT J. TENNANT

REUBEN TERRIS

MARTTIE THOMPSON

JOHN E. THORNE

DONALD G. TOLLEFSON

NEIL J. TOMAN

ARNOLD S. TREBACH

SAMUEL W. TUCKER

IRVING TUKEL

A. P. TUREAUD

HARRY WACHTEL

MATT WADLEIGH

GEORGE G. WALKER

BRUCE C. WALTZER

HORACE WARD

ROWLAND WATTS

DAVID P. WEAVER, JR.

GABRIEL WEBNER

PETER WEISS

THEODORE S. WEISS

JOHN F. WELLS

EARL WHITTE

JERRY L. WILLIAMS

JESSE WILLIAMS

RAY WILLIAMS

ROBERT W. WILLIAMS

CALVIN T. WILSON, SR.

WARREN B. WILSON

HAL WITT

WALTER T. WITTMAN

HENRY WOLFE

HARRY I. WOOD

GEORGE WOODY

MARIAN WRIGHT

MELVIN L. WULF

JACK H. YOUNG

MELVIN ZAHR

SOL ZELZER

ROBERT ZIBILICH

Foreword

BY JAMES FORMAN

Southern courts, Southern judges, Southern laws—the entire fabric of the Southern way of life is designed to humiliate, degrade, and keep in total submission black folk who must live in a white-dominated society. But many people, especially Negro students, have waged a constant struggle against this "Southern" way of life where you "ain't got no rights at all." And they have been aided by a handful of lawyers. Bill Kunstler is one of the lawyers who are trying to change not only the pattern of Southern justice but also that of the ingrained prejudices and legal and structural defects in the entire American way of life.

On February 1, 1960, when four students from North Carolina Agricultural and Technical College decided to remain in their seats at a Woolworth lunch counter until they were served, they ushered in a period of nonviolent protest that has not diminished. They also posed serious problems for those friendly lawyers who did not have precedents on which to defend nonviolent demonstrators. Legal defense was not the problem of the demonstrators. Their role was to force on the American consciousness the shameful reality of a segregated way of life. We had to throw up the dirt in order to start housecleaning, and our objective has not yet been totally achieved.

Southern judges, politicians, newspaper editors, businessmen from the North and South, the Klan, the White Citizens' Councils, and the local Societies for the Preservation of the White Race retaliated in turn. They beat the demonstrators. They killed some. They consistently used the segregated courtroom and unjust Southern laws to make the struggle costly and time-consuming. Arresting four and five hundred people for peacefully picketing or walking toward a county courthouse, placing scores of women and young children in a cell built for four, setting bail from one thousand to ten thousand dollars on charges destined to be thrown out of courts, prejudging trials, setting appeal bonds at high rates—these were just a few of the "legal" tactics employed.

This corruption of the law swiftly became the legal way of life in the South-wide effort to resist any change in race relations. The jailing of the Freedom Riders charged with minor offenses in a maximum security state penitentiary; the arrests of civil rights workers for so-called overtime parking offenses and defective mufflers; the setting of bail at five hundred dollars where the maximum fine was fifty dollars; the stopping of movements through the use of serious felony charges such as inciting insurrections against the states of Georgia or Louisiana—these are examples of how sheriffs, prosecutors and judges tried to maintain the "Southern way of life."

We had to meet this challenge. Many black Southern lawyers worked overtime trying to keep up with the demands on their time. It was not really until the Movement was well under way that a significant number of Northern lawyers began to assist in the legal fight against segregation. The Student Nonviolent Coordinating Committee, formed two months after the sit-ins at Greensboro, always poor, forever in need of free legal services, tried to encourage more and more

Northern lawyers to become involved in the struggle. After all, we were not just suffering, going to jail, receiving licks for ourselves; our struggle was a national struggle.

The influx of lawyers into the South did more than just provide an impromptu legal aid system for the movement. These attorneys, frustrated and dismayed by the perverse uses of the law in such outposts as Albany, Georgia, Jackson, Mississippi, and Birmingham, Alabama, turned to the courts of the United States. Instead of relying on the slow and tedious process of appealing state convictions to their ultimate determination by the Supreme Court, they sought immediate relief from bigotted state courts by advancing to federal courts where, although often biased at the district level, the procedures permitted one to finally reach a federal court of appeals. There the chances for a fair hearing are much better. At least one is not likely to hear: "I am not interested in whether the registrar is going to give a registration test to a bunch of niggers on a voter drive . . . Who is telling these people they can get in line and push people around, acting like a bunch of chimpanzees?" So said Judge Harold Cox of the Mississippi District Court, while sitting on the bench in a voter registration case argued by the United States Justice Department.

An invaluable contribution of Bill Kunstler—and his associates, Arthur Kinoy, Ben Smith, Bruce Waltzer, Morty Stavis, Mike Standard, and Len Holt to mention only a few —has been in forging new tactics in the practice of removals to federal courts. Kunstler and "crew" have also earned the respect of the Movement for filing suits designed to attack basic causes of segregation. They and the people in the Movement are often aware that these suits are not going to win within the present legal structure. But to win is not the sole point. Such cases as *COFO vs. Rainey* and the Mississippi

Challenge force the country and the courts to grapple with certain realities of segregation.

Undoubtedly, Bill Kunstler's book was begun as the personal narrative of one man who became deeply involved in the quickening tide. But *Deep In My Heart* has evolved as something very different from its creator's original intention. In essence, it is not a story of the law or lawyers alone. It is a saga of the Movement itself seen from one vantage point.

James Forman
Executive Secretary
Student Nonviolent Coordinating
Committee (SNCC)

FOREWORD

BY

Dr. Martin Luther King, Jr.

It is common knowledge that I have had a little something to do with lawyers since the 1955 Montgomery bus boycott. I have appeared many times in the criminal and appellate courts; I have served time. I guess I could be described as a "notorious litigant" and "frequenter of jails."

I have a deep and abiding admiration for the legal profession and the tremendous role it has played in the service of the cause with which I have been identified. The road to freedom is now a highway because lawyers throughout the land, yesterday and today, have helped clear the obstructions, have helped eliminate roadblocks, by their selfless, courageous espousal of difficult and unpopular causes.

The freedoms which provide the indispensable undergirding of our civil rights struggle have been won because in all ages there have been lawyers who have heeded and followed the inspiring creed which was once expressed by that great judge, Oliver Wendell Holmes: "A man may live greatly in the law as elsewhere; that there as well as elsewhere his thought may find its unity in an infinite perspective; that there as well as elsewhere he may wreak himself upon life, may drink the bitter cup of heroism, may wear his heart out after the unattainable . . .

"No man has earned the right to intellectual ambition until he has learned to lay his course by a star he has never seen, to dig by the divining rod for springs which he may never reach . . . To think great thoughts you must be heroes as well as idealists."

In pursuit of this star, in seeking the deep, hidden springs, lawyers will continue their efforts to help the civil rights movement keep open the road we must still travel to attain our full citizenship. In truth, we could not be where we are today without the great rights of free speech, free press, freedom to demonstrate, petition and march to the seat of Government—even in Montgomery, Alabama, where redress of grievances may be brought.

As we have fought and demanded our just rights, as we have given witness with our bodies to the existence of evil, lawyers have steadfastly used their professional talents, knowledge and abilities to aid us, to make our plea for dignity heard in the courts of our land.

I do not intend to deprecate these achievements when I make the observation that justice at times proceeds with a halting gait, that at times the law has been slow to speak for the poor, the oppressed, the unpopular, the disfranchised.

It is, in point of historical measurement, only a flicker of an eye since a labor union was, in this country, a criminal conspiracy, a Negro a chattel, a pacifist an anarchist, and any aggressive disciple of the theory of the redistribution of wealth a dangerous radical.

Indeed, we as a nation and as a people, are still suffering from the blows of the haunted 50's.

But it is the strength of America, and more importantly its

people utilizing that indispensable ingredient of relentless and insistent struggle characteristic of American democracy, which causes the evil to be exposed and ultimately overcome. It is these struggles, in the composite, which constitute the finest hours of American history.

The lawyer has played his part. From these struggles there have emerged defenders of great renown; Andrew Hamilton, Clarence Darrow, Wendell Willkie, Thurgood Marshall, Charles Huston, William Thompson, Jack Greenberg, and that Portia, Constance Baker Motley, to mention but a few. For every noted hero, there have been hundreds who have labored humbly and anonymously in the vineyard of freedom.

They defended the runaway slaves, the Scottsboro boys, the victims of the Palmer raids and the McCarthy inquisitions, and are today scouring the South in the defense of liberty against the acts of the Ku Klux Klan, the Sheriffs Clark and Rainey, and others.

Observing and learning from these lawyers, one perceives a strain that runs through all, be he Negro or white, conservative or radical, rich or poor. It is an immutable commitment to the philosophy that, with all of its uncertainties and weaknesses, the law is majestic and the judicial process supreme.

I can recall what may very well have been a turning point in my life as a participant in the Negro struggle in the South. It was the year 1960, in Montgomery, Alabama. The bus strike had been won and the struggle for the implementation of the Brown decision was moving into high gear. The glorious sit-ins at lunch counters had seized the attention of all Americans. The Negro community was restless and determined that every obstacle to full integration should be overcome.

The white Southern power structure, in an attempt to

blunt and divert that effort, indicted me for perjury and openly proclaimed that I would be imprisoned for at least ten years.

The case was tried before an all-white Southern jury. All of the State's witnesses were white. The judge and the prosecutor were white. The courtroom was segregated. Passions were inflamed. Feelings ran high. The press and other communications media were hostile. Defeat seemed certain and we in the freedom struggle braced ourselves for the inevitable.

There were two men among us who persevered with the conviction that it was possible, in this context, to marshal facts and law and thus win vindication. These men were our lawyers, Negro lawyers—Negro lawyers from the North: William Ming of Chicago and Hubert Delaney from New York.

They brought to the courtroom wisdom, courage, and a highly developed art of advocacy; but most important, they brought the lawyers' indomitable determination to win. After a trial of three days, by the sheer strength of their legal arsenal, they overcame the most vicious Southern taboos festering in a virulent and inflamed atmosphere and they persuaded an all-white jury to accept the word of a Negro over that of white men. The jury, after a few hours of deliberation, returned a verdict of acquittal.

I am frank to confess that on this occasion I learned that truth and conviction in the hands of a skillful advocate could make what started out as a bigoted, prejudiced jury, choose the path of justice.

I cannot help but wish in my heart that the same kind of skill and devotion which Bob Ming and Hubert Delaney accorded to me could be available to thousands of civil rights workers, to thousands of ordinary Negroes, who are every day facing prejudiced courtrooms.

I am pleased to give recognition that particularly since the disgraceful events of Birmingham in 1963, there has been an ever-increasing response on the part of the legal profession to the great need for counsel on the battlefield of civil rights in Mississippi, Alabama, and throughout the Southland. Legal services accorded to our non-violent armies of today are like plasma to the wounded in military combat.

The American Civil Liberties Union, the Law Students Civil Rights Research Council, the Lawyers Constitutional Defense Committee, the NAACP Legal Defense and Educational Fund, the National Lawyers Guild and the President's Committee on Civil Rights Under Law have made a fine beginning. But so much more remains to be done. Our needs increase as the final victory over entrenched segregation nears.

As Bill Kunstler's book so graphically points out, there is urgent need for the further extension of this vital, indispensable function, so that the right for all to qualified counsel will become a reality.

Lawyers should be proud of their admirable tradition, which other professionals would do well to emulate. I refer to their willingness to give their time, talents and energies to the advancement of issues and causes outside of their calling.

The lawyers' sense of participation on far-off battlefields is undoubtedly in furtherance of this majestic formulation by Mr. Justice Holmes: ". . . As life is action and passion, it is required of man that he should share the passion and action of his time, at the peril of being judged not to have lived."

So many lawyers, hearing the agonized cry of justice denied, have joined the fray, regardless of consequences. Clarence Darrow, speaking at the bier of a fallen victim, John Peter Altgeld, focused, as only he could, on this quality when he said of the deceased: "He so loved justice and truth and liberty and righteousness that all the terrors that the earth could hold were less than the condemnation of his conscience . . ."

By such involvement lawyers are honoring the truth that all life is interrelated and all men interdependent. They are in the true spirit of the Judeo-Christian tradition recognizing that the agony of the poor diminishes the rich, and that the salvation of the weak enriches the strong; that we are inevitably our brother's keeper because of the interrelated structure of reality.

John Donne interpreted this ennobling truth in graphic terms when he affirmed: "No man is an island, entire of its selfe: Every man is a peece of the continent, a part of the maine: If a clod bee washed away by the sea, Europe is the lesse, as well as if a promontorie were, as well as if a manor of thy friends or of thine owne were: Any man's death diminishes me, because I am involved in mankinde: And therefore never send to know for whom the bell tolls: It tolls for thee . . ."

Quite obviously this book is not the story of any one lawyer but of all lawyers who have refused to remain silent in the face of chronic and systematic injustice. When their voices are joined by those of their brethren at the bar, their thundering insistence will speed the end of our denial, the end of our discrimination, the end of our second-class citizenship, the end of all inferior education. Yes, it will hasten the end of the whole rotten, ugly system of racial injustice which for 350 years has degraded the doer as well as the victim.

If the legal profession would share the passion and action of our time, it has the strength to achieve these magnificent goals.

Martin Luther King, Jr.
President
Southern Christian
Leadership Conference (SCLC)

PART I

JACKSON,
MISSISSIPPI

CHAPTER 1

It All Begins

I don't know how long the telephone had been ringing before its insistency awakened me. As I groped for the receiver, I noticed through a crack in the saffron draperies that lined the window side of my motel room that dawn had come to Sunset Boulevard.

My caller was Rowland Watts, the legal director of the American Civil Liberties Union.

Watts, a tall, soft-spoken ex-Marylander, had recruited me in early 1956 to institute proceedings to renew the passport of William Worthy, an American reporter who had gone to Communist China in open defiance of the State Department's regulations placing that country off limits to United States citizens. Our long collaboration in that case had ripened into a lasting friendship that has managed to survive even early morning telephone calls.

"Rowland," I muttered sleepily, "don't you realize that it's only six o'clock in the morning here?"

"I couldn't wait to call you," he replied. "All hell is breaking loose in Jackson, Mississippi, with Freedom Riders pouring in on every bus and train and only one overworked Negro lawyer to represent them."

He hesitated for a moment. "When do you intend to return East?" he asked.

I had arrived in Los Angeles nine days earlier—June 6, 1961, to be exact—in order to make some radio and television appearances in connection with a book I had just written about Caryl Chessman's original 1948 trial. All that was left on my schedule was an early evening radio interview.

"I've got a reservation on tonight's jet to New York," I replied.

"Would it be possible," Watts asked, "for you to change your flight so that you could stop in Jackson for a day and say hello to Jack Young, the local lawyer who's trying to hold the fort there?"

As I think back, my answer to that question was to alter my life radically, but at that moment all that crossed my mind was that I had only enough money left to return to New York without any side trips. When I explained this to Watts, he said that he would wire $100 to me at once if I would agree to make the Jackson detour.

"All right," I replied, "I'll go, but I would like to know just what it is you want me to do when I get there."

"You don't have to do anything," he explained blithely. "Just introduce yourself to Young and tell him that the American Civil Liberties Union is ready to help him in any way it can. You'll find his office on North Farish Street. When you get back to New York, let me know if there is anything that the Union can do."

Although I didn't realize it at the time, a new life had begun for me.

CHAPTER 2

A Touch of History

The Freedom Rides, as they soon came to be known, were part and parcel of an historical cycle that began when the first African Negroes were sold by their rulers into foreign bondage for a few liters of rum and some Spanish dollars. The buses that were streaming into Jackson were the direct, if reverse, successors to the slave ships of the seventeenth and eighteenth centuries. To understand the pressures and demands of the civil rights movement, some knowledge of the time in between is essential.

The slave trade between Africa and the Americas was systematized shortly after 1520 when Holy Roman Emperor Charles V granted a patent to one of his Flemish subjects authorizing the importation of four thousand Negroes annually into Haiti, Cuba, and Puerto Rico. This franchise was subsequently sold to some Genoese merchants who arranged with foreign traders for a steady supply of African natives.

In 1619, a Dutch ship with a cargo of Negroes bound for

the Caribbean Islands dropped anchor in Jamestown Harbor. Before leaving port, the vessel's captain had sold a handful of slaves to several local tobacco farmers who wished to experiment with such labor. The Africans, however, initially did not prove to be as profitable workers in temperate Virginia as they had in the tropics and, by 1661, there were only two thousand in the colony as compared to four times that number of indentured white servants.

By the beginning of the Revolutionary War, slavery existed in all thirteen colonies. The institution was strongest in the Southern tier where the large plantations with their staple crops of tobacco, rice, and indigo were much better adapted to slave labor than the smaller and more specialized farms of the North.

In 1774, the Continental Congress, cognizant that three hundred thousand Negroes comprising one fifth of the population had been brought into the colonies, recommended the end of the foreign slave trade. For years, Americans both North and South had been urging such a course, and several local legislatures even had passed laws forbidding or heavily taxing the further importation of Negroes. In ordering royal governors to veto such statutes, the British colonial secretary curtly reminded them that "we cannot allow the colonies to check or discourage in any degree a traffic so beneficial to the nation."

In his first draft of the Declaration of Independence, Thomas Jefferson accused George III of "suppressing every legislative attempt to prohibit or restrain this execrable commerce." Although isolated but firm Southern opposition succeeded in eliminating this indictment from the final document, it reflected the feelings of most colonists with the possible exception of a few large plantation owners and those Northern shipowners who, Jefferson caustically observed, "though their people had very few slaves themselves, had been pretty considerable carriers of them to others."

By the time of the Constitutional Convention in 1787, all of the Northern states except New York and New Jersey* had begun the process of abolishing slavery. Indeed, there was strong abolitionist sentiment among many prominent southerners who, on humanitarian grounds, urged an end to the practice. "I tremble for my country," Jefferson said on the eve of the Convention, "when I reflect that God is just and that His justice cannot sleep forever."

George Mason, who had written the Virginia Declaration of Rights, put his opposition on a somewhat more practical basis. "Slavery," he declared, "discouraged arts and manufactures, led the poor to despise labor, prevented immigration of white persons to the State, turned slave masters into petty tyrants, and brought the judgment of Heaven upon the country."

Just prior to the Convention, this widespread dissatisfaction with slavery was reflected by the Northwest Ordinance which prohibited it in what is now the states of Ohio, Indiana, Illinois, Michigan, Wisconsin, and part of Minnesota. However, the debates in Philadelphia were primarily concerned, not with the institution itself, but with the status of the slave under the new government.

Both Northern and Southern interests were in complete accord that slaves should have no political rights whatsoever. The major question was whether they should be counted in determining Congressional representation.

The issue was resolved by a series of compromises. First, every five slaves were to be counted as three free men insofar as legislative apportionment was concerned. Second, Congress was forbidden to end the slave trade until 1808, by which time all Southern planters could have adequately stocked their acreage. Third, escaped slaves were to be "delivered up" to their masters upon demand.

* Shortly after the adoption of the Constitution, these two states promptly followed suit.

Despite the Convention's heated debates over its effect on representation, slavery might well have died a natural death had it not been for the invention of the cotton gin in 1793. With the capacity of the Negro increased overnight more than a hundredfold, cotton rapidly became the chief industry of the South. By 1803, the region was exporting more than thirty-five million pounds of the highly adaptable fiber,* and slave labor had suddenly become an "economic necessity."

With the end of the foreign slave trade on New Year's Day, 1808, its domestic equivalent became spectacularly profitable. Many owners of well-populated Southeastern plantations turned to the breeding of Negroes for sale to settlers in the growing territories. For these flesh merchants, the constant expansion of their Western markets was indispensable to their continued success. Like the cotton planters whose fields they stocked, they strenuously resisted every Northern effort to restrict the spread of slavery.

They had ample opportunity to do so. The next half century was punctuated by recurring crises over the "peculiar institution," each one precipitated by the proposed admission of new states. After those of Louisiana and Alabama had equalized sectional representation in the Senate, Maine and Missouri were admitted under a compromise that forever prohibited slavery in the remainder of the Louisiana Purchase north of the 36° 30' line. Only Missouri itself was exempt from this restriction.

The legal status of slaves who crossed into free territory was the original issue in the *Dred Scott* case. In 1834, Scott, the property of a St. Louis Army surgeon, was taken to Fort Snelling in the Wisconsin Territory. When he returned to Missouri four years later, Scott maintained that his journey to the North where slavery was forbidden by the Missouri

* As compared to fifty thousand pounds ten years earlier.

Compromise had freed him. After being defeated in the state courts, he brought a federal suit.

Shortly after Scott had begun his litigation, a proposal prohibiting slavery in any territory acquired in the Mexican War was appended to an appropriations bill pending in the House of Representatives. Dubbed the Wilmot Proviso, after the Pennsylvania Congressman who introduced it, the amendment was destined never to muster up enough votes to be carried. But it did lead directly to the Compromise of 1850 which was hailed throughout the country as a "final settlement" of the vexing slavery question.

Under the compromise, California entered the Union as a free state while the New Mexico and Utah territories were to decide their own status when they were ready for admission. Moreover, in return for agreeing to the end of the slave trade in the District of Columbia, the South was given a stringent fugitive slave law. The latter was the direct result of the growing success of the Underground Railroad and the enactment by many Northern states of legislation favoring runaway Negroes.

It took only four years to prove that as far as slavery was concerned, no solution could be regarded as final. In 1854, Senator Stephen A. Douglas of Illinois, whose "popular sovereignty" formula had been an integral part of the Compromise of 1850, sponsored a bill for the organization of the Kansas and Nebraska territories. In essence, it repealed the Missouri Compromise and left it up to the individual territories to decide whether they would apply for admission as slave or free states.

The result was the tragedy of "bleeding" Kansas, where rifles rather than reason dictated the "popular" decision.

On Monday, March 5, 1857, while Kansas was still in the throes of civil war, James Buchanan was inaugurated as the fifteenth President of the United States. Two days later, the Supreme Court rendered its fateful decision in the *Dred Scott* case. In an unnecessarily broad opinion, Chief Justice Roger B. Taney held that Congress had no power to regulate slavery in the territories. Accordingly, he declared the Missouri Compromise unconstitutional.

The main point in the case—whether Scott was enough of an American citizen to sue in the federal courts—was decided in the negative. According to Taney, for centuries Negroes had been regarded as inferior beings wholly unfit to associate with white men. They were simply chattels to be bought and sold like any other piece of property, and it had never been intended by the framers of the Constitution that Negroes should enjoy the benefits of citizenship.

The Negro, Taney concluded in one of the most unfortunate asides ever made by an American judge, "had no rights that the white man is bound to respect."

Short of a miracle, the decision made the Civil War inevitable. If Congress could not regulate slavery in the territories, then, according to freesoilers, the institution was destined to spread unchecked. It would only be a matter of time before political control of the country rested firmly in the hands of the slavocracy. For the industrial North, such a prospect, real or imagined, was an intolerable one.

The Lincoln-Douglas debates marked the last substantial effort at a rational approach to the issue of slavery. In the end, however, they resolved nothing except to decide who would represent Illinois in the United States Senate. If anything, they solidified Northern abolitionist sentiment by undermining Douglas' "popular sovereignty" concept as a peaceful and equitable way of determining whether the Western territories would be slave or free.

Two widely separated events following the debates indicated that the age of compromise had indeed come to an end. In the fall of 1858, a recaptured runaway slave was freed by a group of Oberlin College professors and students near Wellington, Ohio. Although forty of the Negro's rescuers were prosecuted for violating the new Fugitive Slave Act, a state grand jury promptly retaliated by indicting the United States marshals who were out searching for the missing slave. The matter was settled by an agreement to drop all charges.

Of far more significance was John Brown's abortive raid one year later. The seizure of the federal arsenal at Harper's Ferry, Virginia, was to be the first step in Brown's plan to provoke a general slave uprising. Although he was quickly captured, convicted of treason, and hanged, he was widely regarded in Northern circles as little less than a saint.

The two incidents convinced the South that the North was dead set on destroying its economy, its traditions, and its way of life. If the Fugitive Slave Act could not be enforced and unbalanced abolitionist zealots were eulogized for breaking the law, there was no longer any point in discussion. The sectional abyss could not be bridged.

Guns finally accomplished what all the combined talents of Clay, Webster, and Calhoun had failed to do. The Thirteenth Amendment, purchased at the cost of four years of civil war and 650,000 battle deaths, finally settled the question of slavery by outlawing it. The amendment's ratification eight months after Appomattox officially closed the first chapter of the Negro's American experience.

At first the new freedom did not carry with it even the faintest promise of equality. To all Southerners and most Northerners, the Negro was and would always remain inferior to the white man. After all, hadn't Mr. Lincoln himself told a Negro delegation in 1862 that "on this broad continent, not a single man of your race is made the equal of a single man of ours"?

Undoubtedly, many freedmen, if they thought about it at all, would have shared Lincoln's view. People who had been denied even the most rudimentary education, the right to marry or own property, and the security of family life, and who had been bought and sold like livestock on the auction block could hardly be expected, because of a new addition to a constitution most of them couldn't even read, to have a sudden high regard for themselves. Two hundred and fifty years of systematic dehumanization had exacted a fearful psychological toll.

Clearly, there was to be no immediate end to trauma. The ex-slave soon found that emancipation meant simply that he was now free to scratch for a living among the ruins of a ruptured and resentful civilization. Otherwise, he was very much as he had always been—a despised and exploited being, separated from all but the most fleeting contact with the meaningful world. The plantation had simply expanded to encompass the horizon.

With a few notable exceptions, most white Americans refused to concede that the end of slavery automatically entitled Negroes to unqualified membership in a free society. "Separate but equal" was a state of mind in the United States long before the Supreme Court raised it to the level of a constitutional principle. As one member of the Thirty-Ninth Congress put it, Negroes were "chiefly fit to black boots and cut hair."

Lincoln probably spoke for most of his contemporaries when, in 1862, he asked Congress for funds for the purpose "of colonizing people of African descent" in what is now Colombia. An outspoken segregationist, he constantly and earnestly urged free Negroes to leave the United States so that their enslaved brethren would follow them. "We should be separated," he said, in the early days of the war. "There is an unwillingness on the part of our people, harsh as it may be, for you colored people to remain with us."

Lincoln's racist views had crystallized long before his election to the Presidency. During the Douglas debates, he constantly assured his audiences that he was no integrationist. "I have no purpose to introduce political and social equality between the white and black races," he said during one of them. "There is a physical difference between the two which in my judgment will probably forever forbid their living together upon the footing of perfect equality; and inasmuch as it becomes a necessity that there must be a difference, I, as well as Judge Douglas, am in favor of the race to which I belong having the superior position."

Andrew Johnson shared his predecessor's cavalier attitude toward Negroes. After beginning his administration with some wild threats to shoot all Confederate leaders, he quickly adopted Lincoln's overconciliatory approach to reconstruction. From the outset, he spared no efforts to restore white political supremacy below the Mason-Dixon line.

One of his first acts after taking the oath of office was the issuance of an amnesty proclamation modeled after one suggested by Lincoln in late 1863. In general, it provided that as soon as ten percent of the adult male population of any Southern state had taken a prescribed loyalty oath, the state was free to reestablish a government that would be recognized at once by Washington. Within weeks, all of these newly approved legislatures had begun to grind out laws which virtually reenslaved the Negro. Known as Black Codes, they prevented Negroes from going to school, working without a license, or leaving the places where they lived.

Fortunately, some members of the postwar Congress, spurred by Charles Sumner and Thaddeus Stevens, were much more perspicacious than the President. Determined to insure the legal equality of the millions freed by the Thirteenth Amendment, they overruled the Black Codes by drafting comprehensive statutes giving Negroes all the rights of citizenship. After passing these laws over Andrew Johnson's

veto, they pushed through the Fourteenth and Fifteenth
Amendments, thus placing them beyond the immediate
reach of any future hostile Congresses.

But convinced that such laws alone would not do the trick,
the Radical Republicans also repudiated the Lincoln-Johnson policy of easy and early reunion and, in 1867, divided the
South into five federal districts, each ruled by an Army
commander. Only by adopting a constitution permanently
perpetuating Negro suffrage could any former Confederate
state shake its military rule and regain representation in the
national legislature. By 1870, all eleven had decided that
readmission was well worth what they were sure would be a
temporary black vote.

During the brief—and remarkable—Reconstruction era,
the Southern Negro, in the midst of one of the most profound social dislocations in the history of any people, proved
that he could use his freedom to constructive ends. Negroes
participated in the writing of the Constitution of Mississippi,
represented seven members of the Old Confederacy in the
House of Representatives, helped to bring progressive legislation to their home states, and worked with a frenzy to educate
themselves and their children. By and large, Negroes proved
far better citizens than many of their white neighbors.

By 1871, it was abundantly clear that given a few more
productive years the erstwhile slaves would be permanently
absorbed into the American community. But the emergence
of the Klan, the panic of 1873, the growing conservatism of
the Supreme Court, and the need for cheap labor which
diminished the principle of human equality all combined to
bring Reconstruction to an abrupt end. By the fall of 1874,
Democrats had replaced Republicans throughout the South,
and only the presence of federal troops kept Negroes voting
in such states as South Carolina, Louisiana, and Mississippi.

The Hayes-Tilden campaign in 1876 brought the period to

a tawdry close. The uncertainty of the vote in four states led to the appointment of an electoral commission to determine which man had been elected. Several days before the commission's vote, Hayes assured the Southern Democrats that if he ever occupied the White House he would withdraw all remaining federal troops and permit white domination of state legislatures.

His offer was quickly accepted. At 4 A.M. on March 2, 1877, the Electoral Commission named him President-Elect. Within two months, the Union soldiers were on their way home, and the great experiment was over. A social and economic revolution of the first magnitude had fizzled out in a Washington hotel room and four million men, women, and children had been tragically betrayed.

As Jim Crow statutes spread across the South, the rest of the country averted its eyes. Secession, civil war, and reconstruction were yesterday's problems, and men now concerned themselves with the questions of economic and industrial development. Even the Fourteenth Amendment, the darling of the Reconstruction Congress, was quickly converted to the preservation of big business.

By 1890, all of the Southern states had succeeded in imprisoning the Negro in another and more insidious form of slavery. Rigidly segregated into a black world from which there seemed no escape, he could not vote, obtain an adequate education, or earn a decent livelihood. He was back where he had started from almost three centuries earlier.

In New Orleans, the Comité des Citoyens, a Creole protest group, decided to make one last desperate stand. Under its auspices, Homer Adolph Plessy, an octaroon, entered a white-only coach of the East Louisiana Railway Company and was at once arrested and charged with violating a Jim Crow law. When his test case, *Plessy v. Ferguson,* reached the United

States Supreme Court in 1896, eight justices ruled that there was nothing unconstitutional in separating whites and Negroes provided that the latter enjoyed equal facilities.

John Marshall Harlan, the sole dissenter, had contributed $50 to the Comité des Citoyens in the early days of the case. He saw the majority's decision as a tragic error. He said sadly, "It seems that we have yet, in some of the states, a dominant race, a superior class of citizens, which assumes to regulate the enjoyment of civil rights, common to all citizens, on the basis of race. Our Constitution is color-blind, and neither knows nor tolerates classes among citizens."

Thirteen years earlier, the Court had invalidated the first attempt by Congress to end segregation in public accommodations. Now it had set its official seal of approval on Jim Crow as a national attitude toward the Negro race. "The road to freedom and equality, which had seemed sure and open in 1868," Thurgood Marshall was to tell the same Court fifty-eight years later, "was now to be securely blocked and barred by a maze of restrictions and limitations proclaimed as essential to a way of life."

The immediate result of the Plessy decision was the destruction of the incipient Populist-sponsored political coalition of Negroes and poor white farmers throughout the South. But its long-range effect was even more disastrous. It made possible the retrenchment and successful maintenance of a caste system in the United States. Just as the invention of the cotton gin had perpetuated slavery by making it essential to a plantation economy, so "separate but equal" attempted to make Negro equality utterly unattainable.

It was fifty-eight years before the Supreme Court reversed its stand.

Monday, May 17, 1954, a Supreme Court decision day, was not expected to produce much in the way of news. When the Court convened precisely at noon, most of the reporters who covered its proceedings were lolling in the basement press room. Suddenly, Banning E. Whittington, the Court's information officer, stood up and donned his coat. "Reading of the segregation decision is about to begin in the courtroom," he announced. "You will get the opinions up there."

Seconds later, a horde of newsmen raced up the long flight of marble steps leading to the imposing courtroom.

As they burst into the august chamber, Chief Justice Earl Warren had just started reading the Court's unanimous opinion. His first sentences marked the end of an era that had begun in New Orleans sixty-two years earlier. "In the field of public education," he said, "the doctrine of 'separate but equal' has no place. Separate educational facilities are inherently unequal. To separate Negro children from others of similar age and qualification solely because of race generates a feeling of inferiority as to their status in their community that may affect their hearts and minds in a way unlikely ever to be undone."

Like *Plessy v. Ferguson,* which was not limited in effect to railroads, the school segregation cases went far beyond classrooms. What the Court was saying was that state-supported segregation itself was beyond the pale of a democratic society. Just one week short of sixty-two years since Homer Plessy's ill-fated attempt to ride in a white-only day coach, racial segregation had been dealt a fatal blow.

True, it would be years and perhaps generations before Jim Crow could properly be called a corpse, but the handwriting was clearly visible on the walls of hundreds of segregated schoolhouses from Washington, D.C., to Miami, Florida, and from Norfolk, Virginia, to Houston, Texas. The Constitution, it seemed, was just what Harlan had said it was—color-blind.

The end of "separate but equal" as a constitutional principle ushered in a new era for the American Negro. Armed with a court decision of the first magnitude, he went into the streets to implement it: first in Montgomery, Alabama, with a boycott of segregated buses; then sit-ins in the lunchrooms of Greensboro, North Carolina, wade-ins on the beaches of Biloxi, Mississippi, and kneel-ins in the churches of Savannah, Georgia; finally, mass demonstrations in countless Southern cities whose names quickly became as well-known as the battlefields of World War II.

With the Civil Rights Act of 1964, the legal circle was to come full round. The newly freed slave who, bewildered and frightened, had walked away from the plantation a hundred years earlier, had finally found his way to freedom. At the start, it had been Sumner and Stevens who had led the way but, when the gates finally swung open, it was a black and not a white hand on the latch.

The Civil Rights Act may have officially ended segregation, but it was the federal courts that kept hope alive along the way.

In the beginning, the Negro could expect little consideration and no help from the judges of the United States. Chief Justice Taney had ruled that Dred Scott had no standing to sue in a federal court because slaves were not American citizens. But a century later, another Supreme Court responded wholeheartedly to the pleas of Negro school children from Kansas, Virginia, Delaware, South Carolina, and the District of Columbia for an integrated education.

Although the Thirteenth Amendment ended slavery, it took the Fourteenth to declare that "all persons born or naturalized in the United States, and subject to the jurisdiction thereof, are citizens of the United States and of the State wherein they reside." With the *Dred Scott* decision effectively nullified by this constitutional change, Negroes were free to ask the federal courts to enforce their newly recognized civil rights.

The Reconstruction Congress enacted a whole battery of protective statutes, most of which are still law. In addition to those that made it a crime for public officials to deprive Negroes of their federal rights, the latter could also bring lawsuits against their persecutors. If they were successful, they would be entitled to damages or an injunction ordering the defendants to cease their discriminatory conduct.

Moreover, Negroes who were sued or prosecuted in state courts because they attempted to exercise their civil rights or who could show that they could not get a fair trial in such cases, were specifically authorized to transfer them to the nearest federal court. Unfortunately, like so much of the other Reconstruction legislation, this safeguard was emasculated by the federal courts themselves after Hayes' surrender to the Southern Democrats in 1876.

The sad fact is that federal judges, like their fellow citizens, had little if any interest in the plight of the Negro after the end of Reconstruction. In 1881, for example, the Supreme Court invalidated the country's first public accommodations law on the grounds that Congress had no power to forbid discrimination by private persons. In case after case, the freedmen were bluntly told that they must look only to the courts of their home states for relief from the oppression to which they were being subjected.

Yet despite more than six decades of callous disregard by the judicial branch, Negroes began, in the middle thirties, to turn to it again. With the help of the newly formed NAACP Legal Defense and Educational Fund, they brought a plethora of suits under the Reconstruction laws seeking court orders restraining racial discrimination on a broad front.

Finally, in 1938, the first significant breakthrough came. The Supreme Court, in reversing an adverse decision in one of these suits, held that the "separate but equal" rule was not applicable where Missouri did not provide a law school for Negro students. "The fact remains," it said, "that instruction in law for Negroes is not now afforded by the State . . . and that the State excludes Negroes from the advantage of the law school it has established."

Twelve years later, the Court made its bent even clearer when it held that the establishment by Texas of a separate Negro law school did not provide an "equal" legal education. Without any contact with the judiciary, the bar associations, and other law schools, the Court reasoned, prospective Negro lawyers would be denied a significant part of their training. "Few students and no one who has practiced law would choose to study in an academic vacuum, removed from the interplay of ideas and the exchange of views with which the law is concerned."

Now it was only a matter of time before "separate but equal" was as dead as the reasoning which gave it birth.

But even while the main attack on *Plessy* was taking place, major victories were being won on related fronts. In rapid succession, the Supreme Court outlawed segregation in interstate travel, condemned racial discrimination in housing and employment, and invalidated a score of devices designed to prevent or restrict Negro voting. Case by case, in theory at least, it was eradicating the color line.

Before the turning point in 1938, the usual way for Negroes to protest discriminatory laws was to violate them and then defend the resulting criminal prosecutions in the local trial courts, either municipal or county. When all of the state's appellate procedures had been exhausted, the defendant was then free to apply to the United States Supreme Court for help. Since that tribunal has the power to pick and choose the cases it will consider, a bare handful managed to be heard—and then long years after the initial deprivation of civil rights.

With each new and encouraging decision from Washington, the legal techniques for attacking segregation became more effective. Instead of waiting to be prosecuted, increasing numbers of Negro plaintiffs began lawsuits in the federal trial courts seeking to have one or another form of racial discrimination declared unconstitutional. When they lost, as they invariably did, they appealed at once to the appropriate United States court.

These three-judge courts, known informally as circuits, handle most appeals from the federal trial courts. Since the Supreme Court accepts only a few hundred cases a year, a circuit's decision is usually final. All but one of the eleven circuits cover a number of states, the exception being that for the District of Columbia which is limited in area to Washington.

The Fourth Circuit (Maryland, North Carolina, South Carolina, Virginia, and West Virginia) and the Fifth Circuit (Alabama, Florida, Georgia, Louisiana, Mississippi, and Texas) quickly became the major appellate battlefields for these legal clashes. As the Supreme Court accelerated its output of favorable decisions, the judges of these circuits began to apply them to the innumerable civil rights cases on their dockets. At long last, the Constitution began to filter down to the grass roots.

The litigation course was now clear. As soon as the district court rendered an adverse decision, civil rights lawyers appealed at once to the appropriate circuit. If the latter affirmed the trial judge, the Supreme Court was asked to review the matter. When it would not do so, the attorneys started all over again with a new case involving similar issues in the hope that eventually the votes necessary to insure Supreme Court review would be obtained.*

This route is infinitely simpler and less time-consuming than proceeding in the state courts. In Mississippi, for ex-

* It takes the concurrence of four justices to obtain a hearing.

ample, a defendant who is prosecuted for any one of a number of misdemeanors used by that state to prevent integration is normally tried first by a justice of the peace. Since no record of this trial is kept, an appeal consists of a new trial in the county court. When he is again found guilty, he must ask the circuit court to reverse his conviction. If he is unsuccessful there, he may appeal to the Supreme Court of Mississippi. Only after that court's decision is he free to seek review in the United States Supreme Court. It often takes more than three years for such a case to reach Washington.

The Freedom Rides themselves soon inspired the use of two more dynamic legal approaches. Shortly after the first arrests, a halting attempt to resuscitate the 1866 civil rights removal statute, which had lain dormant for more than eighty years, took place in Jackson, Mississippi. As has been previously indicated,* this provision had been all but destroyed by restrictive federal court decisions.

About the same time, an application for a writ of *habeas corpus* was filed on behalf of a Freedom Rider who was being held in a Mississippi state prison. Since the purpose of such a writ is to obtain the release of a person who is illegally imprisoned, it was hoped that it would be issued. If anything was certain, it was that all of the Riders were being held in total violation of their federal rights.

Both legal experiments proved failures. But they did reveal the potential sweep of federal procedures which might, with an assist from the courts, help to abort paralyzing state prosecutions. Long before the Civil Rights Act of 1964, each technique had received substantial judicial approval and was in regular—and effective—use throughout the South.

In 1963, Supreme Court Justice Arthur Goldberg,** in

---

* See Page 19.
** Goldberg resigned from the bench in the summer of 1965 to accept appointment as United States Ambassador to the United Nations.

ordering the City of Memphis to desegregate its public parks, observed that "the basic guarantees of our Constitution are warrants for the here and now." Even before he said it, however, both the Fourth and Fifth Circuits, by providing avenues for immediate appellate hearings when delay would cause irreparable injury to Negro plaintiffs, had made speedy constitutional vindication reasonably available.

Finally, in the spring of 1965, the Supreme Court provided a significant adjunct to the legal arsenal of civil rights attorneys. In a landmark decision, it ruled that a federal court had an obligation to stop state criminal prosecutions based on unconstitutional laws when their very purpose was to punish defendants for the exercise of civil rights. In any such case where permanent damage was deemed inevitable, federal judges could no longer refuse to intervene.

Some of this history and much of this legal development was still a long way off as I left Los Angeles on the night of June 15, 1961. I was concerned only with the immediate future and spent the entire flight reading about the Freedom Riders in every newspaper and magazine I could find on the plane.

Suddenly, I was interrupted by the voice of the stewardess. "We are now making our descent to Jackson Municipal Airport," she announced. "Please fasten your seatbelts and observe the 'No Smoking' sign when it appears on the forward panel."

As the orange lights of the runway came in sight, I wondered what lay ahead for me.

CHAPTER 3

The Freedom Rides

I must admit that I came into Jackson with a chip on my shoulder. Like millions of Americans, I had been following with avid interest the newspaper accounts of the perilous tour across the deep south of a band of whites and Negroes who had taken seriously the Supreme Court's frequent pronouncements that racial segregation in interstate travel was unconstitutional.

The Freedom Rides had started on May 4, 1961, in Washington, D.C., when six whites and seven Negroes, ranging in age from eighteen to sixty-one, boarded an Atlanta-bound Greyhound bus. Sponsored by the Congress of Racial Equality, a New York-based civil rights organization known as CORE, the thirteen Riders announced to the few reporters who saw them off that they intended to test segregated travel facilities in Virginia, the Carolinas, Georgia, Alabama, Mississippi, and Louisiana.

For the first three days, their journey was uneventful. On May 8, however, a Negro Rider was arrested in Charlotte, North Carolina, and accused of entering an all-white barbershop in that city's bus terminal. Two days later, he was acquitted of trespass and rejoined the bus in South Carolina.

On May 9, Negro John R. Lewis, a student at the American Baptist Theological Institute, attempted to enter a segregated restroom in the depot at Rock Hill, South Carolina. Lewis, who in 1963 was to be named chairman of the militant Student Nonviolent Coordinating Committee (SNCC), was attacked by a group of whites and narrowly escaped serious injury.

The next day, two Riders were arrested in Winnsboro, South Carolina. Henry Thomas, a young Howard University student, was charged with trespassing when he tried to buy a sandwich at a segregated restaurant along the route. White James Peck, a forty-seven-year-old pacifist and the editor of CORE's newsletter, was arrested when he attempted to intercede for Thomas. After being held for forty-eight hours, both men were released and caught up with their bus at Sumter.

When they reached Atlanta, the Riders split into two groups for the trip westward through Alabama to Jackson. One group, composed of five Negroes and four whites, boarded another Greyhound while the other group bought passage on a Trailways bus. Both vehicles were headed for Birmingham.

No trouble was encountered until Sunday, May 14, when the two buses reached Anniston, a town of thirty thousand, twenty-nine miles inside the Alabama border. Just west of the city, the Greyhound, which had been forced to stop because of a mysterious flat tire, was destroyed by a fire bomb thrown through one of its rear windows. The few Riders who did not require medical treatment for smoke inhalation left at once for Birmingham on another bus.

A few minutes later, the Trailways bus pulled into town, only to be met at the station by an angry mob. Although Jim Peck was beaten so badly that he had to be hospitalized, the bus was not attacked and, after a short delay, continued its journey westward.

In Birmingham, the Ku Klux Klan had issued a call for volunteers to meet the two buses, which were expected to arrive in the Steel City in mid-afternoon. A large crowd responded to the appeal and, by four o'clock, the street in front of the Greyhound depot was packed with shirt-sleeved men. The news that one of the buses had been destroyed at Anniston caused the mob to rush to the Trailways station three blocks away where it waited in ominous silence.

"Here she comes!" a man shouted as the big red and white Vista View bus turned the corner. When the vehicle pulled into the parking area behind the station, the crowd pressed forward eagerly until the terminal was filled to overflowing.

Suddenly, a Negro youth appeared at the head of the passageway that led into the white waiting room.

"The nigger waiting room is back that way!" one man yelled at him.

When the Negro hesitated momentarily, another man pushed him back into the passageway. A third punched him in the face, dropping him to the floor. Each time the boy staggered to his feet, an assailant struck him again.

A white Rider who attempted to come to his fellow passenger's rescue, was also brutally beaten. The two men were then pushed back to the parking area. Some newsmen who tried to enter the station in order to observe what was taking place inside were themselves savagely attacked by the tremendous crowd that now completely surrounded the station.

Three days later—Wednesday, May 17—eight Negro college students from Nashville arrived in Birmingham. At two-thirty that afternoon, they entered the white waiting room in the Greyhound station and purchased tickets for the three o'clock bus to Montgomery. When they arrived on the loading platform, they were informed by the bus driver that he was afraid of violence.

"If you get on," he warned, "I will not drive the bus."

As the students walked back to the waiting room, they were met by Police Chief Jamie Moore.

"I am placing you under protective arrest," he told them. "It is dangerous for you and for others for you to stay here."

When Reverend Fred L. Shuttlesworth, one of Birmingham's most militant Negro leaders, protested, Moore arrested him, too.*

"These students came here to ride out on a regularly scheduled bus," Shuttlesworth told Moore. "That is our irrevocable position. The challenge has to be made. This is a continuation of the Freedom Ride which was stopped temporarily here in Birmingham. When it is proven people can ride through Birmingham without molestation, it will all be over here."

Although the minister was soon released on bond, the students remained in jail where they promptly started a hunger strike. At eleven-thirty Friday night, two days after their arrests, they were taken from their cells by Police Commissioner Eugene (Bull) Connor.

"You people came here from Tennessee on a bus, and I'm taking you back to Tennessee in five minutes under police protection," he told them. "In view of your stand, this is the only way for the police to protect you and the citizens of Birmingham."

The eight Negroes were then spirited out of the city in a black limousine escorted by three unmarked police cars. Some four hours later, the little caravan pulled into the tiny town of Ardmore, some 125 miles north of Birmingham.

* Shuttlesworth was later convicted of interfering with the police. On March 9, 1964, his conviction was unanimously reversed by the United States Supreme Court.

"This is the Tennessee line," Connor informed his charges. "Cross it, and save this state and yourself a lot of trouble."

As the portly police commissioner entered his car for the return trip to Birmingham, Lucretia Collins, a pretty, vivacious girl who was the unofficial spokesman for the group, voiced her companions' defiance.

"We'll see you back in Birmingham about noon!" she shouted after Connor's disappearing back. His only response, noted the reporters who had followed the four-car convoy to the state line, was a loud laugh.

But like the rest of the country, Alabama was beginning to take the Rides seriously. Ten hours earlier, Circuit Judge Walter B. Jones had issued an injunction forbidding Freedom Riders from testing travel facilities in the state. His sweeping order, which was granted at the request of the state's Attorney General, prohibited CORE from "entry into and travel within the state of Alabama and engaging in the so-called 'freedom rides' and other acts or conduct calculated to provoke breaches of the peace."

Some Alabamians, however, were not content to rely on court orders. At 10:15 the next morning, a howling mob of more than one thousand men and women attacked eighteen Negroes and three whites who had arrived in Montgomery on a Greyhound bus. The twenty-one Riders who, after waiting almost an entire day in the white waiting room in Birmingham, had finally been sold tickets to the state capitol, were beaten as they left their bus and attempted to make their way to Reverend Ralph D. Abernathy's First Baptist Church.

As the Riders scurried for safety, women in the crowd screamed "Get those niggers!" White men, armed with metal pipes, clubs, baseball bats and sticks, attacked their quarry in successive waves until the streets around the station were littered with unconscious and bleeding victims.

Two white girls, who had arrived on the Greyhound, escaped serious injury by running into a nearby church and then vanishing into an adjacent office building. John Siegenthaler, a personal representative of Attorney General Robert Kennedy, and later the editor of the Nashville *Tennessean*, was knocked unconscious as he tried to aid one of the girls.

It took fifteen minutes for the Montgomery police to arrive on the scene. By this time, the mob had assaulted reporters and photographers who were covering the incident, had broken the leg of a Negro bystander, and had tried to burn one Negro boy alive.

"Hit 'em, hit 'em again!" encouraged onlookers as wild-eyed white men, seemingly unnoticed by the police, attacked everyone in sight who appeared to be sympathetic to the Riders' plight.

Most of the bus passengers had dropped their suitcases as they ran for their lives. While a Negro girl wept uncontrollably, the luggage was gathered together on the street outside the station and ignited. As the flames leaped higher, reporters noticed that an English composition book belonging to one of the student Riders was on top of the pyre.

Reaction in Washington was swift. The President issued a statement in which he said that the situation in Alabama was "a source of the deepest concern to me as it must be to the vast majority of the citizens of Alabama and all Americans." He called upon Governor John Patterson and other state officials "to exercise their lawful authority to prevent any further outbreak of violence."

Patterson gave half-hearted assurances that he would try to preserve the peace.

"While we will do our utmost to keep the public highways clear and to guard against all disorder," he said, "we cannot escort busloads of rabble rousers about our state from city to city for the avowed purpose of disobeying our laws, flaunting our customs and traditions, and creating racial incidents."

The next evening, Dr. Martin Luther King, Jr., addressed a mass meeting of Montgomery Negroes at the First Baptist Church. While the Atlanta minister, whose leadership of the successful Montgomery bus boycott during 1955–1956 had won him national attention, was declaring that Alabama had "sunk to a level of barbarity like Hitler's Germany," several hundred infuriated whites gathered in an open park across the street.

Shortly before ten o'clock, after burning an automobile being used by author Jessica Mitford,* the mob began to move toward the church. Inside the red brick building, there was near panic as the angry shouts outside became clearly audible.

Suddenly, a clear baritone voice singing "Leaning on His Everlasting Arms" was heard above the moaning of frightened women and, in a matter of seconds, order was restored.

As his now calm audience began singing hymns, Dr. King left the rostrum and entered the pastor's office where he placed a call to Robert F. Kennedy.

"They're moving in on the church," the minister informed the Attorney General.

"The marshals will stop them," Kennedy said confidently.

King left the telephone for a moment to look out of the church's front door.

"You're right," he told Kennedy.

It took the combined efforts of five hundred federal marshals, most of Montgomery's police force, and scores of highway patrolmen to restore order. As the church's besiegers started across the street, the marshals hurled tear gas bombs into their midst.

* Miss Mitford, who had come to Montgomery to do an article on Southern society for *Esquire*, had gone to the church to hear King for the first time.

When this failed to disperse the jeering crowd, which was growing larger by the minute, armed marshals on foot began to herd it back toward the park. In addition, federal agents in automobiles raced up and down to the street to prevent would-be attackers from reaching the beleaguered church.

Despite the fact that, earlier in the day, Governor Patterson had curtly informed Attorney General Kennedy that "we don't need your marshals," the state's director of public safety pleaded for reinforcements. In a telephone call to the federal command post at nearby Maxwell Air Force Base, he urged Byron R. White, Kennedy's chief assistant,* to "commit your reserves—this is an ugly situation!" He was informed that every marshal in the area had been sent to Montgomery.

By midnight, the streets around the First Baptist Church were clear. Inside the building, the fifteen hundred Negroes who had attended the mass meeting were asked by James F. McShane, the chief federal marshal, to remain overnight. Toward dawn they were escorted to their homes in small groups while mobile units patrolled the entire area.

With Montgomery under martial law, James Farmer, CORE's national director, announced that despite the violence the Rides would continue.

"Many students are standing by in other cities to serve as volunteers if needed," he said. "We don't want a large delegation and will not call on these volunteers unless those in Montgomery waiting to make the trip are prevented from going."

Farmer proved to be an able prophet. At 9:12 A.M. on Wednesday, May 24, a Trailways bus with twelve Riders, some Alabama National Guardsmen, and about twenty newsmen aboard, pulled out of the Montgomery terminal. Escorted by a squad of motorcycle policemen, the vehicle sped to the city limits where it was met by sixteen highway patrol

---

* Now an Associate Justice of the United States Supreme Court.

cruisers, each carrying three combat-equipped National Guardsmen and two state troopers. As the bus headed westward on Route 80 toward the Mississippi line, three L-19 reconnaissance planes and two helicopters hovered overhead.

Although there was no trouble along the route, the Riders were cursed by roughly dressed whites when the bus passed through Selma. At Demopolis, the jeers of a crowd along the highway were accentuated by a rock which struck the side of the bus. But its occupants did not seem particularly disturbed by their unfriendly reception. When they weren't singing freedom songs, they were conducting back-of-the-bus workshops on nonviolent action.

At the Mississippi line, the vehicle was turned over to officials of that state who escorted it to Jackson. Minutes after Reverend C. T. Vivian of Nashville's Cosmopolitan Community Church had led his fellow passengers into the Trailways station, they were all under arrest. Four were seized when they tried to enter the white restrooms while the other eight were taken into custody in the white men's room.

A second busload of Riders from Montgomery, which included CORE's Jim Farmer, pulled into the terminal at 6:47 P.M. As soon as its fifteen passengers had debarked, they lined up in front of the entrance to the station's white cafeteria. Captain J. L. Ray of the Jackson Police Department, who was shortly to become a familiar figure to hundreds of their successors, asked the members of the interracial group to leave the terminal. When they refused, he ordered them arrested.

From his cell, Farmer issued a call to action.

"The time to act is now," he said. "Throughout the nation we can end segregation in bus, train, and airline terminals if we are willing to make the sacrifices needed. These are sacrifices of your time, your money, and your safety. The decision to act must be made calmly and deliberately, with full knowledge of the risks and opportunities."

The response was immediate. Before the Rides ended in late July, people from all over the United States had arrived in the Mississippi capital with the avowed purpose of desegregating the Illinois Central Railroad Station, the Municipal Airport, and the two bus depots. Unlike Montgomery and Birmingham, there was no violence; each integrated group was promptly arrested by Captain Ray and his officers who performed their duties with all the skill and polish of a West Point drill team.

By the time of my arrival on the morning of June 16, 111 Riders had been introduced by Captain Ray into the mysteries of Mississippi prison life. Before I left in late August, that number had swelled to almost four hundred.

CHAPTER 4

A Toe in the Water

As I rode into Jackson that first day, I was fully conscious of the tension that gripped the city. My cab driver, a short, stocky man in a large Western-style gray stetson, lost no time in berating "niggers" and "nigger lovers" who, in his opinion, were fast giving Jackson a bad name across the country.

"They all ought to be strung up," he ranted.

When I informed him that I would like to be taken to North Farish Street, he shifted in his seat and looked back at me suspiciously.

"That's a colored district," he said. "You sure that's where you want to go."

When I assured him that I did, he became quite agitated.

"Say, you ain't one of them mixers," he drawled.

"Not yet," I replied.

He hesitated a long moment while he mulled over the significance of my answer.

"Well, I'm sure glad to hear that," he finally said.

After a fifteen-minute ride, I found myself standing on the

sidewalk outside of a nondescript two-story building, sadly in need of painting. Nailed to the right side of its entrance was a small sign which proclaimed "Jack H. Young, Lawyer." As I walked up the creaking stairs, I began to wonder whether I had been in my right mind when I consented to visit Jackson. What could I possibly tell this Negro attorney who had been in the thick of things for three weeks?

But my doubts soon disappeared. When I entered Young's sparsely furnished office, the warmth of his greeting left no room to doubt that he was overjoyed to see another lawyer. A tall, thin man with a slight stoop who had given up a steady job as a postman to take up the precarious profession of the law, he quickly briefed me on what was happening on the legal front.

The Riders were being tried as fast as they were arrested in Municipal Court where Judge James L. Spencer, Jr., meted out $200 fines and four-month jail terms for breach of the peace, the charge uniformly employed by Captain Ray and his "antimix" squad. At first the convicted defendants were kept in Jackson jails but, as their number grew, they were taken two hundred miles to the north to the state penitentiary at Parchman.

"There must be some way to stop this persecution," Young told me, "but I just haven't had time to do anything more than appear in court each day. Is there anything that we can do to take the play away from the city?"

I had not expected to be asked for any legal advice and murmured that I would have to think it over.

"While you're doing that," he said, "why don't you go down to the Greyhound bus station. I've heard from CORE that a new shipment of Riders from Memphis will be in today."

Minutes later, I was sitting at the lunch counter in the depot. It was obvious that Young was not the only one who expected trouble. The station was filled with policemen and reporters who kept peering at their watches and looking toward the passageway that led to the loading ramp. While I waited, I sat down at the lunch counter and ordered a hamburger.

Suddenly, I was aware that the policemen in the waiting room had stiffened to attention. One officer approached me and several other men at the counter and ordered us to leave the stools on which we were sitting. As I strolled over to one side of the room, I saw three white girls, a white man, and a Negro youth enter the station from the direction of the ramp.

When they noticed the roomful of policemen and newspapermen, they hesitated for a moment, then walked over to the side of the lunch counter which I had just vacated. An officer, who I later discovered was Captain Ray, met them as they sat down on the empty stools.

"I'll ask you just once," he said firmly, "to leave the station. If you do not, you will be arrested."

There wasn't a word from the quintet. Ray waved at his men. "O.K." he barked, "take 'em away!" In a matter of seconds, the five Riders were escorted out of the station and into the waiting paddy wagon. The incident was over.

As I walked back to Young's office, my head was whirling. For the first time in my life I had been privileged to watch total human commitment and I sensed that I would never be quite the same again. The sight of five frightened young people who had traveled long and far in order to offer their bodies as a witness to the equality of all men, quietly but forcefully, had taught me what I had never known before— that only by personal involvement can one justify his existence, either to himself or to his fellows.

By the time I turned back into Farish Street, I had decided to take Jack Young at his word. I wasn't quite sure what could be done or whether the American Civil Liberties

Union would approve, but I was determined to join the protest against racial segregation that had just been so eloquently demonstrated to me. Just how I would go about doing this wasn't quite clear to me, but that didn't seem particularly important at the time.

Young gave me the answer. Did I think that a federal writ of *habeas corpus* would lie? Although I had never applied for such a writ, I felt certain that arrest and imprisonment for daring to sit at a lunch counter in a place devoted to furthering interstate commerce was patently unjustified. If that wasn't an object of national concern, I didn't know what was.

Looking back I don't think that Jack Young knew any more about writs of federal *habeas corpus* than I did, but I imagine that anything was better than the dreary course he was pursuing. With his consent, we had two eager lawyers. All that we now needed was a client.

We didn't have to look far for one. Ensconced in the Hinds County Jail was Elizabeth Porter Wyckoff, a former professor of Greek at Mount Holyoke College. Dr. Wyckoff, who had the singular distinction of being the first white woman Rider to be arrested in Jackson, was delighted to retain Young and myself as her attorneys and willingly signed the application for the writ that we had put together with the help of a federal form book that afternoon.

It was too late to file our papers that day, but Jack promised to do so the next morning. In the interim, I decided to return to New York. When I reported to Rowland Watts what I had done in Jackson, he assured me that the American Civil Liberties Union would stand behind me.

District Judge Sidney C. Mize, who was then holding court in Biloxi, promptly set Dr. Wyckoff's hearing down for June 21 in that Gulf Coast resort city. For the first time since my admission to the bar in 1948, I was to argue a case outside the state of New York.

On June 20, I flew to New Orleans where I was met by Bob Collins and Lolis Elie, two young Negro lawyers who represented CORE in Louisiana. Early the next morning they drove me to Biloxi where I joined Jack Young at the ultra modern Federal Building. The medium-sized court-room on its second floor was packed with spectators and, as I walked to the counsel table with Young, I could feel the hostility that was immediately directed our way. I later became accustomed to such receptions, but I must admit that, for the first few times, they were hard to take.

After I had been introduced to Judge Mize, a small, wizened man with strong segregationist leanings, Young and I launched into our argument. Among other things, we pointed out that Dr. Wyckoff had every right to use interstate travel facilities on an integrated basis and that a federal court had a duty to release her. She was being prosecuted, we said, for attempting to exercise rights guaranteed to her by the Constitution and not, as the State of Mississippi claimed, for causing a breach of the peace.

Although Mize seemed to be listening attentively, he did not ask a single question. In the main, the audience in the courtroom was quiet and orderly. The only exception occurred when I made a reference to the recent burning of a cross on the lawn of the home of one of the Riders in Rye, New York. "It is an indecency," I said, "that the symbol of Christianity should be used to sanctify segregation and discrimination."

At this moment, a man in shirtsleeves stood up in the rear of the room. "Why don't you shut your goddamned mouth," he shouted, "and stay the hell out of Mississippi!" He subsided at once, however, when Judge Mize ordered him to sit down or be ejected from the room.

The state of Mississippi had brought down a sizable legal battery from Jackson, headed by Attorney General Joseph T. Patterson. A thin, dour man with a marked predilection for dark suits and oversized hats, Patterson regarded any courtroom as a forum for the airing of views favored by his constituents. Federal courts, he warned, were duty bound to avoid catering to "outside agitators" who were invading Mississippi in order to destroy the pleasant relations that had existed for generations between its white and Negro citizens.

The general's five aides, however, stuck to the law. They insisted that Dr. Wyckoff had no right to federal assistance because she had not first exhausted her remedies in the courts of the state. Unfortunately, the law on this point had not developed to the point it was to reach two years later when the federal courts began to recognize that emergency situations called for emergency measures.

We could only point out that, since Dr. Wyckoff would have to be bailed out before the end of forty days in order to safeguard her right to appeal her conviction, her application for a writ of federal *habeas corpus* would shortly be moot if she had to proceed in the state courts first.

When the arguments were finished, Mize uttered the first words he had spoken since welcoming me to his court.

"I will reserve decision until I have had a chance to study the briefs," he said. "The prisoner is remanded to prison to await my ruling."

As soon as the judge had left the bench, Young and I walked over to where Dr. Wyckoff was sitting. A pleasant-faced, gray-haired woman in her mid-forties, she had followed the arguments with great interest.

"I didn't understand everything you said," she commented, "but after three weeks in jail, it is comforting to hear someone standing up for you."

Ten days later, as had been expected, Judge Mize refused

to grant the writ of *habeas corpus*. Dr. Wyckoff, he ruled, had failed to exhaust her state remedies. After the Fifth Circuit had affirmed his decision, I filed a new application for a writ directly with Supreme Court Justice Hugo L. Black.

In the middle of July, Black denied the writ.

Although I was bitterly disappointed, I had, at the very least, bought myself two cents worth of involvement.

CHAPTER 5

Legal Gymnastics

Just before leaving Jackson on June 17, I met Charles R. Oldham, CORE's National Chairman. Oldham, a white St. Louis lawyer, had defended the first Riders arrested in the Mississippi capital.

Over breakfast, Oldham asked me if I was available to assist Jack Young who had been hired by CORE as its local counsel. Between mouthfuls of the first hominy grits I had ever tasted, I told him that I would think it over.

Strangely enough, it was Governor Ross R. Barnett who made up my mind for me. After the Wyckoff hearing in Biloxi, I had driven to Jackson with Jack Young. My purpose was to check on the condition of Price Chatham, a Texas Rider who was deep into a hunger strike at Parchman. Chatham's wife, who was worried about her husband's health, had called me before I left New York on June 20 and asked me to look into the situation.

On Thursday, June 22, I entered Mississippi's imposing Capitol Building. Walking past drinking fountains that were restricted to white lips only, I ascended a magnificent stair-

41

case to the second floor. When I arrived at the governor's office, an attractive receptionist asked me if I had an appointment. I replied that I did not but that I wanted to speak to the governor on an extremely urgent matter.

To my surprise, I was immediately ushered into Barnett's office. When I explained that I was there to discuss Price Chatham, the governor appeared disinterested. "If he doesn't want to eat, that's his lookout," he said laconically.

After he had refused my request to release Chatham, I informed him that the prisoner's wife had authorized forced feeding if necessary to save his life. "I'll see that the warden gets that information," he drawled.

As I turned to go, he stopped me.

"Just why are you mixed up with these trouble makers?" he asked abruptly.

Although I was totally unprepared for such a question, I managed to stammer out some sort of an explanation which, as I remember, was filled with clichés about brotherhood, equality, and human dignity.

He looked at me quizzically. "Mr. Kunstler," he asked, "do you have any children?" I nodded. "Two girls," I replied.

His tone hardened. "Mr. Kunstler," he snapped, "what would you think if your daughter married a dirty, kinky-headed, fieldhand nigger?"

It was my turn to raise my voice. "I think that such a step would be her own responsibility. She has a right to select her own husband."

The governor looked stricken. "Mr. Kunstler," he roared, "that sounds like some of the Eleanor Roosevelt junk. If it were my daughter, I'd disown her."

I tried to point out to him that I didn't think that marrying white women was the goal of Negroes involved in the integration movement, but he would have none of this. "That's all the niggers want," he retorted. "Besides there hasn't been a single society yet where they integrated and the society hasn't collapsed."

When I pointed out that he was about to attend the Governors' Conference in Hawaii where he would find a fully integrated society, he launched into ancient and inaccurate history.

"Take the example of Egypt," he said. "That was a pure white society. But when the niggers came up the Nile and they intermarried and integrated, that caused the collapse of the greatest white civilization we'd known up to that time."

I ventured the opinion that, as I remembered my history, the Romans had something to do with the Egyptian decline. At this, the governor exploded. "I never heard a white man give me an answer like that in my life!" he retorted.

"Isn't it possible, Governor," I continued, "that some Negroes have contributed a great deal to the world. I seem to remember George Washington Carver. I recall his experiments with peanuts did a lot for the country."

Barnett acknowledged that Carver had been "one of our *good* Nigras."

But the governor was adamant that he would never appoint any Negro, no matter how well qualified, to a post in his administration. "You should never put a nigger in a position of responsibility," he said. "They're not capable of it."

"We have a Negro—Dr. Robert C. Weaver—sitting in virtually a Cabinet position in Washington," I reminded him. "Doesn't that impress you in any way?"

He shook his head. "No, he should never have been appointed. I didn't vote for either Kennedy or Nixon because of their racial stands."

As our conversation drew to a close, Barnett reminded me that Khrushchev was "taking these racial incidents down here, which are provoked by outsiders, and hurting us abroad." My observation that Mississippi's treatment of the Freedom Riders might have given the Russians considerably more grist for their propaganda mill ended the interview.

As I walked to the door, the governor followed me. "Look," he said in a confidential tone, "when you go out of this office don't you dare tell anyone sitting out there anything about your racial theories because we've had too much bad publicity, and I don't want you lynched right here in the state capital."

The ten-minute conversation had been both depressing and revealing. If this was the way the state's chief executive felt, I thought, then how much more virulent must be the attitude of the mass of Mississippians who, presumably, did not have at least the restraint of public office to curb them.

As I walked down the Capitol steps, I wondered: how could the principles of nonviolence and brotherly love ever succeed with men like Barnett who were blinded by prejudices so deep and so strong that they shut out all history, all logic, and all reason? Was any progress doomed to founder on ignorance and stupidity? Was hope in this area as deceptive as the governor's own historical perspective?

Before I reached the sidewalk, I knew that I couldn't leave Mississippi without irrevocably aligning myself against everything Barnett stood for. Minutes later, my mind was made up. No sooner had I reached Jack Young's office than I put in a call to Oldham in St. Louis.

"Charlie," I said when he came on the line, "if you still want me, I'm available."

The next two months were to be the most active I had ever spent. When I wasn't busy boning up on the law affecting the right of all Americans to integrated travel, I was practically commuting between New York and Jackson. It was a rare week that I didn't spend some time in Jack Young's office, and his two tiny rooms became as familiar to me as my own Fifth Avenue office suite.

During July and most of August, Young and I were preparing for the County Court trials of the first Riders in late summer. Under Mississippi law, a person charged with a misdemeanor must be tried initially in Municipal Court. Should he be convicted there—as all our clients had been—he could post an appeal bond and obtain a new trial in the County Court.

All of the Riders had been charged with violating Section 2087.5 of the Code of Mississippi. This statute, which had been enacted by the legislature in 1960 in order to prevent "wade-ins" by Negroes desiring to use the segregated beaches of Biloxi, made it a misdemeanor to do anything that might provoke a breach of the peace. The punishment: $200 fine or four months in jail or both.

Early in August, Jack Travis, the city prosecutor, informed us that he expected the first two hundred Riders who had been arrested and who were all now free on bail* to return to Jackson for their arraignments in County Court. When we explained to him that it would cost about $25,000 to do this, and that Mississippi law permitted a lawyer to answer "not guilty" for a person accused of a misdemeanor, Travis said that he would ask for bond forfeitures if any defendant failed to appear.

It was obvious to both Young and myself that Travis was reflecting a state policy to make the assertion of constitutional rights by our clients as costly as possible. Although we were sure that we would be unsuccessful, we were determined to try every legal maneuver we could think of in order to prevent the return to Jackson of the Riders, many of whom lived as far away as California, New York, and Illinois.

* At least two hundred others who had been arrested later were still in jail.

The arraignments* were scheduled for Monday, August 14. A week earlier, accompanied by Carl Rachlin, CORE's general counsel, I had visited County Judge Russel D. Moore, III, who was to try all the cases and asked him to permit us to answer for our clients. Moore, an ex-Louisianian whose crew cut and pink cheeks gave him the appearance of a college boy, promptly refused our request, claiming that he was bound by a 1960 court rule.**

We then asked for a hearing before Mississippi Supreme Court Justice William N. Ethridge, Jr., in order to seek an order prohibiting Moore from enforcing this rule. Ethridge, a polio victim who has to use a wheel chair whenever he appears in public, informed us that under Mississippi law we had to apply to the local circuit judge first.

On Thursday, August 10, we appealed to Circuit Judge Leon F. Hendrick† to prevent what we called an abuse of Moore's discretion. Hendrick gave us short shrift. "If Judge Moore should order the bonds forfeited because the defendants did not appear," he told us, "you would have the right to resist forfeiture by appeal. I can't tell Judge Moore how to run his court."

We then called Justice Ethridge and informed him what had happened in Hendrick's court. When Ethridge insisted that he did not have the power to reverse the circuit judge, we realized that we had reached the end of our rope.

"This is it," we told the small army of reporters who had been following us from court to court. "There are no more appeals. We've called CORE in New York and told them to have all the defendants here for the opening of the term."

---

* An arraignment is a *pro forma* proceeding in which a person accused of crime informs the court how he intends to answer the charge.

** We had heard rumors that Moore was actively connected with the White Citizens Council, Mississippi's more "sophisticated" version of the Ku Klux Klan. Two and a half years later, his racial bias was dramatically revealed by his association with Byron de la Beckwith during the latter's trial for the murder of Medgar Evers.

† In early 1964 Hendrick presided at Beckwith's first trial for Evers' murder.

All over the United States, our clients were preparing to return to Jackson. What the United Press had referred to as "an endurance race" between Rachlin and myself on one side and City Prosecutor Jack Travis on the other had ended with the state the winner of this round. The experience had taught us one valuable lesson—the state of Mississippi was not going to give an inch in its determination to teach all "outside agitators" that equality was very expensive business indeed.

Because he feared mob violence, Jim Farmer asked the Justice Department to provide federal marshals to protect the returning Riders. Deputy Attorney General Byron R. White refused his request, stating that there was "no basis to assume that the people of Mississippi will be lawless or that responsible law enforcement officers will be unable or unwilling to maintain law and order."

Governor Barnett, who had declared that his state "wants no federal marshals and needs no federal marshals," was "elated" by the decision.

Starting on Saturday, August 12, the Riders began to stream back into Jackson. They arrived by plane, train, bus, and private car. Most of the out-of-town defendants were quartered at Tougaloo Southern Christian College, an American Missionary Association school some three miles north of the capital, and at Campbell College, one of Jackson's two Negro institutions of higher learning.

I had never met most of my clients, so on Sunday afternoon, with the mercury hovering near 100°, I was driven out to Tougaloo by Aurelia Young, Jack's energetic wife, whose impromptu but excellent meals had been welcomed by scores of half-starved Riders after their release on bond from Parchman.

When we arrived at Tougaloo, the campus had a homecoming atmosphere. Riders who had shared prison cells were greeting each other like long lost friends. In a grove of moss-mantled oak trees, a group of boys and girls sang to the accompaniment of two guitars. If it had not been for the ubiquitous reporters and cameramen, it could have been a scene at almost any American college.

At four o'clock, the bells of Woodworth Chapel began to toll and, in a matter of minutes, the building was filled with Riders. While they waited for the meeting to begin, they sang freedom songs, many of which had been born in Parchman, under the direction of Guy Carawan, one of the finest folk musicians in America. This was the first time that I had heard many of the songs, and I must say that, although I have listened to them many times since, they never meant as much to me as they did at that moment.

After Jim Farmer had movingly welcomed his codefendants back to Jackson, Reverend C. T. Vivian laid down the ground rules for the Riders' behavior. There was to be no interracial dating off campus. Anyone going into town was to be dressed in conventional street costume. Nothing was to be done or said that would give the authorities any excuse for arrest.

"In short," Vivian said, "the word is dignity."

I was asked to say something about the legal situation. I could only add that I hoped that everyone would dress neatly for court, and that Young and I would be there the next afternoon to represent everyone at the arraignment. As for the normally segregated courtroom, I recommended that the Riders take whatever seats were available and that no attempt be made to adhere to any seating plan which the city of Jackson might try to implement.

"You rode into town together," I concluded, "and there's no reason why you can't sit in court together."

After the meeting, I strolled around the open campus and tried to match up some of the names I had on my lists with the human beings they represented. The variety was awesome. There were rabbis, ministers, and seminarians; lawyers and legislators; married couples and teenagers; students and professors; brothers and sisters; and fathers and sons. They hailed from as far away as Los Angeles and Maine and as near as from Jackson's Lynch Street. They were, in short, a cross section of a troubled and uneasy national conscience.

Although it was impossible to do more than say hello to each one, I did take special note of a few of the Riders. There was, for example, Reverend Vivian who had led the first bus into Jackson on May 25. A proudly erect man in his early thirties who was known to everyone as C. T., he was one of the two persons I had met since my involvement who could clearly and adequately explain the simple but overwhelming power of the doctrine of nonviolence, the philosophical bulwark of the Rides.

The other was James M. Lawson, Jr., a young Methodist preacher who had conducted a workshop on nonviolence in the back of Vivian's bus during the trip from Montgomery to Jackson. Both men were instrumental in convincing me that it was possible to superimpose the Gandhian concept of passive resistance on the Negro struggle for equality.

"We can win," Lawson insisted, "if we return love for hate and if we really believe that turning the other cheek is the only answer to brutality and degradation."

Lastly, there was Wyatt Tee Walker, Dr. Martin Luther King's executive assistant, who had left the pulpit of his Virginia church to join the freedom movement. A slender, handsome man who was usually meticulously attired. Walker, with his wife, Anne, had been arrested for trying to integrate the Trailways bus terminal. Although I didn't know it at the time, he was to have a major role in shaping my future commitment.

That evening, there was a mass meeting at the Negro Masonic Temple on Lynch Street. Despite a violent thunder-

storm, more than fifteen hundred people turned out to hear
Jim Farmer answer Governor Barnett's complaint that "outside agitators" were ruining his state.

"There are no outsiders in America," Farmer said. "That's
what makes America great."

Much to my later regret, I did not attend this meeting. I
was too new to the movement to be a part of it, and I still felt
that my place was in the courtroom alone. I have since
learned that a lawyer is just another worker with special skills
and that he should be wherever his clients need his presence.
But this was a truth only the future could teach me.

The arraignments were scheduled for one o'clock the next
afternoon in the Hinds County Courthouse. Of the 198
Riders who had been ordered to appear, four were in jail in
Louisiana and five others had not been located. In order to
prevent the forfeiture of the latters' $500 bonds, we tried a
new gambit—removal of their cases to the federal court.

Early in my Jackson stay, I had met William L. Higgs, a
young Jackson attorney who had recently graduated from
Harvard Law School. Higgs, whose great-great-grandfather
had signed the articles of secession that took Mississippi out
of the Union in 1860, was strongly interested in the use of
federal power to end segregation. For some time, he had been
urging me to remove some of the Riders' cases to the federal
court.

In 1866, the Reconstruction Congress had enacted a statute
which made it possible to transfer civil rights cases from state
to federal courts. The theory behind this statute was that it
might be difficult if not impossible for ex-slaves to secure
justice in courts controlled by their former masters.

On the morning of the arraignments, I went to see Higgs.
The lawyer, who had been evicted from his office in the
Barnett Building when he became a little too interested in
civil rights for his own good, conducted his dwindling prac-

tice from a private home near the Capitol. Together, we drew
the removal petitions for the five missing Riders.

When they had been typed, we filed them with Loryce
Wharton, the clerk of the United States District Court. As
soon as she had given them a docket number, the cases were
automatically transferred to her court. Now it was up to the
state of Mississippi to make a motion for their remand to the
County Court.

But for the time being, at least, five bail bonds were safe.

CHAPTER 6

Days in Court

The Hinds County courthouse was virtually sealed off from the rest of Jackson that afternoon. As the buses containing the Riders began arriving at the gray stone building with its rooftop statue of Hammurabi, two dozen policemen saw to it that no trouble ensued. Traffic was cleared in front of the courthouse, and groups were not permitted to assemble on the adjoining sidewalk.

Judge Russel Moore's courtroom was on the building's second floor. When we reached the landing, we were delightfully surprised to see that the two restrooms whose doors usually bore the legends "White Men" and "White Women"* had been desegregated for the day at least. During the morning, workmen had covered them with temporary signs which read "Male Defendants" and "Female Defendants."

The arraignments took two hours and twenty minutes. As burly Jack Travis, the city prosecutor, read off his or her name, each Rider approached the bench and said "not

---

* The Negro toilets were located in the basement.

guilty." While their pleas were being entered by the court clerk, Assistant Prosecutor Bob Nichols compared their faces with photographs which had been made at the time of the arrests.

"We don't want any ringers standing in for anyone," he explained when we protested this time-consuming process.

When the formalities had been completed, Moore announced that the appeals, which consisted of new trials, would be held on a two-a-day basis starting with Tuesday, August 22. At that rate, it would take well into the New Year for this batch of Riders to be processed. The first trials—those of Henry Thomas and Julia Aaron—were set for the morning and afternoon of Tuesday, August 22.

While we waited for Thomas' trial to begin, we had plenty to do. On Friday, Young and I appeared before United States District Judge William Harold Cox, who had the distinction of being Kennedy's first appointment to the federal trial bench. Cox had ordered a hearing when Mississippi had asked him to return the cases of the five missing Riders, which we had removed Monday morning, back to the Hinds County court.

A heavy-set man with ponderous jowls whose low-pitched voice made him exasperatingly difficult to hear, Cox listened impassively to the arguments of both sides. This was my first of many appearances before him and, although I had no way of knowing then that he was destined to have one of the worst records in the country in civil rights cases, I was soon brought face to face with the realities of Southern "justice."

We pointed out to Cox that these cases properly belonged in his court since they involved the denial of constitutional rights under the patently transparent dodge of maintaining civil order. "It is not a breach of peace law," we argued. "It is a segregation law—pure and simple."

Attorney General Patterson, with his usual stump oratory,

insisted that our removal petition was "just a blatant attempt to nullify action in the state court by coming in the back door."

As I listened to Patterson's bombast, I had a chance to study the courtroom, which is located on the fourth floor of the Post Office Building. I was immediately struck by a huge mural that occupied almost the entire wall behind the bench. Perhaps more than anything else I had seen in Jackson, this painting symbolized the sorry state of race relations in Mississippi.

It is probably an accurate, if highly stylized, picture of life in the Magnolia State, but to one seeing it for the first time, it is shocking.

It portrays a group of whites, all of whom reflect complete Caucasian domination of industry, business, the arts, and the professions. There is the architect, the engineer, the minister, the builder, the plantation overseer and other authoritarian figures. Their stately ladies and blonde, blue-eyed children look as if they had just stepped out of the pages of an antebellum *Ladies' Home Journal.* Painted in bright and virile colors, they suggest a strength and dignity that one would easily associate with the doers and movers of this world.

To their left are four or five faceless Negroes of both sexes who are picking, baling, or hauling cotton. The only excepton is a gray-haired, barefooted Negro man who, all smiles, is squatting on the ground and picking at the strings of a banjo. The Negroes are all poorly dressed and, in contrast to the whites in the scene, are sketched in drab browns and grays.

A more blatant—and meaningful—disparity could not be imagined. It is a disgrace to this federal building.

Cox promised a prompt ruling, and he was as good as his word. A week later, he remanded the five cases back to the state court. In an unnecessarily scathing opinion, he castigated the Riders as "criminals" whose only purpose in coming to Jackson was to cause trouble. As far as he was concerned, the prosecutions involved nothing more than garden variety breaches of the peace without any federal significance.

By this time, we were deep in the Henry Thomas trial which had opened as scheduled on Tuesday, August 22. Thomas, a nineteen-year-old Howard University student from St. Augustine, Florida, had arrived in Jackson on May 24 on the second bus to leave Montgomery that day. Like everyone else, he had been convicted of breach of the peace in Municipal Court.

Our opening maneuver was to attack the Hinds County jury system. The list of fifty-three prospective jurors included only two Negroes. Yet, according to the 1960 census, Hinds County had 31,548 white and 16,139 Negro males of voting age. The disparity between the two ratios was so great that we were certain that it could not possibly be the result of sheer coincidence.

Under Mississippi law, only men of good character over the age of twenty-one are eligible for jury duty. Prospective jurors are selected from the voting rolls by the county supervisors. If we could show that qualified Negroes had been systematically excluded, we would have raised a constitutional issue as to whether Thomas or any other Rider could get a fair trial.

First, we called a number of local Negroes who met all of the state qualifications. Dr. A. H. McCoy, a dentist, had been a registered voter for thirty years. Reverend R. L. T. Smith's name had been on the rolls for all of thirty-six years and that of high school teacher M. J. Lyell, for fourteen years. Yet none of them had ever entered a Hinds County jury box.

Then we interrogated a dozen white Jackson lawyers who specialized in criminal trials. Former District Attorney Julian Alexander was typical when he swore that both sides in criminal cases usually agreed to reject Negroes without being charged with a preemptory challenge. District Attorney William Waller agreed with the other lawyers we had called that he had never witnessed a criminal trial in which Negroes sat on the jury.

After three Hinds County supervisors stated that they did not discriminate in the selection of jurors, Judge Moore ruled that we had failed to prove our point. "Some of the members of the colored race," he said, "testified that they had not been called to serve on a jury. The court does not find this to be uncommon among the Caucasian race."

On Wednesday morning, we went through the motions of selecting a jury. Just before the noon recess, the all-white, all-Protestant panel was complete. We quickly used up our six allotted challenges and had to accept their replacements at face value. The two lone Negroes in the *venire facias* never reached the jury box.

After lunch, Jack Travis, who was one of four lawyers representing the state, made his opening statement.

"The defendant," he began, "came into Mississippi in a group for one purpose: to cause trouble, to create a disturbance, to cause violence. Ten days before, he did the same thing. He was on a bus at Anniston, Alabama, that was burned. When he went to the bus station at Jackson, there was a large crowd—a dangerous situation—and police ordered him to move on twice and he refused. That, gentlemen," he concluded, "is a breach of the peace!"

Carl Rachlin, CORE's general counsel, handled our opening. "We're not here to discuss bus burnings in Alabama," he told the jury. "We are here to discuss circumstances in the Trailways bus station in Jackson." The defendant had "committed no other act but entering a waiting room of a bus terminal.

"The only question is whether this defendant could have

possibly committed a breach of the peace with all the high-way patrolmen, city policemen, and National Guardsmen who were in that station on May 24."

As the state began to put in its case, it became obvious that we were in for a long trial that was certain to upset Moore's two-a-day schedule. To our surprise, the prosecution had subpoenaed a host of Alabama law enforcement officers. Apparently, the purpose of their presence was to show that the Riders' activities in that state during May had caused great tension and unrest among Mississippians.

But there was another and more insidious aim. This became quite clear when Detective-Sergeant T. H. Cook of the Birmingham Police Department, a self-styled investigator of "un-American activities," testified that the CORE letterhead contained the names of "known Communists." Even though our objection was sustained, the significance of the remark was not lost on the jury.

But neither Cook nor any of the other Alabamians could testify to a single illegal act on the part of Thomas or any of the other Riders. Cook, for example, had observed the defendant in the Birmingham bus terminal.

"As far as I was concerned," he said, "he was a law-abiding citizen."

Eli M. Cowling, a state investigator, had ridden the Greyhound bus that had been burned at Anniston from Atlanta to where it was destroyed.

Q. Did you see Thomas do anything illegal from Atlanta to Anniston?
A. I did not.

Cowling's description of the murderous crowd at Anniston was a graphic one. "They cursed and beat on the outside of the bus," the investigator recalled. "They were mad. They called them Communists and Nazis and told them if they didn't like it here they could leave. The crowd was mad and angry. They were acting like they wanted to whip somebody. About the time two other officers arrived, somebody threw an incendiary or smoke bomb into the rear window."

W. M. Stanley, Montgomery's assistant police chief, stated that martial law had been declared after the arrival of the Freedom Riders had set off two riots in the Alabama capital. "They were caused," he drawled, "because the Riders came to integrate and the people resented it."

On cross-examination, however, Stanley readily conceded that the Riders had done nothing to provoke the attacks.

When he finished with his Alabama witnesses, Travis began to call Mississippians whose testimony was designed to show the extent of the tension caused as soon as the Riders crossed the state line on May 24. Highway patrolmen, city policemen, newspapermen, and Jackson businessmen followed each other with monotonous regularity, each trying to outdo his predecessor in depicting the fear generated by the approach of the Riders.

As I listened to them, it seemed as if they were describing a Martian invasion rather than a few busloads of peaceful American citizens.

But when the last one finally stepped down, there was not a shred of evidence in the record to justify their dread. Neither Thomas nor any other Rider had breached the peace of Alabama or Mississippi.

Just before the supper break, Judge Moore announced that he was thoroughly dissatisfied with the time the trial was taking and that we would go on all night if necessary. From 9 P.M. on, I made periodic motions to adjourn, but it was not until almost eleven o'clock, when we were well into the session's fourteenth hour, that the judge decided to call it a night.

Rachlin and I were dead tired, but we were to get very

little sleep that night. When we reached our motel, we were surprised to find Rabbi Perry Nussbaum of Jackson's Temple Beth Israel waiting for us. He had come, he explained somewhat self-consciously, to beg us to keep Jewish clergymen out of the Freedom Rides. He was afraid that their continued participation would cause a wave of anti-Semitism in Mississippi.

I was extremely depressed by Nussbaum's plea. As a Jew, I had been very proud of the many rabbis like Joseph H. Gumbiner and Allan Levine who had joined the Rides. It seemed to me then, as it does today, that religious leaders, of all people, have an obligation to put into practice the principles that fill their sermons. Simply saying the right things regularly was not enough for this or any other age.

And Jews, who for centuries have known discrimination at first hand, should be among the first to protest when others are its victims. If suffering is redemptive, and I believe that it is, it must unite those who have borne it.

It was almost three in the morning when Nussbaum left. Although we had made it quite clear to him that we could not, as a matter of principle, comply with his request, he asked us to think it over. "You have an obligation to your fellow religionists," he warned.

All told, it had been a long and hard day.

The *State of Mississippi v. Henry Thomas,* which had already earned the distinction of being the longest misdemeanor trial in the state's history, ended the next afternoon. After his fifteenth witness, a Jackson detective who had interviewed Henry Thomas on the afternoon of his arrest, had testified, Travis conferred briefly with his three aides. He then approached the bench.

"The state rests," he informed Moore.

Because we were convinced that the prosecution had not established any breach of the peace on Thomas' part, we saw no need to call any witnesses. We did want, however, to read into the record a decision of the United States Supreme Court banning segregation in interstate commerce.

But Moore would have none of it. "As I have previously ruled," he said sharply, "this is not a segregation case. Only evidence relating to a breach of the peace will be received."

"In the light of your Honor's ruling," Rachlin replied, "we have nothing further to offer. The defense rests."

The summations were brief. We maintained that a peaceful citizen could not be arrested "merely because a policeman ordered him to move on." Travis, on the other hand, insisted that the jury's verdict would decide "whether we will have law enforcement or whether there will be a complete breakdown of law enforcement."

The jury retired at 2:55 P.M. Forty minutes later, it filed back into the courtroom. The not unexpected verdict was guilty as charged.*

Moore immediately sentenced Thomas to a fine of $200 and four months in jail, the same penalty prescribed in Municipal Court exactly three months earlier. Then in a completely unexpected gesture, he raised the defendant's bond to $2,000, four times the amount set in the lower court.

It was clear that Mississippi had no intention of relinquishing its dollar defense to desegregation.

* On April 26, 1965, the United States Supreme Court unanimously reversed Thomas' conviction, as well as those of the other Riders.

CHAPTER 7

Goodbye for Now

Henry Thomas' trial was destined to be one of the most bitterly fought of the Rider trials. Although litigation was to continue for many more months, the prosecution normally limited itself to one witness—the indefatigable Captain Ray—who had begun to spend more time on the stand than he did on the streets. Few actors have ever enjoyed longer runs than Jackson's "antimix" expert.

As the trials wore on, CORE decided that it was far cheaper to interpose *nolo contendere* pleas* than to fight each case out on the merits. The organization could not afford the exorbitant appeal bonds that Moore was requiring, and we felt that a favorable decision by the United States Supreme Court in the *Thomas* case would inure to the benefit of all the Riders.

In addition, it had become impossible to bring more out-of-state attorneys into Jackson. Shortly after the arraignments,

---

* With such a plea, the defendant, although not admitting guilt, offers no defense to the charge against him.

we had publicly asked for volunteers to help us meet Moore's two-a-day schedule. Although the response was substantial, we were able to bring into Mississippi only two young attorneys—Ernst H. Rosenberger of New York City and William Harrell of Macon, Georgia.

No sooner had they begun to appear in court than Judge Moore announced that, because of complaints he said he had received from the Hinds County Bar Association, only Rachlin, Harrell, Rosenberger, and I would be permitted to try the remaining Rider cases.

Without such outside assistance, Jack Young, Carsie Hall, and R. Jess Brown, who comprised three quarters of the state's Negro bar, could do little more than put in a perfunctory defense.

I left Jackson on August 26. As I checked in at the Delta counter at Municipal Airport, I saw once more the "White" and "Colored" signs that distinguished the four restrooms in the terminal. Some day, I said to myself, such signs will come down everywhere, and what we have done here this week may have contributed to their welcome appearance.

They were to start coming down sooner than I expected. Three weeks after the Rides had started in May, Attorney General Kennedy had urged the Interstate Commerce Commission to issue regulations "to remove doubts as to the rights of passengers and obligations of carriers." On September 22, the commission complied with his request.

"We find," it reported, "that in a substantial part of the United States many Negro interstate passengers are subjected to racial segregation in several forms. On vehicles, they continue to be subjected to segregated seating based on race. In many motor passenger terminals, Negro interstate passengers are compelled to use eating, restroom, and other terminal facilities which are segregated."

Beginning on November 1, 1961, all interstate buses would

have to display a sign stating: "Seating aboard this vehicle is without regard to race, color, creed, or national origin." By the New Year, all tickets for interstate travel would have to bear the same legend. In additon, all terminal facilities were now to be operated on a nonsegregated basis.

It had taken the United States just four months to catch up with morality. A few hundred intrepid souls who loved freedom more than they feared arrest and imprisonment had forced their government to face up to the unpleasant reality that it required more than a few favorable Supreme Court decisions to destroy Jim Crow.

But the victory had not been without sacrifice. A Southern jail in the middle of summer is hardly anyone's prototype of an ideal vacation spot. Crowded into steaming cells, often with fewer bunks than occupants, the Riders patiently endured drab surroundings, monotonous food, and inadequate sanitary facilities.

At Parchman Penitentiary, women prisoners were forced to sit around in their underwear in full view of passing male guards. The toilets in each cell were easily visible to the corridor, a condition hardly calculated to make prison life more tolerable. To add to the general misery, unnecessary vaginal examinations were conducted almost every day.

The men were not treated any better. Confined in the penetentiary's maximum security section, a flat one-story building surrounded by a high wire fence topped with rolls of barbed wire, they were rarely permitted out of their cells. Only several letters a week, not exceeding two pages, could be received or sent by them, and they were not allowed to have any printed material. Smoking was strictly prohibited.

On June 18, CORE's Charles R. Oldham visited Parchman. "Under Mississippi law," he wrote the next day, "it is illegal to put individuals convicted of a misdemeanor in the state penitentiary, yet here we are in the maximum security prison normally reserved for hardened criminals. Despite this, the Riders' spirits are high; they are convinced that their example and their willingness to protest the illegal action of Mississippi is worthwhile and is a significant step in the fight to eliminate discrimination."

It would take more than physical discomfort to halt the great adventure that had begun in Washington on May 4.

PART II

MONROE, NASHVILLE,

AND BIRMINGHAM

CHAPTER 8

Another Call

I was not destined to stay home long. Just one week after the Thomas trial ended, I received a call from Wyatt Walker. He told me that serious trouble had developed in Monroe, North Carolina, and that he would like me to join him there. I didn't need persuasion—my Mississippi summer had more than opened my eyes.

Monroe, the county seat of Union County, lies some twenty-five miles southeast of Charlotte. Boasting a population of eleven thousand persons, this farming community was reported to be the southeastern regional headquarters for the Ku Klux Klan. It was also the home of Robert F. Williams, the past president of the Union County branch of the NAACP, whose firm belief in armed self-defense had resulted in his expulsion by the national office.

Williams had first sprung into national prominence in the fall of 1958 when he had come to the aid of two Negro boys, aged eight and nine, who had been sentenced to indeterminate sentences in the reformatory for kissing a seven-year-old white girl. Because of his help, the "Kissing Case," as it came to be known, had ended with the release of the two boys.

After the arraignments of the Riders in Jackson, Williams had wired for volunteers to stop in Monroe on their way home. Seventeen accepted his invitation and, on August 21, arrived in Charlotte. At Williams' suggestion, they moved into a vacant dwelling on Boyte Street in Newtown, Monroe's Negro section, just two doors away from Williams' residence.

The following Tuesday—August 22—the Riders, reinforced by local Negroes, began to picket the Union County courthouse for an end to racial discrimination. Organized into twenty-man units, the demonstrators picketed from eleven in the morning until five at night. They took great pains to observe the provisions of an ordinance regulating picketing which had been hastily passed by the City Council the night before.

Reaction from the white community was swift. The following day, a counter-picket line, composed of young Negro boys who had been hired at twenty-five cents an hour, marched around the courthouse. On Thursday afternoon, cars bearing vicious racist signs such as "Birds Don't Mix—Why Should We?" and "It's Open Season on Coons" patrolled the area. In addition, physical attacks on the Riders began to occur with alarming regularity.

By Friday night, it was obvious that serious trouble was not far off. One Rider was shot in the stomach from a passing car; another was beaten up across the street from the courthouse; a third was cornered by twenty white youths and slammed against a store window. Many were spat upon.

Richard Griswold, a Rider who had been arrested on Tuesday for taking pictures of the demonstration at the square, was savagely beaten in his cell, by Howard Stack, a fellow prisoner who was awaiting trial for passing a bad check. Stack later admitted that he had been instructed by the authorities to attack Griswold.

"The Monroe police and deputy forces of the city of Monroe," he said, "put to me a proposition if I would by force assault one of the Freedom Riders, Griswold, they would see I went free of my charges."

After picketing had ended on Saturday afternoon, the Riders and their supporters marched from the courthouse to Newtown. When they left the square, they were followed by a large crowed of jeering whites. As the demonstrators passed one house, a woman emerged, steak knife in hand, and tried to slash them while her husband threw Coca-Cola bottles into their midst. On the outskirts of Newtown, there were several shots.

Picketing was resumed at three o'clock Sunday afternoon. By 4:30 P.M. the crowd around the courthouse had become so unruly that the Riders called for three Negro-driven taxis to take them back to Newtown. Just as the cabs arrived at the square, several white men in the crowd attacked the pickets. In the melee that ensued, one Monroe policeman was shot in the thigh and a number of demonstrators were mauled.

It took the combined efforts of the city's entire police force and seventy-five state troopers to restore order. Before the square was cleared, thirteen Freedom Riders and thirty-five other persons were under arrest. Charged with inciting to riot, the Riders were held pending the posting of $1,000 bonds.

When news of the clash at the square reached Newtown, Boyte Street was filled with panic-stricken Negroes who expected a momentary attack from the Ku Klux Klan, similar to one which had taken place four years earlier. Outposts were stationed at both ends of the two-way thoroughfare with instructions to stop all cars containing whites. Despite these orders, however, one such vehicle managed to drive the full length of the street shortly after the guards were posted.

Five minutes later, a black Ford Galaxie turned into Boyte Street. When it reached Williams' house, it was stopped by a solid wall of armed Negroes which stretched from one curb to the other. Its passengers—a Mr. and Mrs. G. Bruce Stegall of nearby Marshville—were escorted into Williams' house where they sought refuge for several hours before leaving.

During the night, sporadic gunfire was heard along the Newtown perimeter. With heavily armed white and Negro residents of Monroe roaming around, state troopers carrying rifles and submachine guns patrolled the darkened streets all night. Their presence helped to maintain the uneasy truce that had followed the rioting at the square.

On Monday, August 28, the Union County Grand Jury, which was in regular session, returned indictments charging Williams with kidnapping the Stegalls. When police went to the Negro leader's house to arrest him, they found that he, his wife, and two children had fled. An avowed admirer of Fidel Castro, Williams later managed to escape to Cuba despite an intensive FBI manhunt.

By Tuesday morning, four more true bills were found by the Grand Jury. One of the new defendants, a thirty-four-year-old Negro woman named Willie May Mallory, managed to escape to Cleveland, Ohio. The other three—a white Freedom Rider and two local Negro youths—were taken into custody by the police and held without bond.*

I arrived in Charlotte on Thursday evening. Wyatt Walker, who met me at the airport, drove me to Monroe after we had supper at the bus terminal, one of the few places in the city where whites and Negroes could eat together. It was dark when we arrived in Newtown, the only illumination on most streets being that cast by the dome lights on the state troopers' cars that prowled throughout the area.

The trials of some of the Riders arrested on Sunday, all of whom had been released on bond, were scheduled for Friday morning in Recorder's Court. Since I knew almost nothing

* For the outcome of their joint trial, see Chapter 28.

about the factual situation, Walker had scheduled a meeting between me and my new clients in the home of Dr. Albert E. Perry, a Negro physician who was vice-president of the Union County NAACP branch.

Perry had had his own troubles in Monroe long before the Riders' arrival. A practicing Catholic, he had been charged in 1958 with performing an abortion on a white woman. He was convicted solely on the uncorroborated testimony of the woman involved. After his conviction, he was not permitted to practice medicine in Union County and was forced to move his office to Charlotte.

We met in Dr. Perry's basement, where I spent most of the evening interviewing the Riders. As I questioned them, they seemed most interested in having Len Holt, a Negro lawyer from Virginia who had visited them in prison, assist me during the trials. I assured them that I could use all the help I could get and that I looked forward to working with Mr. Holt.

It was after 1 A.M. when Walker and I drove back to Charlotte where we had reserved a room in a Negro-patronized hotel. Early the next morning, we returned to Monroe and went at once to the Union County Court House. The antique, red-brick structure, which is topped by a grotesque neon cross, is situated on a square block in the heart of town. Legend has it that its construction was financed by money received by a Monrovian as a reward for killing a runaway slave.

Three days earlier, Walker had been thrown down the concrete steps at the west entrance to the courthouse when he tried to enter the building with two Negro reporters. Massive Vann M. Vickery, a Monroe restaurant operator, had blocked the door to the building and, when Walker tried to pass, had picked up the slight minister and hurled him through the air. Walker, who was miraculously unhurt, landed at the base of a granite Civil War monument thirty feet away from the steps.

Vickery, who struggled violently with the police before he was handcuffed and bundled into a patrol car, was charged with public drunkenness and resisting arrest.

As I entered the second-floor courtroom, a handsome, well-built Negro in his early thirties accosted me. "I'm Len Holt," he announced.

This was my first introduction to a most interesting man. Known all over the South as Snake Doctor, Holt plunged into civil rights litigation as soon as he was admitted to the Virginia bar in 1957. Shrewd, articulate, and histrionic, he quickly achieved an almost legendary status as a courtroom performer.

"I'm very happy to work with you," I told him.

The trials of the Riders and their local supporters took most of the day. In addition to the inciting-to-riot charges, the defendants were accused of violating the picketing ordinance, resisting arrest, destroying property, and using profanity. Much to our surprise, Holt and I were successful in obtaining acquittals in the picketing ordinance cases. The measure had been so hastily drafted by the City Council that it contained a sizable loophole.

Everybody else was found guilty by Judge James E. Griffin, a young Harvard Law School graduate whose family ranks high among Monroe's officialdom. The sentences were identical—six months in the county jail, suspended, provided that the defendant "did not engage in or be involved in picketing or any other activity calculated or liable to cause a riot or disturbance for the next two years in Union County."

Although some of our clients thought that appeals should be taken from Griffin's rulings, I felt that discretion was the better part of valor. Two years later, I might not have come to the same conclusion, but in 1961 I could not see the sense of appealing suspended sentences.

An hour after informing Griffin that there would be no appeals, I was on my way to the CORE convention in Washington. But my thought that I had seen the last of Monroe was a sadly mistaken one.

CHAPTER 9

Martin Luther King

After spending the next day at the CORE convention, where I renewed my acquaintance with Charlie Oldham, I returned to New York. Two days later, my secretary buzzed me on the office intercom. "Reverend Walker from Atlanta wants to talk to you," she announced.

Characteristically, Wyatt came right to the point. "First, we want you to defend John Lowry, the white Freedom Rider picked up in Monroe on a kidnapping charge," he said. "Secondly, Dr. King wants to know if you would speak on the legal aspects of the Freedom Rides at the annual convention of the Southern Christian Leadership Conference in Nashville late this month."

Without hesitation, I agreed to both requests. After my experiences in Jackson and Monroe, I knew that I had been hooked. The opportunity to work in a field of law attuned to a surge of history was too much for me to resist. For the first time since my law school days, I sensed the power of the law to help bring about significant and dynamic social change. I devoutly wanted to be part of that process.

I was also deeply interested in meeting Martin Luther King. Naturally, I had heard of the young Baptist minister who had sparked the successful 1955–1956 bus boycott in Montgomery, Alabama, but I knew very little about him. I was only dimly aware that he was the president of the Southern Christian Leadership Conference, a newly formed organization of Negro ministers banded together to end racial discrimination below the Mason-Dixon line.

During the noon recess in Monroe, I had visited John Lowry in his second-floor cell in the Union County Jail. I had gone to see him at the request of his fellow Riders who were worried about his treatment. After I had satisfied myself that he was suffering nothing more than the usual discomfort of Southern jails, I did take a statement from him about the situation in Newtown on the day of the riot.

Since Lowry's trial was not scheduled until October 30,* I concentrated on preparing my remarks for the SCLC convention. I must say that I was more worried about this assignment than I had been about the hearings in Jackson and Monroe. It seemed to me that it was a little presumptuous for someone as new in the field as I was to explain its legal ramifications to people who had been on the firing line for many years. But I had committed myself, and I was determined to do as good a job as I could.

I arrived in Nashville with my wife, Lotte, early on the evening of Wednesday, September 27. We were met at the airport by I. M. Augustine, SCLC's prematurely gray general counsel, who drove us to the Holiday Inn where reservations had been made for us.** After depositing our luggage in our room, we were taken to the Negro-patronized Eldorado Motel for supper.

When we entered the dimly lit dining room, Walker

* It was destined not to be tried until February, 1964.
** Looking back, I wonder why I consented to stay at a white-only motel.

greeted us. "Before you sit down," he said, "I want you to meet Dr. and Mrs. King." With that, he escorted us over to one of the booths where a young Negro couple were eating their supper.

They looked up as we approached. "Mr. President," Walker began, "I'd like you to meet Bill and Lotte Kunstler." With the warm smile that I later learned was so characteristic of him, Dr. King welcomed us to his table.

To say that I was surprised at his appearance would be an understatement. From all that I had read and heard about him, I had expected someone with the guise of an Old Testament prophet. Instead I found myself across the table toward a pleasant-faced, youthful-looking Negro immaculately dressed in a well-tailored business suit. His most distinguishing features were a small, neatly trimmed moustache, high cheekbones, and slightly slanted eyes that gave his face a somewhat Mongolian cast.

I don't remember what we discussed that night but, during our conversation, I was very much aware that I was in the presence of a most unusual man. It wasn't so much what he said to us but the manner in which he expressed himself that conveyed this impression.

Possessed of a soft, low-pitched voice of unusual resonance, Dr. King manages to give the most routine remark a dignity far beyond its importance. I don't know whether it is his inflection or his facial expression but, in some indefinable way, he makes his listener feel that what is being said at the moment is vitally significant.

The main event of the convention's first evening was to have been a Harry Belafonte concert at the Ryman Auditorium. Unfortunately, Belafonte had been hospitalized the day before in New York and, even though his troupe had arrived in town, the hall was half-empty at curtain time. Despite the absence of the star attraction, however, such performers as Miriam Makeba and the Chad Mitchell trio saved the evening.

The next morning, we went to the Clark Memorial Methodist Church, where most of the business of the convention was to be conducted. The keynote address was given by Reverend James M. Lawson, Jr., one of the leading apostles of nonviolent direct action, whom I had met in Jackson four months earlier. I was tremendously impressed by Lawson's insistence that a new social order, not just the improvement of the old one, was necessary for the salvation of the United States.

The following evening I had my first opportunity to hear Dr. King address a mass audience. The scene was Nashville's War Memorial Building, a neo-classic structure that sits on one of the city's many hills. When Lotte and I arrived at 8 P.M., the giant auditorium was already packed although King was not scheduled to speak for several hours.

As soon as we entered the building, the ubiquitous Walker was there to greet us. After assigning someone to escort Lotte to a seat, he led me to the rostrum where I joined some three dozen persons who, for one reason or another, had been selected to surround Dr. King. I was delighted to find Spotswood Robinson, III, the dean of the Howard University Law School and a member of the United States Civil Rights Commission,* in the chair to my right.

The theme of the convention was "The Deep South in Social Revolution." In a moving address, King called for a massive voter registration campaign to "change the political structure of the South and the nation." He outlined a plan for a comprehensive door-knocking campaign to be conducted by SCLC and other civil rights organizations.

"One of the most significant steps a Negro can take," he concluded, "is the short walk to the ballot box."

---

* Robinson later became a federal judge in Washington, D. C.

When Dr. King first started to speak, I must admit I was very disappointed. I don't know quite what I expected to hear but, looking back on that night, I imagine that I had anticipated the Montgomery bus boycott leader to be a cross between Jehovah and William Jennings Bryan. He was neither.

He started out in a low, almost timid voice. As he slowly and methodically transmitted his message to the two thousand people in front of him, I began to wonder why he had been referred to so often as a great orator.

I soon had my answer. Almost before I knew it, I had fallen under the spell of one of the most persuasive voices I had ever heard. Imperceptibly, its cadence quickened and its volume increased as Dr. King, with perfect timing, swept on majestically toward his conclusion.

In anybody else, his choice of language might have been too flowery and his metaphors too far fetched. But with Dr. King, these became virtues rather than faults. Long before he had finished that night, I was convinced that he was using the finest—and clearest—prose ever uttered.

I wasn't the only one who felt this way. Every eye in the War Memorial Building was glued to this medium-sized, stocky man as he stood on tiptoes, clutching the lectern with both hands for emphasis. His capacity audience was transfixed and, except for an occasional involuntary shout of "Yes, Sir!" or "That's right!" there wasn't an audible sound in the hall.

When he finished, King stepped back and dropped his hands to his sides. For one breathtaking second, the mammoth hall was still. Then pandemonium broke out. As wave upon wave of applause reverberated around the amphitheatre, everyone was on his feet. The conquest was complete.

Later that night, Lotte and I discussed the speech in our motel room. "I've never heard anything like it," she said. "At first, I thought it was corny, but as it went on, it changed into something powerful and challenging. I now know what people mean when they say that Dr. King can inspire everyone, from Harvard professors to Georgia tenant farmers."

"Amen," I murmured as I dropped off to sleep.

CHAPTER 10

Shuttlesworth v. Moore

Late in January, 1962, Wyatt Walker called me once more. This time, I was to go to Birmingham, Alabama, on behalf of Reverend Fred L. Shuttlesworth, the former pastor of Bethel Baptist Church and one of the Steel City's most militant Negro leaders.* Since the early fifties, there has seldom been a racial incident in Alabama which did not, in one way or another, involve this outspoken minister.

On October 27, 1958, he and several other Negroes had been arrested for violating Section 311 of the Birmingham City Code, a routine breach of the peace statute. Early that morning, they had met at the office of a loan company in downtown Birmingham and gone in a body to board a Birmingham Transit Company bus at Second Avenue and Nineteenth Street.

Although Shuttlesworth did not enter the bus, his companions did. When they seated themselves in the front section of the vehicle, its driver, I. M. Daniel, immediately

---

* Although Shuttlesworth had just accepted the pastorship of Cincinnati's Revelation Baptist Church, he was destined to remain an integral part of the Birmingham scene.

returned to the barn where he ordered the Negro passengers to move to the rear. Those who refused to do so were arrested by Captain W. J. Haley of the Birmingham Police Department. When they arrived at headquarters, they were joined by Shuttlesworth who had been taken into custody at the bus stop.

All of the defendants were convicted that day in Recorder's Court. A month later, having appealed their cases, they were given an automatic new trial in the Circuit Court of Jefferson County. The evidence indicated that on October 16, 1958, they had met at Shuttlesworth's church and adopted a resolution protesting bus segregation and a new city ordinance which gave common carriers the right to formulate rules for the seating of passengers.

Eleven days later, they had assembled at the loan company office for the avowed purpose of testing this ordinance. Before going to the bus stop, each defendant had received a typewritten sheet warning those about to board buses "to be always orderly, mannerly, courteous, and good citizens." Moreover, they were advised that they were legally free to sit in vacant seats anywhere in the buses of Birmingham.

The uncontradicted testimony at the 1958 trial clearly indicated that there had been no breach of the peace by any of the defendants. Julian A. Gordon, a reporter for the Birmingham *News,* testified that he had witnessed no "loud or boisterous noise" at the loan company office.

Q. And when they came out on the street did you notice any disorder or loud or profane talk on the part of Reverend Shuttlesworth?

A. No, I didn't.

According to Police Officer W. W. Gamble, there had been no offensive conduct by the group when they walked from the loan company to the bus stop.

Q. And even these people walking were not disorderly at the time, were they?

A. No.

Q. They were acting nice and decent, weren't they?

A. They were acting normal.

W. H. Webb, the assistant superintendent of the Birmingham Transit Company, observed no violence at the car barn. Bus driver Daniel confirmed this testimony.

Q. Were they creating any disturbance of any kind?

A. No.

Q. And the only thing those passengers did was just to take seats that were designated for white passengers, is that right?

A. That's right.

Captain Haley, who made the arrests, stated that "there was some singing but no profane language." The reason for the arrests: "They did refuse when the operator asked them in my presence to seat from the rear."

Despite the total absence of any evidence against them, the defendants were found guilty and fined $100 each. On January 8, 1962, after more than three years of appeals, the United States Supreme Court, because of a technicality, refused to overturn Shuttlesworth's conviction. Two weeks later, the minister, who had been free on bail, surrendered himself.

When Walker called me, Shuttlesworth had just begun to serve ninety-two days in the Birmingham City Jail, fifty-two of which represented his failure to pay the original $100 and the balance being accumulated court costs.

Shortly after his surrender, through Arthur D. Shores and Orzell Billingsley, two Negro attorneys, he had applied for a federal writ of *habeas corpus.* A hearing on his application had been scheduled for Wednesday, February 2, before United States District Judge Hobart H. Grooms.

I arrived in Birmingham on Sunday. Shores, who met me at the airport, took me directly to his office in the A. G. Gaston Building. The striking fact about the case which dominated our discussion was that the *very* statute under which Shuttlesworth had been convicted in 1958 had since been declared unconstitutional by Judge Grooms himself.

By late Tuesday evening, we had agreed on a trial strategy. All of our confidence, however, vanished abruptly when we walked into court the next morning. Because the main court-room was being repaired, we had been assigned to the smaller bankruptcy one. This made it impossible to seat the hundreds of Birmingham Negroes who wanted to witness the proceedings.

To enter the room, we had to walk down a corridor jammed with Shuttlesworth's supporters, all of whom looked at us as if we were a cross between Sir Galahad and St. Jude. Such open trust made me feel as if I was an imposter who had come into town under false colors. Lord help us, I whispered to myself, if we couldn't convince Grooms to issue the writ of *habeas corpus!*

No sooner had we sat down at the counsel table than guards brought Shuttlesworth in. Since I had never seen the Birmingham minister, except through the medium of a tele-vision screen, I walked over to him and introduced myself.

"I hope that we'll be able to do something for you, Rev-erend Shuttlesworth," I said.

"Hope is all I live on," he answered. "Just do the best you can."

In order for Judge Grooms to grant our writ, we had to prove to him that there was nothing more we could do in the state courts. Both the Alabama and United States Supreme courts had taken the position that Shuttlesworth's failure to file the transcript of his trial with the Jefferson County Circuit Court within sixty days after deciding to appeal his conviction was tantamount to a deliberate avoidance of available state procedures.

To establish that the failure to file the transcript was not Shuttlesworth's fault, we called the court reporter who had prepared it. He testified that he had transcribed his shorthand notes in plenty of time to have it filed within the requisite sixty-day period. However, he had delayed filing it because he had miscalculated the time in which to do so.

Despite the reporter's testimony, however, Judge Grooms dismissed our petition on the ground that we had not exhausted our state remedies. As Shuttlesworth was led from the courtroom, he stopped at the counsel table for a moment.

"Don't worry," he said to us with a broad smile, "you'll find a way."

As I watched his proud and erect figure leave the courtroom, I felt much better than I had at any time since leaving New York.

It took us six days to "find a way." On February 8, we filed an original writ of *habeas corpus* directly with the United States Supreme Court. We pointed out that, since both Judge Grooms and a federal appellate judge had refused to issue certificates of probable cause of appeal, we would be unable to test Grooms' ruling. Moreover, we felt that the case contained many important questions of law which merited the Supreme Court's attention.

For eighteen days, there was no news from Washington. Suddenly, on Monday, February 26, the same day that it ruled unanimously that no state could require racial segregation of transportation facilities, the Supreme Court acted on our petition. In a brief, unsigned opinion, the nine justices ordered Judge Grooms to release Shuttlesworth on bail within five days if the Alabama courts failed to do so.

Of even more significance was the Court's direction that

Grooms should, after setting bail, "consider all state remedies exhausted and proceed to hear and determine the cause." In other words, he was now free to consider our case on the merits.

Shores and Billingsley got to work at once. Within the five-day period set by the Supreme Court, they applied to every appropriate Alabama court for bail. When one after another refused to act, Grooms ordered Shuttlesworth released on $300 bail.

A testimonial dinner to celebrate Shuttlesworth's victory was held on March 23 at Cincinnati's Netherland Hilton Hotel. Dr. King, as the principal speaker, praised the Supreme Court for its decision. Shuttlesworth was more direct. "Bull Connor almost had my neck," he said, "but God wouldn't let him pull the string!"

Although the minister was free on bond, it was to take almost two years before the case ended officially. After the Supreme Court's decision, Shores and Billingsley asked Judge Grooms to dismiss the charge on the grounds that the evidence in the Circuit Court indicated that no crime had ever been committed.

On December 12, 1963, the case finally reached the end of what Grooms himself called its "devious course." In a nine-page opinion, he held that there was "no evidence whatever in the record to support the conviction."

Since I first met Fred Shuttlesworth in that Birmingham courtroom in the winter of 1961–1962, I have been closely associated with him on many fronts. I now know that I was privileged to represent one of the great men of the civil rights movement.

A year and a half later, when I presented the first annual Back Our Brothers Award to him before a glittering New York City audience, I couldn't help but remember his first words to me—"Hope is all I live on."

Hope has taken him a long, long way.

PART **III**

ALBANY,

GEORGIA

CHAPTER 11

The Gandhi Society for Human Rights

At the SCLC Nashville convention, I had met Clarence B. Jones, a young Negro attorney who represented such diversified clients as James Baldwin, Adam Clayton Powell, and Lorraine Hansberry. When Lotte and I boarded our flight home, he was one of our fellow passengers. As our plane headed northward, Jones asked me to read a typewritten document.

More than one hundred pages in length, it was a draft of a new Emancipation Proclamation that attempted—quite successfully, I thought—to point out that only by the elimination of all forms of segregation was it possible to bring slavery to an end at last.

Jones told me that Dr. King and his associates had been working on the draft for many months. By the time we landed in New York, I was convinced that it was one of the most remarkable documents I had ever read.

The next seven months were so busy that I didn't have any time to think about the draft. Not only was I occupied with the *Shuttlesworth* case and my own neglected practice, but I had picked up a baker's dozen of new civil rights matters. At the request of Melvin L. Wulf, who had just replaced Rowland Watts as legal director of the American Civil Liberties Union, I was involved in defending peace demonstrators in New York City who had been arrested while protesting the resumption by the United States of nuclear testing.

In late April, however, Jones invited me to come to Washington for the presentation by Dr. King of a final version of the document to President Kennedy. The ceremony was to take place at the White House on the morning of May 17, the eighth anniversary of the historic Supreme Court decision outlawing public school segregation.

After the presentation, Jones said, there was to be a luncheon at the Sheraton-Carlton Hotel where King would announce the formation of the Gandhi Society for Human Rights. The idea of the society had originated a few months earlier with some of us who had witnessed at first hand the practical application of Mohandas K. Gandhi's *satyagraha* or "truth-force" to the Southern grass roots protest movement. It was hoped that the new organization could furnish legal and other aid to individuals and communities willing to accept a nonviolent discipline in their quest for fundamental human rights.

No one symbolized the philosophy of the Indian leader better than Dr. King. Because of his efforts in the Montgomery bus boycott, the concept of passive resistance was no longer regarded as alien or bizarre. After Montgomery, non-violent persuasion was firmly and irrevocably established as a primary and meaningful social force within our constitutional, social, and political systems. It was wholly natural that

King had been selected as the society's honorary president.

The new version of the draft, bound in morocco leather with each page encased in cellophane, was delivered to the President on the morning of May 17. Referring to the document as "a landmark contribution in the struggle for civil rights," King asked Kennedy to use the full power of his office to eliminate segregation and discrimination throughout the United States.

"As the hundredth anniversary of the Proclamation of Emancipation draws near," it concluded, "we along with millions of our fellow citizens and the peoples throughout the world are watching and waiting to see whether America has at long last fulfilled the hopes and dreams arising from the abolition of slavery.

"We appeal to you because we love so dearly this great land of ours. We appeal to you because we yearn for the time when we can join hands with our white brethren—North, South, East, and West—and sing in joyous hallelujah, 'Sound the loud timbrel o'er Egypt's dark sea, Jehovah hath triumphed—His people are free!'"

At noon, the Gandhi Society was launched at the Sheraton-Carlton. Before some ninety persons, including the Liberian Ambassador, the Sierre Leone Chargé d'Affaires, five United States Senators, and a number of churchmen, educators, and trade unionists, Theodore W. Kheel, the society's first president, announced its formation.

"We propose," he said, "in the manner of Dr. King and in the manner of that great spiritual leader whose name the society bears, to seek our goals through the ethical course of nonviolent persuasion."

Dr. King was almost lyrical. "Nonviolence is now woven into the fabric of American life in hundreds of boycotts across the South," he said. "It is marked on the jail walls of thousands of cells of Freedom Riders. It sits in majestic, democratic dignity upon thousands of lunch counter stools. It may well mark a new stage for mankind in which his conduct acquired a more civilized quality even as he continues a bitter struggle for broader democratic freedoms.

"We know where we were one hundred years ago—we know where we are today. Where will our nation be one hundred years from now? We can bend its moral arc towards justice if we unroot the twisted tangle of evil statutes which unlawfully deprive Negroes of elementary rights.

"To that noble task nearly twenty million Negroes are dedicated—millions of sincere white Americans stand with us—the invincible will of justice and democracy undergirds our struggle. All of the armies of the earth—all of the parliaments—all of the presidents, prime ministers, and kings—are not stronger than one single moral idea which tenaciously demands fulfillment.

"That fulfillment will come because from the first day an American farmer shouldered a musket for liberty to this day, a national character was being formed, which could grow only if it lived in a climate of decency and fair play. That fulfillment will come because America must do it to remain American in the next one hundred years."

Victor Reuther, who was sitting to my left, leaned over as King finished. "It's too bad," he said, "that more people couldn't have heard that kind of talk."

Fifteen months later, countless millions were to listen breathlessly to "that kind of talk" delivered from a rostrum in front of the Lincoln Memorial.

CHAPTER **12**

First Blood

One of the major functions of the Gandhi Society was "to provide front line emergency legal assistance in lower courts, particularly where nonviolent demonstrations involve mass arrests and imprisonment." As a member of a board of directors which included Joseph Curran, president of the National Maritime Union, Dr. Frank Graham, the former Secretary of the Army, and Dr. Mordecai Johnson, president-emeritus of Howard University, I had enthusiastically voted that we assume this role.

I had no idea that it would soon affect me so intimately. In June, Clarence Jones, who was serving as executive director *pro tem* of the society, called me.

"Bill," he began, "would it be possible for you to go to Albany, Georgia, with me? Trouble is developing there fast, and I've offered the Albany Movement our help on the legal front."

Without even knowing exactly where Albany was or much about the racial situation there, I agreed to accompany Jones.

Albany, which is pronounced All-benny by its residents,

lies 175 miles due south of Atlanta. Its fifty-six thousand inhabitants are fiercely proud of their wide-avenued, clean city which serves as the commercial center of a large farming region of southwest Georgia. According to its Chamber of Commerce, it is the "tenth fastest booming city in the U.S.A."

Although Negroes made up almost forty percent of its population, Albany was a rigidly segregated town. Even when the Interstate Commerce Commission issued its celebrated order of November 1, 1961, desegregating all transportation facilities throughout the United States, Albany police continued to arrest any Negroes who attempted to use the white facilities at the Trailways bus terminal on Broad Street.

It was this refusal to obey the law of the land that led to the first massive demonstrations in December, 1961. Shortly after the ICC order went into effect, five students from the all-Negro Albany State College were arrested by Chief of Police Laurie Pritchett for attempting to use the restaurant in the Trailways terminal. On December 10, eight Freedom Riders were arrested by Pritchett for entering the white waiting room at the Union Railway Terminal.

Three weeks earlier, Albany's Negroes, influenced by the Riders' direct-action approach, had formed the Albany Movement. Dr. William G. Anderson, a local osteopath, was named president; Slater King, a real estate broker, vice-president; and retired railroad man Marion Page, secretary.

"The kids were going to do it anyway," Anderson said. "We didn't want them to have to do it alone."

After the arrests at the railroad station, the Albany Movement went into high gear. Mass meetings were held in most of the Negro churches, and hundreds of demonstrators were arrested for marching down to City Hall to protest the imprisonment of the Freedom Riders. On December 16, the tension was heightened by the arrival of Dr. King and Reverend Ralph Abernathy, SCLC's vice-president.

That night, the two ministers, who had responded to an invitation by the Albany Movement, addressed a mass meeting at Shiloh Baptist Church. When Dr. King started to speak, the medium-sized building was jammed to overflowing. Outside, the sidewalks were packed with people who had been unable to push their way into the church.

Following his speech, King led a mass march downtown. Before the demonstrators could reach City Hall, Chief Pritchett ordered them arrested. They were charged with parading without a permit, obstructing the sidewalk, and disorderly conduct. As they were being booked, someone calculated that 737 persons had been arrested in Albany since the ICC order had gone into effect on November 1.

Just as it appeared that the city was about to become a racial battleground, a truce was declared. After negotiations between Pritchett and C. B. King and Donald L. Hollowell, two attorneys for the movement, all of the imprisoned Negroes were released on property bonds and an early consideration of their grievances by the seven-man City Commission was promised.

This promise was never fulfilled. On January 23, Dr. Anderson appeared before the City Commission with a petition asking for the desegregation of certain public facilities. One week later, the commission bluntly dismissed the petition.

"The demand for privileges," it stated, "will scarcely be heard, wherever and whenever voiced, unless arrogance, lawlessness, and irresponsibility subside."

Albany's Negroes were urged to raise their own moral and ethical standards before seeking equality.

To his credit, Mayor Asa D. Kelley dissented from his colleagues' ruling.

"In my judgment," he said, "the city of Albany has got to recognize that it has a problem and cannot solve that problem by sticking its head in the sand and ignoring that problem. No solution can be reached unless there are lines of communication."

With the December truce fast dissolving, Albany decided to begin the trials of the 737 persons arrested in November and December. On February 27, Dr. King and Reverend Abernathy, along with two local Negroes, appeared in Recorder's Court to answer charges growing out of the December 16 protest march. They were defended by Don Hollowell and C. B. King.

The two lawyers maintained that the arrests had been motivated by Albany's desire to maintain segregation and were therefore unconstitutional. The city countered with the argument that the defendants were being prosecuted solely for parading without a permit and not because they were Negroes.

When Hollowell asked Chief Pritchett to define a parade, the burly police officer replied that he had no ready definition.

Q. Then it's anything you want to make it?
A. In my opinion, yes.

After a three-hour trial, Recorder A. N. Durden reserved decision.

A month later, violence erupted in the Albany Superior Court where the Freedom Riders who had been arrested at the railroad station on December 10 were being tried. When a Negro spectator attempted to sit in the white section of the courtroom, he was knocked to the floor by a deputy sheriff and dragged to the rear of the chamber. Four white sympathizers who tried to join him on the back seats were ejected from the courtroom.

As the spring wore on it was obvious that, just below the surface, Albany was seething. During the first week in April, Dr. Anderson and three other movement leaders were convicted of disorderly conduct for picketing a downtown store. Several weeks later, twenty-six people were arrested for sitting in at an all-white lunch counter.

On April 21, twenty-nine demonstrators were taken into custody for assembling at City Hall to protest the death of Negro Walter Harris. The latter had been shot to death by a policeman who claimed that Harris was resisting arrest. In early June, nine young Negroes were arrested for picketing downtown stores.

The tinder was plentiful and dry. All that was lacking was the spark.

The Battle Is Joined

On July 10, Recorder Durden finally announced his decision in the King-Abernathy case.

Both men were sentenced to forty-five days' imprisonment and a fine of $178 for their part in the December 16 demonstration. Characteristically, they elected to go to jail rather than pay their fines.

The spark caught at once.

The next day—a Wednesday—thirty-two Negroes, led by Tallahassee's diminutive Reverend C. K. Steele, started the long walk downtown. Two blocks from City Hall, they were stopped by Chief Pritchett and two squads of Albany police. As the newly arrested Negroes were being marched to the city jail, they began to sing "We Shall Overcome," an old Negro church song whose modern version had become the anthem of the Freedom movement throughout the South.

Clarence Jones and I arrived in Albany on Thursday afternoon, only to find that King and Abernathy had been mysteriously released that morning. According to Pritchett, an unidentified, well-dressed Negro had suddenly appeared at

Police Headquarters and paid the fines in cash. The two ministers, who were anxious to remain in jail as a symbol of Negro resistance, were forcibly ejected from their cells.

At Shiloh Baptist Church that night, Abernathy expressed his bewilderment at the morning's events.

"I've been thrown out of lots of places in my day," he said wryly, "but never before have I been thrown out of jail."

Early Sunday morning, Wyatt Walker asked me to drive to Camilla, twenty-five miles south of Albany, where some of the previous Wednesday's demonstrators were imprisoned. Because of a shortage of jail space in Albany, many of those arrested in the city had been farmed out to other communities which had available cells. Reverend Steele and two dozen of his followers had been sent to Camilla after their arrests near City Hall.

Despite the fact that it was very early, we were able to get into the squat two-story structure and talk to Steele. He assured us that he was willing to remain in jail as long as the movement wished him to do so. As we left, he asked us to call his wife in Tallahassee and make sure that arrangements had been made to fill his pulpit for that day's eleven o'clock services.

When we left the jail, we walked around to the other side. The Albany women and girls who had been arrested with Steele were confined in a large cell on the second floor, and Wyatt wanted to talk to them before we left Camilla. They crowded to the one window in the room and shouted so many requests at Walker that he had difficulty in writing them down on the clipboard he habitually carried with him.

One woman asked him to make sure that her children were being adequately cared for by a neighbor. Another, an agent for a mail-order cosmetics firm, was worried that her monthly shipment would arrive at her empty house. Several school-girls who were supposed to take make-up examinations in early August were anxious to have their books sent to them. There were two telephone booths across the street from the jail. Walker, who wanted to call Mrs. Steele in Tallahassee, gave me his clipboard and asked me to get in touch with Dr. Anderson in order to expedite the women's requests. Just as I dropped a dime into the coin slot, I noticed four white youths lounging on a bench in front of a garage across the street.

I had just completed my call when they rose and started to walk slowly toward the booths. Instantly, I realized that they must have seen us talking to the imprisoned women and that they were up to no good. I opened the door to my booth and rapped on the glass wall of the other one. When Walker looked up, I pointed to the youths who, by this time, were only thirty feet away.

"Put your foot up against the door so that they can see it," he said. "That way, they'll know that the only way they will be able to get at you is to break the glass and risk cutting an artery."

I did as he suggested.

His advice proved sound. When the four boys sauntered up to the booth, they pushed against the door. Finding it securely barred by the leverage exerted by my foot, they contented themselves with spitting against the glass. After doing the same to Walker's booth, they walked off down the street.

"That was good advice," I told the slim minister.

"I learned that in Alabama," he replied. "A few tricks like that make it possible to stay in civil rights work and out of the hospital."

With the City Commission steadfastly refusing to negotiate with "law violators," the movement decided to test all "white only" public facilities and accommodations in Albany. Between Tuesday, July 17, and Friday, July 20, attempts were made to desegregate the Carnegie Library, five downtown lunch counters, the swimming pool, athletic fields and a picnic area at Tift Park, and the bus station restaurant. The result: further mass arrests.

Jones and I, who had left town late on Sunday, returned a week later. As we walked through Atlanta's green-glass airport terminal toward our Southern Airways flight to Albany, we ran into an excited Don Hollowell. He informed us that United States District Judge J. Robert Elliott, a longtime political ally of the Talmadge dynasty, had just issued a sweeping injunction which barred Albany's Negroes from "unlawful picketing, congregating or marching in the streets, and from any act designed to provoke breaches of the peace."

Hollowell was en route to New Orleans to find Chief Judge Elbert P. Tuttle of the United States Court of Appeals for the Fifth Circuit. Tuttle, who was rumored to be vacationing near the Louisiana city, had the power to set aside Elliott's order.

After seeing Hollowell off, we boarded our flight. Wyatt Walker, who had flown from New York with us, was the only major defendant on Elliott's order who had not been served. Because of this, we fully expected to be met by a federal marshal when we landed at Albany Municipal Airport.

Our fears proved groundless—for the time being, at least. The small airport looked deserted when we touched down and Reed Collins, a reporter for a New York radio station, remarked that it reminded him of a Western ghost town. The sign, "Welcome to Albany, Georgia," that faced the runway seemed strangely out of context with what we knew was happening in the strife-torn town.

We were driven to Dr. Anderson's house on Cedar Avenue, an unpaved road whose red clay surface must have been impassable for wheeled vehicles after a heavy rainstorm. Inside, we found Dr. King and the entire high command of the Albany Movement. From the expression on their faces, it was obvious that they were deeply concerned with the effect of Elliott's injunction.

"I don't mind violating an unjust state injunction," King was saying, "but I won't violate a federal one."*

Just as I asked to see a copy of the order, the front door burst open. A man who never bothered to remove his hat entered, and in a gruff voice announced that he was a federal marshal looking for Reverend Walker. When Wyatt identified himself, he was handed a copy of the injunction. Without a word, he turned and gave it to me.

As soon as I had read the stiffly worded document, I was convinced that Elliott's restraining order was unlawful. Not only did it forbid conduct which was protected by the First Amendment, but it did so for the most specious of reasons. The demonstrations by Albany's Negroes, Elliott had decided, violated the civil rights of the city's white residents.

That evening, followed by two of the detectives who were always stationed around the Anderson house, Dr. King and several of us took a long walk around the neighborhood. During our stroll, I constantly stressed the fact that I considered the injunction illegal. While I did not advise King to violate it, I made it quite clear that I did not think he was bound by it.

But he was adamant. Since the restraining order bore a federal imprimatur, he was determined not to flaunt it.

"The federal courts," he said, "have given us our greatest victories and I cannot, in good conscience, declare war on them. Elliott may be a segregationist, but he is still a United States District Judge, and I'll rely on the upper courts to reverse him."

It was eight o'clock when we returned to Anderson's house. Although King had decided that, because of the injunction,

* Two-and-a-half years later, in Selma, Alabama, he was to take the same position.

he would not attend the regular Saturday night mass meeting, he was not able to remain away. At eight-thirty, he asked Dr. Anderson to drive him to Shiloh. Minutes later, accompanied by his wife, Coretta, Jones and myself, he arrived at the rear entrance to the church.

It was obvious that Dr. King was extremely troubled over the passive role forced upon him by the injunction. Determined not to violate its terms, he remained in the pastor's study listening to the impassioned speeches being delivered from the pulpit to an overflow audience. For the first time since our meeting in Nashville, I felt sorry for him.

Suddenly, we were conscious of a new voice out front. Reverend Samuel B. Wells of nearby Williams Springs Baptist Church, whose courage easily outran his formal training as a clergyman, was speaking.

"I've heard about an injunction," he shouted, "but I haven't seen one. I heard a few names, but my name hasn't been called. But I do know where my name is being called. My name is being called on the road to freedom. When shall we go? Not tomorrow! Not at high noon! Now!"

At this point, he was drowned out by his listeners. "Freedom! Freedom! Freedom!" they roared.

"We will go to the City Hall," Wells continued when the cheering had subsided, "and we will protest peacefully the evils that have been grinding the life out of our spirits for ninety-nine years!"

At his last words, the audience surged to its feet. When the short, dark minister walked down the center aisle of the church and out the building's front door, almost two hundred people, most of whom were teen-agers, were in his wake.

The injunction had failed.

King was jubilant. "They can stop the leaders," he exulted, "but they can't stop the people."

He insisted on following the marchers downtown. As soon as they had left the church, we piled into Dr. Anderson's station wagon and drove after them. Strung out behind Wells, they were singing "I Ain't Gonna Let Nobody Turn Me 'Round" as they headed for City Hall. A green police sedan kept pace with them as a detective radioed their location and route to headquarters.

A block from their destination, the Negroes were met by Chief Pritchett and two squads of Albany police.

"Well, Rev," Pritchett asked, "you got a permit?"

Wells' answer was blunt and to the point.

"I have no permit," he replied calmly. "We're going to City Hall to pray."

The police chief lifted his electric bullhorn to his lips.

"Does anybody in this group have a permit?" he shouted. "I want to tell you you are in violation of the city ordinances!"

There was no answer from the marchers. At a signal from Wells, they fell to their knees in the center of the street and bowed their heads in silent prayer.

"Arrest them all!" Prichett ordered.

A minute later, the demonstrators were being led by their captors to jail.

We had just started to drive back to Anderson's when two Negroes in a Volkswagen flagged us down.

"Be careful," one of them yelled. "We heard that there are four white men with rifles looking for Dr. King."

The small frame house was dark when we pulled into the driveway. Because of the warning we had just received, we decided to leave it that way. After pulling down all the shades, we located a candle and set it on top of the upright piano that stood against one wall of the living room.

The minutes began to drag by slowly. Just as I felt that the tension was becoming intolerable, Dr. King stood up and walked over to the piano. "Would anyone care to sing?" he asked quietly. As if we were one person, we rose and formed around the upright.

All at once, a young woman who proved to be an excellent pianist emerged from nowhere. From the moment that she began to play "This Little Light of Mine," the fears and discouragements of the long day disappeared, to be replaced by a transcendental feeling of love and hope for all humanity.

As we sang, I wished that there was some way to remove the roof above us so that the whole world could witness what I was witnessing and feel what I was feeling. I wanted everyone everywhere to listen to five Negroes and one white man singing freedom songs by the light of a single candle in a darkened house on a dirt road in southwestern Georgia.

An hour after we began singing, we ended with "We Shall Overcome." We linked hands together as we raised our voices. We ended with a prayer. While we hummed the melody, Dr. King asked for our protection from those who would do us harm. When he said Amen, we joyously finished the refrain. "Oh, deep in my heart, I do believe, we shall overcome some day."

After breakfast the next morning, Clarence Jones and I went down to C. B. King's law office in Harlem, Albany's Negro business district. C. B. King, a Western Reserve graduate, is a stocky, intense man in his early thirties whose bitterness at the white man's treatment of the Negro is hardly concealed by a tendency to pontificate on racial matters in lofty philosophical terms. I have the deepest respect for him and have always felt privileged to work with him.

Since Dr. King and Dr. Anderson were having an early afternoon press conference, we were anxious to give them a report as soon as possible on what we hoped to do about Elliott's injunction. Fortunately, it did not take us long to find the necessary precedents to support our earlier feeling that the restraining order was totally invalid. Our research concluded, we hurriedly prepared a request to Judge William A. Bootle, Elliott's immediate superior, for a vacation of the latter's order.

The press conference, which was being held in Anderson's backyard, was already in progress when we returned from C. B. King's office. We managed to slip a note to Dr. King, reiterating that, in our opinion, the injunction was illegal and that, if we could not convince Elliott of this, we would try to locate Bootle in Macon.

After scanning our note, Dr. King began talking about the injunction to the yardful of newsmen. "It is a continuation of a pattern that is developing in many areas of the Deep South," he said. "Injunctions and temporary restraining orders are being used to stifle and block the movement to exercise and achieve the constitutional rights of Negro people."

He expressed his deep regret that some Southern federal judges were "engaged in a conspiracy with state and local political leaders to maintain the evil system of segregation." But this did not mean that he or his associates would violate their orders.

"Out of respect for the leadership the federal judiciary has given," he concluded, "we have agreed to obey the order issued by Judge Elliott and to work vigorously in higher courts to have it dissolved."

We spent the rest of the day trying to locate Judge Elliott. Toward evening, we learned that he had gone to visit his daughter in North Carolina shortly after issuing the injunction at midnight Friday. Our next step was to apply to Judge Bootle in Macon.

That evening, a most unusual conference took place in Slater King's backyard. The brother of C. B. King and vice-president of the Albany Movement, Slater lived in a modern one-story house near Dr. Anderson. Because of some dissatisfaction with top strategy in Albany by members of the Student Nonviolent Coordinating Committee (SNCC), Dr. King had agreed to meet with them and thrash out any differences of opinion.

SNCC, which grew out of the Greensboro, N.C. sit-ins in early 1960, had been organized several months later through the efforts of Ella Baker, then SCLC's executive director. Composed, for the most part, of unmarried white and Negro college students, its personnel, many of whom quickly adopted a uniform of blue denims and sneakers, were singularly free from the day-by-day responsibilities that plagued adults in the movement. What SNCC considered a lack of militancy on the part of Dr. King and his aides had resulted in some friction between the two organizations.

Although no decisions were reached that night, the discussion did serve to clear the air. In the main, Dr. King listened patiently to the grievances of such veterans of the Southern struggle as Cordell Regan, Charlie Jones, William Hansen and Charles Sherrod who were sprawled on the lawn around him. In a sense, the gathering had many of the aspects of a group therapy session with catharsis and not action being its immediate result.

It was still going strong when I tore myself away. C. B. King, Clarence Jones, and I had arranged to drive to Macon early the next morning in the hope that we would be able to persuade Judge Bootle to dissolve the injunction. Suddenly, sleep seemed more compelling than even the fascinating outdoor conference that showed no signs of abating.

CHAPTER 14

A Victory and a Loss

We had planned to leave for Macon early Monday morning. At six-thirty, Dr. Anderson's wife, Norma, padded into the tiny bedroom I was sharing with Ralph Abernathy and Vincent Harding, a Mennonite minister, and shook me awake.

"C. B. will be here in an hour," she whispered. "Hurry up and get dressed. I've got coffee on the stove."

Promptly at seven-thirty, C. B. King called for me. Emanuel Jackson, the movement's treasurer and an excellent driver, had volunteered to chauffeur us the eighty miles to Macon. Jackson, known to everyone as Bo, is a giant of a man who once enjoyed a responsible position as Negro circulation manager of the *Herald,* Albany's only daily newspaper. He had been fired by publisher James D. Gray, a transplanted New Englander with pronounced racist views, when he became active in the movement.

Despite a flat tire a few miles out of Albany, we arrived in Macon just after ten o'clock. When we went to Bootle's chambers in the post office building, we were met by a young man who announced that he was the judge's law clerk. "The judge is on vacation," he informed us, "but I will read any papers you may have over the telephone to him."

We handed him the request to set aside Elliott's order which we had prepared the day before in C. B. King's office. When he left to call the judge, we sprawled on the hard-backed chairs in the anteroom. It was a brutally hot day and only Bo's discovery of a Coca-Cola dispensing machine in the corridor made the waiting tolerable.

Twenty minutes later, Bootle's clerk returned. From the expression on his face, we knew that we had failed. "I read your petition to the judge," he said, "but he refused to disturb the ruling of another district judge. I'm very sorry."

As we left the building, we passed a telephone booth on the first floor. For some reason, we decided to put in a call to Judge Tuttle's office in Atlanta. We knew that Hollowell had not been able to locate the judge in New Orleans and, if we were willing to reach for straws, it was just possible that he might have returned to the Georgia capital.

To our surprise, he was in his chambers. After we had explained the situation to him, he suggested that we drive to Atlanta at once. "I don't know what I can do," he said, "but I'm willing to look at your papers and discuss the situation with you." We told him that we would come to Atlanta as fast as we could get there.

With almost two hours of driving ahead of us, there was plenty of time in which to think out our strategy. As we sped northward, C. B. King and I mulled over the main legal question that Tuttle had to resolve. Did a federal judge have the power to enjoin Negroes from demonstrating for their constitutional rights because he felt that they were violating those of the white community?

The more we thought about it, the more convinced we became that the question had to be answered in the negative.

The Fourteenth Amendment and the Civil Rights Acts*
were designed to protect minority groups and it seemed
grotesque to us that they could be used against them. We
were sure that if Tuttle gave us an opportunity to argue the
point, he would see it our way.

When we arrived in Atlanta, Bo drove us to the Old Post
Office Building. While he parked the car, C. B., King, Jones,
and I went at once to Tuttle's fifth-floor office where we
found a sizable group of reporters already waiting for us.

This was my first meeting with the Chief Judge of the
Fifth Circuit. A slender, ascetic-looking man in his late
sixties, he had emigrated to Georgia from New York more
than thirty years earlier. Like so many of the South's better
federal judges, he had been named to the bench by Eisenhower.

It is tragically ironic that Kennedy's judicial appointments
in the deep South included so many outright racists. The
political necessity of clearing appointments to the federal
bench with such Democratic stalwarts as Eastland, Russell,
and Byrd has resulted in a surfeit of district judges devoted to
the continuation of segregation. Lacking the necessity of
observing such protocol, Republican Presidents have normally had a much freer hand in the selection of judges.

Tuttle was extremely gracious. After ushering us into his
inner office, he listened patiently to the saga of our long trek
from Albany to Atlanta. When we had finished our tale, he
sat in silence for a moment. "I'll give you a hearing in the
morning," he finally said. "Make sure that you notify the
Albany officials that it will be held in the Court of Appeals at
ten."

Before we left, he directed us to brief three points of law.

* Adopted in 1868, The Fourteenth Amendment forbids the states to deny
the equal protection of the laws to any person; the Civil Rights Acts refer to
federal legislation enacted in 1866, 1870, and 1875 to grant Negroes legal and
political status equal to that of white persons.

First, he wanted to know whether he should sit as a circuit or a district judge in considering the validity of Elliott's restraining order. Second, he needed to be sure that, in either capacity, he had the power to dissolve the injunction. Last, was the injunction as invalid as we claimed it was?

When we left the Old Post Office Building, we were exuberant. We knew that getting a hearing was half the battle and we were certain that we would be able to answer all of Tuttle's questions to his satisfaction. But we still had a whole night of work before us. Not only did we have to do a thorough job of research, but we had to put together the necessary legal papers with which to make a good showing the next morning.

After sending a telegram about the Tuesday hearing to the Albany City Attorney, we got down to the work of the evening. In order to make sure that nothing was overlooked, we gave every lawyer we could jam into Don Hollowell's office a different assignment. Although Don himself was out of town on a murder case, Horace Ward and Howard Moore, Jr., two of his associates, were available and worked through the night with us.

About two in the morning, Constance Baker Motley of the NAACP Legal Defense and Educational Fund arrived in Atlanta. Mrs. Motley, whom I had known slightly at Columbia Law School, is an extraordinarily gifted attorney who has had a large role in the landmark test cases that did so much to set the stage for the Negro protest movement of the sixties. A tall, handsome woman with an imperious mien, she recently became the first woman President of the Borough of Manhattan.

Mrs. Motley and I divided the main argument between us. I was to answer Tuttle's first two questions while she was to discuss the invalidity of Elliott's injunction.

It was seven in the morning when we finished our preparation. All of the necessary papers had been typed, and we had even drafted a long overdue federal lawsuit to desegregate all of Albany's public facilities. Bo Jackson, who had done yeoman service all night, drove Mrs. Motley to a friend's house and then dropped the rest of us off at the only integrated motel in the city.

Sleep was out of the question, but we did find time to take showers and change our shirts. Mrs. Motley even managed to squeeze in a hairdresser's appointment before court opened.

The courtroom was crowded when we walked in at 9:45 A.M. We had asked Dr. King and the other leaders of the movement to come to Atlanta for the hearing, and we were glad to see them sitting in the first row of the spectators' section. We didn't know whether Tuttle intended to take any testimony, and we thought that it would be wise to have some prospective witnesses present if he decided to do so.

Because we represented the moving parties, we were directed by the bailiff to the counsel table on the right of the bench. To our left sat the lawyers for the City of Albany. There were Henry Rawls, the portly city attorney, Mayor Asa D. Kelley, Jr., and Freeman Leverett, a state deputy assistant attorney general.

When Tuttle mounted the bench, I stood up. "If the court please," I began, "I believe that we have the answer as to whether your Honor can sit as a district or a circuit judge."

He raised his hand. "You don't have to go on any further, Mr. Kunstler," he said in his quiet crisp voice. "I have decided that it is perfectly proper for me to sit as a circuit judge."

He then proceeded to ask me a flurry of questions relating to the background of the case. Where was Judge Elliott? Had I tried to contact him in North Carolina? Had I spoken to Judge Bootle? When had the injunction been issued? Had all the defendants named in it been served? Had we applied to any other circuit judge for relief?

Then it was Mrs. Motley's turn. During an interlude in Jackson a year earlier, I had watched her trying the James Meredith case. I was very much impressed with her competency then, and she more than lived up to my remembrance of her. Skillfully and with infinite precision, she outlined the applicable law and concluded with the convincing proposition that Elliott's order was completely illegal.

Albany's case was presented by Freeman Leverett who prefaced his argument with the statement that he was appearing at the request of Governor S. Ernest Vandiver. This was no surprise to us as it was an open secret that the governor's legal staff had conceived the plan of applying to Elliott for the injunction. Leverett's rationale: The city's white residents had been denied equal protection of the laws because policemen had been withdrawn from their regular assignment to prevent violence.

As soon as the arguments were concluded, Tuttle announced his decision from the bench. "The trial court had no jurisdiction to enter this order at all," he said bluntly. The reason: Judge Elliott had based his decision on two Reconstruction statutes that could only be used to control unlawful state action which violated the civil rights of individuals.

I was so excited by Tuttle's decision that I tried to shake Mrs. Motley's hand before he had finished speaking.

"Shhhh," she whispered to me, "wait until he leaves the bench!"

My jubilation was shared by the people of Albany when the news of the injunction's dissolution reached them. Mass meetings were immediately scheduled for that very night at Shiloh and Mount Zion Baptist churches. Dr. King and his staff left Atlanta at once in order to be present at both meetings which were set for 8 P.M.

Although I flew back to New York with Mrs. Motley, I soon learned that violence had broken out shortly after the meetings began at the two churches. As soon as Dr. King had spoken at Shiloh, a group of forty demonstrators marched out of the building and headed toward City Hall. They were arrested as soon as they reached the downtown area.

In Albany's Harlem, an angry crowd of two thousand Negroes gathered in the streets to protest the new arrests. When more than a hundred policemen and state highway patrolmen attempted to clear the area, the air was filled with flying rocks, bricks, and soda pop bottles. One trooper was struck on the cheek by a rock and taken to the hospital. According to Pritchett, the wounded man lost two teeth.

The next day, Dr. King canceled plans to lead a mass demonstration and declared a day of penance because of the violence in Harlem. He spent the day visiting the shops, poolrooms, and taverns on South Jackson Street, urging every Negro to remain peaceful.

"We abhor violence so much," he told reporters who followed him from place to place, "that when it occurs in the ranks of the Negro community we assume part of the responsibility for it."

We had won a great victory in Atlanta, but the bricks and bottles that punctuated it had cast a blight on it. I couldn't help but recall Gandhi's prophetic words when, in 1936, he told a visiting American clergyman that "it may be through the Negroes that the unadulterated message of nonviolence will be delivered to the world."

Nothing, I fervently hoped, would stand in the way of the prophecy's fulfillment.

CHAPTER 15

In the Right Court

On Friday, July 27, Dr. King and Dr. Abernathy, who for almost two weeks had been trying without success to talk to the City Commission, decided to adopt a more direct approach. At two-fifteen that afternoon, the two ministers, accompanied by Dr. Anderson and seven other Negroes, arrived at City Hall in a station wagon. As they piled out of the vehicle, Chief Pritchett barred their way.

"We would like to speak to the mayor and the commissioners," demanded Dr. Anderson.

Pritchett replied that none of the city officials was in City Hall. "I'm asking you to leave and go about your business," he told the group. When Anderson repeated his request, the police officer informed him that he would have to arrest everyone who did not leave.

Abernathy stepped forward. "We'll just pray until they see fit to see us," he said. Pritchett pointed to a handful of curious white men on the sidewalk who had been attracted by the scene. "You're creating a disturbance as you can see," he told the minister. "Move on!"

At this point, Dr. King intervened. "Dr. Abernathy, would you lead us in prayer," he asked. The Negroes bowed their heads. "We pray, oh God," Abernathy began, "that Thou would touch the hearts of the people and let them know that there will be no peace in this community until we talk over our differences."

When Abernathy had finished, Pritchett stepped forward. "All right," he said quickly, "you've had your prayer. You've made your point. Now move on or you're under arrest."

The demonstrators stood fast.

The chief waved to his waiting men. "Take them all into City Hall," he ordered. King and his companions were led into the stone structure where they were booked on charges of disorderly conduct, congregating on the sidewalk, and disobeying the command of an officer. When they refused to post $200 cash bonds, they were taken to cells at the rear of the building.

Two hours later, with Mayor Kelley watching from the steps, fourteen youths and four girls knelt on the sidewalk in front of City Hall. "We are praying for our white and black brothers all over the South who are not yet free," one of them said as the others bent their heads.

At the prayer's conclusion, Pritchett ordered the group to leave the area. When they refused, he placed them under arrest and told them to walk into the building.

Eleven did so, but the rest remained on their knees. "Walk or be toted in there," the chief said. No one moved. Pritchett turned his head. "Bring out the stretchers!" he ordered. At his words, policemen rushed out with green litters, and the Negroes were picked up one by one and dropped heavily onto them. They were then carried into City Hall.

For the next two weeks, Albany seethed with excitement. On July 28, William Hansen, a white SNCC field worker from Cincinnati who had been arrested in front of City Hall the day before, was severely beaten by a trusty at the county jail. His jaw was broken, his lip was split, and a number of his ribs were broken. According to Hansen, a deputy sheriff had encouraged the trusty to attack him.

The following day, C. B. King was caned by Sheriff Cull Campbell when he tried to check on Hansen's condition. One observer later stated that Campbell had ordered the lawyer to leave his office.

"As Mr. King was about to reply, Mr. Campbell picked up a walking stick out of a basket containing several, and hit Mr. King viciously over the head, breaking the cane."

Pritchett, who called C. B. King's beating "very regrettable," was busy arresting people by the score for praying in front of City Hall. On the very day that the lawyer was caned, the chief took twenty-eight sidewalk worshipers into custody. A few days later, thirty more, including Elizabeth Porter Wyckoff, the former Mount Holyoke professor of Greek who had been my first client in Jackson a year earlier, were on their way to jail.

As August began, the total number of demonstration arrests since December edged toward twelve hundred.

On July 31 hearings began before Judge Elliott on Albany's petition for a permanent injunction against the Albany Movement. Although Tuttle had dissolved the temporary restraining order of July 20, he had not dismissed the case. For seven straight days, city officials paraded to the stand in an attempt to prove that, as Pritchett put it, "racial tensions have reached a boiling point."

When testimony ended on August 7, the Justice Department, which had been conspicuously silent since December, finally took a cautious stand. It intervened in the injunction proceeding and asked Elliott to dismiss the city's petition. Albany, it argued, had shown such bad faith that it did not merit federal relief. The judge replied that he wasn't sure when he would decide the case. He was destined never to do so.

The Justice Department's long belated action followed close on the heels of a meeting on the Albany crisis held by Attorney General Robert F. Kennedy in his office late on the afternoon of August 2. SCLC was represented by Reverend Walter Fauntroy of Washington and myself; CORE, by Richard Haley; the American Civil Liberties Union, by Melvin L. Wulf; and the NAACP, by Roy Wilkins and Clarence Mitchell. Burke Marshall, the Attorney General's assistant for civil rights, also sat in.

Robert Kennedy, whom I had never met before, impressed me as a youthful, almost boyish man. With his rolled-up shirtsleeves, his unbuttoned collar, and his unruly hair, he reminded me of a daring office boy who was trying out the boss' chair in his absence. Despite the seriousness of our visit, I could not shake the feeling that the real Attorney General would walk in at any moment.

Even the magnificence of the beautiful vaulted office could not make me believe that I was just a few feet away from the second most powerful man in the United States. My inability to accept this reality was heightened by the score of finger paintings and crayon sketches that were scotchtaped to the long wall facing Kennedy's cluttered desk. I later learned that they were the creations of his many children who used their father's office for exhibition purposes.

Throughout our discussion, the Attorney General seemed extremely distracted and ill at ease, not at all the coolly calculating political being who, barely two years earlier, had helped maneuver his brother into the Presidency. I sensed that his mind was elsewhere and that it was only with the greatest of effort that he forced himself to remain with us.

At one point, he received a telephone call, following which he announced, almost gleefully, that he had to leave us for a while to make an appearance at a reception for Anthony J. Celebrezze, the newly appointed Secretary of Health, Education, and Welfare.

Only once did Kennedy show any animation. When Clarence Mitchell bitterly criticized the Justice Department for its inaction in Albany and elsewhere, the Attorney General became extremely agitated.

"You know as well as I do, Clarence," he said sharply, "that we have done what we can do under existing law. We could do a great deal more if our hands weren't tied."

I did not return to Albany until Thursday, August 9. I had spent the early part of the week defending foreign correspondent William Worthy against a charge that in late 1961 he had entered the United States from Cuba without a passport. Since the State Department had refused to renew his passport because he had defied it by going to Communist China in 1956, Worthy had traveled to Cuba without one.

His trial had taken place in a federal court in Miami on August 8 and he had been found guilty of violating a statute that made it a crime for any American citizen to return home without a valid passport. He faced a possible penalty of five years in jail, a fine of $5,000, or both. Fortunately, his conviction was eventually reversed when the statute upon which it was based was declared unconstitutional.

After the trial, Worthy, Lotte and I flew from Miami to Tallahassee. In the Florida capital, we rented a car and drove the seventy miles to Albany. When we entered the city, I became hopelessly lost while trying to find Dr. Anderson's house.

It was almost dinner time, and the streets in the Negro section were deserted. Finally, we saw a white man in clerical garb walking along the road. We stopped near him and asked if he knew the way to Anderson's home. "I'm going there myself," he answered, "and I'd be happy to direct you."

In the car, he introduced himself as Reverend Forrest Johnson, the pastor of the Edgehill Congregational Church in Riverdale, New York. A tall, strikingly handsome man in his middle thirties, he had come to Albany to demonstrate Northern religious support for the movement. He proved to be an excellent guide and in a matter of minutes we arrived at our destination.

The house was all but empty as almost everyone had gone to the Shiloh Baptist Church for a mass meeting. Norma Anderson managed to scrape up enough fried chicken to assuage our hunger, and then she drove Lotte and Worthy to the church. I headed for the city jail to see Elizabeth Wyckoff.

She was overjoyed to see me. After we had brought each other up to date on our goings and comings since Jackson, she asked me whether I would consider instituting another *habeas corpus* proceeding for her. Since I had harbored the same thought myself, I didn't need much urging.*

I then drove to Shiloh where the mass meeting was in full swing. Most of the speakers reminded the overflow audience that King and Abernathy, who were starting their third week in jail, would be tried in Recorder's Court the next morning. Since it was not likely that they would be released, mammoth protest demonstrations were being planned.

Coretta King, for example, was scheduled to lead a mothers' march to City Hall after the trial. When I returned to Anderson's house later that evening, I found that Lotte had volunteered to join the march. A briefing session for all interested women had been set for Friday morning at Shiloh.

I did not attend King's trial because I was busy preparing and filing Dr. Wyckoff's *habeas corpus* application in federal

* Shortly after Dr. Wyckoff's petition was filed, she was released, thus mooting her application.

court. When I arrived at Recorder's Court, I met the defendants leaving the building.

"We were given $200 fines and sixty-day jail sentences," Dr. King told me, "but they were all suspended."

With King and Abernathy suddenly free, the protest demonstrations that had been planned were canceled. Instead, the movement turned its attention to testing the truth of City Attorney Rawl's insistence during the trial that there was no segregation in Albany. Small interracial teams were organized and instructed to visit various facilities.

That night I accompanied the first of these, a group composed of white and Negro ministers, which attempted to integrate the "white only" Beck's Cab Company. While the Negro member of the team hid behind a telegraph pole, his white companions flagged down a passing taxi. As soon as the vehicle had come to a halt, all four clergymen piled into it before the surprised driver knew what was happening. The ruse was successful as the ministers managed to ride downtown and back without incident.

While I was serving as "official witness" to the cab integration project, my wife and Penelope Patch, a young white girl from Swarthmore College who was spending the summer with SNCC, were asked to inspect a segregated bowling alley across the street from Central Baptist, the largest Negro church in Albany. As they left the church, they were accosted by a medium-sized white man who asked them whether they had been inside the building. When they replied that they had, his face reddened with anger.

"Why would people like you want to get mixed up with niggers?" he demanded harshly.

The two women pushed by him, crossed the street, and entered the bowling alley where they proceeded to note the location of the assignment desk, the alleys, and the restrooms.

When they left the building, they found the same white man waiting for them on the sidewalk.

"I suppose you'd sleep with niggers, too," he snarled.

Although Lotte did not answer him, Penny was not so reticent.

"I would if I felt like it," she retorted.

The man's rage knew no bounds. "God damn you!" he roared as he raised his clenched fist. A scream rose to my wife's lips but she was determined to be nonviolent and nonresistant in the best Gandhian tradition.

She closed her eyes and waited silently for the blow to fall. Miraculously, it did not. Mystified by the apparent willingness of a tiny white woman to be beaten for what she believed in, the man could not bring himself to strike her. With a muttered oath, he dropped his hand and walked away into the night.

On Saturday morning, integrated teams were sent out to test most of the city's public facilities. Toward noon, I found myself on my way to play tennis at all-white Tift Park with Reverend Henry Elkins, a white clergyman who assisted Dr. King at his Atlanta church, and Reverend Joseph Smith, the Negro pastor of Salem Baptist Church in Albany. As we headed toward the park in Elkins' Volkswagen, we were followed by a caravan of newsmen.

When we arrived at the courts, we discovered that the nets had been removed. Nothing daunted, we started to volley back and forth. We had only time to hit one or two balls before Chief Pritchett interrupted us.

"You're in the wrong court, counselor," he told me. "I'll have to ask you and your friends to leave."

Since we had been warned to avoid arrest if possible, we walked off the netless court.

When we got back into the car, Elkins said that, if we couldn't play on the white courts, then surely there could be no objection if we resumed our game at Carver Park, on the Negro side of town. We immediately headed in that direction.

When we pulled up in the parking lot, we were immediately aware that trouble was brewing. As we scrambled out of the Volkswagen, two Negro boys, armed with shears, raced toward the tennis courts. Before we could stop them, they had cut the cords holding the nets to their supports and again we were confronted with the prospect of netless tennis. But we were never to strike a ball.

No sooner had we walked on the court than two burly deputies ran after us.

"This park's been closed down," one of them said. "If you're not out of here in twenty seconds, you'll be under arrest."

Elkins, Smith, and I walked off the court as slowly and as nonchalantly as we could. Just as we reached the car, I hit one of the tennis balls into the air as high as my anger would take it. All that the gesture did was to stimulate a crowd of young Negro boys who scrambled for the descending ball.

Before the day ended, almost every public facility in Albany had been shut down. The white Carnegie and the Negro Monroe Branch Libraries closed their doors shortly after small integrated groups had tried to enter both buildings. Despite the 90° weather, all swimmers were ordered out of the municipal pools in both Tift and Carver Parks. Choctaw State Park, two miles north of Albany, was closed during the afternoon, minutes before a group of integrated picnickers could open their lunch baskets.

In the early afternoon, Dr. King left by car for Atlanta. It was his hope, he told reporters, that his absence would give the city commission a chance to open good faith negotiations with local Negroes.

However, City Manager Stephen A. Ross, who welcomed

"the leaving of this recognized agitator," insisted that city officials had no intention of meeting with the leaders of the Albany Movement.

Several hours after Dr. King's departure, Lotte and I, who hoped to hear him preach the next morning at Ebenezer Baptist Church, headed for Atlanta with Hank Elkins and Edwina Smith, Wyatt Walker's secretary. When Elkins' Volkswagen pulled into Americus, a hamlet some thirty miles due north of Albany destined to become a focal point of the civil rights movement in 1965, it was just beginning to get dark and we realized that we had better find a place to spend the night.

Because Edwina was a Negro, it was obviously impossible for us to stay at any motel or inn along the way. Accordingly, we decided to stop at Koinanina, an interracial farm near Americus whose name, in Greek, means together. Run by Clarence Jordan, a white Georgian, the thousand-acre farm specialized in pecans.

Jordan had founded Koinanina some twenty years earlier in order to promote better racial understanding. It was his objective to have the farm worked by Negro and white families who would live together in the small bungalows that were clustered behind the big main house. Despite a bitterly hostile community, Koinanina had managed to become a nationally known symbol of brotherhood and equality.

Since none of us knew exactly where the farm was, we stopped at a gas station just outside of Americus. When Elkins asked for directions, the attendant was immediately suspicious.

"What do you want to go to that nigger-loving place for?" he asked.

With amazing equanimity, Elkins repeated his question.

"Take the Dawson Road," the man replied brusquely.

Ten minutes later, we arrived at the farm. The Jordans had just finished dinner but there was enough left to feed four more mouths. After supper, Clarence took us on a guided tour of his acreage. It was a delightful walk and, as we followed the path of the setting sun, it was hard to believe that, just thirty miles away, a city had shut down its parks and libraries because Negroes and whites might use them together.

After breakfast the next morning, we headed north once more. We had 140 miles to go in three hours if we wanted to get to church by eleven, and Hank Elkins didn't spare the gas. At 10:30 A.M., we pulled into Atlanta and stopped at Edwina's apartment where we had just time enough to freshen up before driving across town to Ebenezer.

It was almost eleven o'clock when we arrived at the church. This was Dr. King's first service since his arrest two weeks earlier and the building was jammed with people. The crowd was so large that the overflow had to be accommodated in a basement room where what was going on in the church proper could be heard through the medium of a loudspeaker.

After turning us over to an usher, Elkins disappeared into the robing room. We were escorted down the right side of the church where we found standing room next to the wall. I was destined to remain on my feet throughout the entire service, however, while two gentlemen of the congregation gallantly surrendered their choice seats to Lotte and Edwina.

After the formal part of the Baptist Sunday morning service had been completed, there was a period of meditation. As the members of the congregation bowed their heads, a solitary contralto without any musical accompaniment sang Stuart K. Hine's "How Great Thou Art," a beautiful hymn I had first heard in Albany. There, it had been sung by a teen-aged Negro choir from Hartford, Connecticut, which had ridden almost two tiring days on a bus to spend a few hours with the movement.

I can no longer listen to this hymn without the most

intense emotion. Its lilting melody and simple but expressive lyrics symbolize for me the fervor and passion that underlie the tortuous struggle for human liberty that is so sorely testing our national ability to exist as a democratic society.

> O Lord my God!
> When I in awesome wonder
> Consider all the worlds Thy hands have made,
> I see the stars,
> I hear the rolling thunder,
> Thy pow'r throughout the universe displayed . . .

As the contralto's rich voice filled every corner of the hushed church, I stole a glance at the man next to me. I was startled to see that tears were streaming down his face.

> Then sings my soul, my Savior God to Thee;
> How great Thou art, how great Thou art!
> Then sings my soul, my Savior God to Thee;
> How great Thou art, how great Thou art!

Even Dr. King's sermon was something of an anticlimax. But I was moved by his father who, as Ebenezer's associate pastor, is responsible for the daily operation of the church. The senior King's ingenuous delight in his famous son is so irrepressible that he cannot resist punctuating Martin's sermons by rapping his cane on the floor or shouting out such encouragements as "Make it plain!" or "You hear that, deacons!"

After the service, we were invited by the Kings to have dinner with them in the basement of the church. In spite of a persistent radio reporter who insisted on interviewing Dr. King throughout the meal, we thoroughly enjoyed ourselves. It was somehow comforting to realize that Martin, despite his asceticism, is very much a family man.

Hank Elkins drove us to the airport later that afternoon. Before leaving the Kings' modest home on Johnston Avenue,

Lotte had reached an entente with Martin as to the date of a fund-raising benefit to be held in White Plains, New York, later in the year. Westchester County in December seemed far removed from Atlanta in August but the connection was much closer than any of us realized at the time.

It had been an exciting and rewarding week. As our Convair 880 headed north, I relaxed by leafing through the pages of the New York *Times* which we had picked up at the airport newsstand. Suddenly, I was brought up short by a United Press International picture of Reverend Smith, Chief Pritchett, and myself on the Tift Park tennis court.

As I stared at the photograph, I recalled that exactly one year earlier I had refused to appear at a Freedom Rider rally in Jackson because I thought that a lawyer's place was only in the courtroom. I realized that I had come a long way since then.

Pritchett was wrong. I had been in the right court.

CHAPTER 16

Postscript

In mid-September of 1963, I returned to Albany. It was a far cry from the city I had left a little more than a year before. In place of the enthusiasm and exuberance that had characterized the movement during the summer of 1962, were only disillusionment and despair. Even the children reflected the bewilderment that enervated their elders.

On the integration front, little had changed. True, Negroes could now use the Carnegie Library on a stand-up basis but, in almost every other respect, the city was as rigidly segregated as ever. The great effort that had once fired the world's imagination was now just a bitter memory.

"It's as if nothing ever really happened here," one nineteen-year-old veteran told me.

Because Dr. Anderson had moved to Detroit, Slater King was now president of what was left of the Albany Movement. When he asked me to address that evening's mass meeting at Shiloh, I readily agreed. I might have refused if I had known how painful it would be to stand up in a half-filled church and talk to an apathetic and spiritless audience about the glories of another day.

As I sat on the platform awaiting my turn to speak, I tried to analyze what had happened to the movement that for months had dramatized the Southern Negroes' determination to destroy the humiliating and degrading indicia of slavery which had only technically ended one hundred years earlier.

Were any victories possible in the face of obdurate power structures? Was the law capable of attaining and preserving basic constitutional rights and guarantees? Could only federal intervention save the situation?

The Albany Movement had failed, it seemed to me, because it had demanded too much from an unprepared Negro community and produced too little. Its defeat proved that gigantic local efforts, even with significant outside help, often exact too great a toll in exhaustion, deprivation, and retaliation to amount to anything more than a momentary dramatization of what all men know but few understand.

The experience had convinced me that solely by dint of a massive unrelenting effort on every level could any significant progress be made. This means detailed local organization, the awakening and sustaining of national concern and the active interest of every branch of the federal government.

But in Albany not only did Washington remain aloof, it joined the ranks of the persecutors. On August 9, 1963, the Justice Department announced that it had obtained indictments against Dr. Anderson, Reverend Wells, Slater King, and six other persons who had been active in the movement. The charges were perjury before a federal grand jury and interfering with the administration of justice.*

They grew out of the picketing of the store of Carl Smith, an Albany grocer. He had served on a federal jury which, in a civil damage suit brought by a Negro who claimed that he had been beaten and shot by Baker County Sheriff L. Warren

* There is even some evidence to indicate that the indictments were the result of an Administration decision to placate Georgia just before an election year.

Johnson, had exonerated the law enforcement officer. The government claimed that the picketing was retaliation against Smith for the quality of his jury service and not, as the defendants insisted, because the grocer refused to upgrade his Negro employees.

The indictments were the last straw. Worn down by twenty months of protest with all their attendant economic and emotional consequences, the Negroes of Albany could not survive the shattering of their last great hope for deliverance. The impassioned voices that, one year earlier, had proclaimed that they weren't going "to let Chief Pritchett turn us 'round," were now silent.

Laurie Pritchett was one foe; Bobby Kennedy was quite another.

Just before Slater King introduced me, his audience went through the motions of singing "This Little Light of Mine," one of the most stirring of freedom songs. As I listened, my mind went back to another night when, in this same church, an eager and inspired crowd had pledged that they were "gonna let it shine" forever.

Unfortunately, it had all but been extinguished, and vanishing along with it were the hopes and aspirations of almost twenty thousand people.

The next morning I left for Americus with C. B. King for a bail hearing on behalf of four civil rights workers who had been charged with insurrection for leading an antisegregation demonstration in that city. Since the crime carried the death penalty, they had been held without bail for more than a month.*

After the hearing, we returned to Albany where Slater King and Reverend Wells asked to talk to me for a few minutes.

* The statute they were accused of violating had been declared unconstitutional by the Supreme Court almost thirty years earlier. In November, a federal court at the urging of CORE attorney Morris B. Abram ordered their immediate release.

Both men wanted to get something off their chests.

"Is everyone turning against us?" Slater asked. "For almost two years, we have been subjected to every possible kind of brutality, and the federal government does nothing more than take statements. Now, we who constantly asked for help find ourselves indicted by our own government. It just doesn't seem right!"

Wells, who had led the march downtown shortly after the issuance of Elliott's ill-fated restraining order, was equally bitter. "I just don't understand it," he complained. "Why don't they arrest those who persecute us? Why have we who want nothing but our freedom been singled out like this?"*

* All of the defendants were subsequently convicted, and their appeals are presently pending in the Fifth Circuit.

PART **IV**

MISSISSIPPI

REVISITED

CHAPTER 17

My Daughter Becomes Involved

With Albany behind me, I tried to return to private practice. For a brief time, I was able to remain in New York and resume what I still believed was my normal life. As the weeks rolled by, I became quite used to returning home every night and to making appointments with some sort of reasonable assurance that I could keep them.

At the beginning of September, my oldest daughter, Karin, who was about to begin her sophomore year at Connecticut College, suddenly announced that she wanted to spend her first semester at Tougaloo Southern Christian College. She had first heard of the school when it became the headquarters of the Freedom Riders who returned to Jackson for their arraignments in the summer of 1961.

Tougaloo had been started in 1869 when the American Missionary Association of New York purchased five hundred acres near Jackson and established a school "to be accessible to all, irrespective of their religious tenets, and conducted on the most liberal principles for the benefit of our citizens in general."

For a time, the new school was known as Tougaloo University, but in 1916 the name of the institution was officially changed to Tougaloo College.

In 1875, the Home Missionary Society of the Disciples of Christ obtained a charter from the state legislature for a private elementary school. As time went on, the new school, which was known as the Southern Christian Institute, developed a fully accredited high school and a junior college which was recognized by both the state of Mississippi and the Southern Association of Colleges and Secondary Schools.

Tougaloo College and the Southern Christian Institute had similar ideals and objectives. Not only did they maintain biracial faculties and administrative staffs, but the children of their white employees who attended the two institutions made them the only integrated schools in the state. It was only natural that they merge, and they did so in 1954 under the name of Tougaloo Southern Christian College.

The college, which is located three miles north of the Jackson city line, is situated on a rolling wooded campus. While its plant could hardly be compared to that of Connecticut College, it is adequate. Although many of its buildings date back to the turn of the century, it does have a few extremely modern structures. For example, its well-appointed Commons Building, which is the center of student social life, was erected in 1962.

But it is its attitude and approach to life that give Tougaloo its distinctiveness. From the moment a visitor drives through the wrought iron arch that straddles the main entrance to the college, he is in a world totally different from the rest of Mississippi. It is as if that arch marked the dividing line between bigotry and what the college catalogue refers to as "a spirit of outgoing goodwill toward all men."

Although I did not reveal it to Karin, I was intensely disturbed by her decision. I had learned at first hand how deep and bitter was the resistance to integration in the Mississippi capital. I also knew that anyone with the name of Kunstler would be a prime object of hatred. Karin was certain to have a hard time.

Moreover, the James Meredith case was fast reaching its inevitable climax. By the time Tougaloo opened for the fall semester, the state was certain to be in the midst of a monumental turmoil over the prospective admission to the University of Mississippi of its first Negro student. It was hardly the most propitious time for a white girl to be attending a nominally integrated college near Jackson.

Karin left for Jackson at noon on Sunday, September 16. As we drove her to Newark Airport, it was obvious that something was troubling her. But it was only when we reached her flight gate that she lost her composure. Bursting into tears as she kissed us goodbye, she fairly raced to her plane, pausing only to look back once as she entered the aircraft.

I had some idea of what was going through her mind. Mississippi may be within the continental limits of the United States, but it is a dark and strange place corrupted by fear and paralyzed by distrust. Dedicated to the continuation of slavery in a somewhat more refined and insidious form than in its antebellum days, its political leaders will do anything to perpetuate its plantation mores.

For a young girl to leave an environment in which the doctrine of white supremacy is hardly significant and enter one where it dominates every area of life is not an easy task. To witness the relentless destruction of every effort at racial integration, to endure a calculated and blatant disregard for human dignity and aspirations, to experience daily a hundred shocks to every sensibility is a frightful burden for anyone to bear, especially a sensitive and impressionable college student.

Fortunately, I saw Karin eleven days later. I was invited to attend the 1962 SCLC convention in Birmingham and I decided to take advantage of the opportunity and go to Jackson first. The flight from Atlanta was an ordeal of anticipation for me. The two-hour trip seemed to take ages and by the time we were fifty miles out of Jackson I was as nervous as a cat. I could hardly contain my excitement when the stewardess finally announced that we were about to land at Municipal Airport.

As the plane rolled to a halt, I could see Karin standing behind the barrier. We met in the middle of the boarding area and, to my surprise, I discovered that I was trembling. I had not realized how deeply I had missed her and how moving our reunion would be.

I had not been back to Jackson since early December of 1961 when, with Carl Rachlin and Derrick Bell of the NAACP Legal Defense Fund, I had participated in the unsuccessful attempt to dissolve Judge Cox' injunction against civil rights demonstrators in McComb, Mississippi.* When Karin and I walked through the terminal building, it was exhilarating to see that the four restrooms were no longer marked by white and colored signs. Henry Thomas had triumphed at last.

I had a wonderful half day at Tougaloo. Not only did I get a chance to meet many of Karin's friends and instructors, but I was able to spend some time with Dr. A. D. Beittel, the college's white president,** and his wife Ruth. Fortunately, they reflected a glowing serenity that managed to make even

* The injunction was later dissolved by the Fifth Circuit on much the same grounds that Judge Tuttle had invalidated the Albany restraining order.

** Beittel was replaced by a Negro in 1964 when Tougaloo entered into a working relationship with Brown University. He is now employed in Jackson by the American Friends Service Committee.

the periodic sniper bullets which are very much a part of the Tougaloo scene seem almost nonexistent.

The Beittels lived in a large, modern, one-story building near the entrance to the college. In a very real sense, this house had become one of the centers of whatever intellectual ferment there was in Mississippi. At any one time you were liable to meet Norman Thomas, Allen Knight Chalmers, or Ralph Bunche sipping tea in its spacious living room. And Ruth Beittel's breakfasts made even the most harassed visitor forget momentarily that he was deep in what editor P. D. East has so aptly labeled the Magnolia Jungle.

After supper at the Beittels', I left for Birmingham and the SCLC convention. I arrived at 8 P.M. and went at once to the Sixteenth Baptist Church in which, just one year later, four young Negro girls were to be blown up by a terrorist's bomb. The evening's program was in full swing when I entered the imposing gray stone building.

As always, Wyatt Walker was there to greet me. "There's a seat for you on the platform," he said. "Get up there quickly because you'll be on in a minute or so."

I raced down the center aisle and took the first empty seat I could find. The man on my right looked familiar to me, but I just couldn't place his face. As I wrestled with the problem of identifying him, Dr. King, who was at the podium, came to my rescue.

"I want you to meet someone," he told the crowd, "who has found the humor we need to keep us going. I give you Dick Gregory."

What the comedian said that night will always remain in my memory, not because it was either eloquent or inspiring, but because he himself was so soon to give it the lie. "I admire all of you," he said, "but demonstrating and all that is not for this cat. The nearest I want to be to a jail is to fly over one. I'll do my complaining where people are willing to pay good money to listen to it."

In less than six months, Dick was to be much nearer to more jails than even he would have thought possible. In this very city, he was soon to find that there is no substitute for commitment and that words are often not enough to communicate social protest. When that first cell door closed behind him, he later told me, he felt far freer than he had at any time in his life.

Because I had arrived so late, I had to share a room at the Gaston Motel with Gregory and Walker. The three of us spent the night in a double bed that groaned under our combined weight. Gregory, who monopolized the center of the bed, kept up a steady stream of chatter throughout the night. Whenever Wyatt and I dozed off, he would shake us back into consciousness.

"Wake up, baby," he said, "I've got a new story for you."

I flew out the next morning. On my plane were Senators Richard Russell, Lister Hill, and John Sparkman who had been attending a Democratic conclave at the Tutwiler Hotel. When we arrived in Atlanta, the three legislators were met by a horde of newsmen who were anxious to get their views on the recent decision by the Fifth Circuit that Governor Ross R. Barnett was guilty of contempt in interfering with James Meredith's admission to Ole Miss.*

As I left the plane, I was recognized by an American Broadcasting Company reporter whom I had met in Jackson in 1961. To my surprise, he asked me to join Russell, Hill, and Sparkman in commenting on the action against Barnett. The senators gave me puzzled looks when I walked over to where they were standing in front of a portable microphone, and no one bothered to make any introductions.

---

* Almost three years later, the same court, by a four-to-three vote, dismissed the contempt proceedings against Barnett.

Their opinions ranged from Russell's outspoken hostility to the court's determination to Sparkman's cautious disapproval. I minced no words. Not only did I thoroughly condone the contempt decree but I said that Barnett was a subversive influence on our national life.

"Who the hell is he?" hissed Russell as I finished.

I had left the convention early in order to fulfill a commitment I had made to Barry Gray, whose late evening interview program over radio station WMCA has been a New York fixture for many years. Gray, who was on a European vacation, had asked me to stand in for him, and I had a recording session scheduled for that afternoon on the subject of interracial marriage. I had just started to interview Malcolm X, one of my guests, when Judy Tarlo, Gray's producer, signaled to me from the control booth. It seemed that there was a telephone call for me from Birmingham.

My caller was Dora McDonald, Dr. King's secretary. Hysterically, she told me that King had just been assaulted by a member of the American Nazi Party. Roy James, a six-foot, two-hundred-pound native of Arlington, Virginia, had leaped on the stage of the L. R. Hall Auditorium and punched King on the left side of his face.

The police had taken James to headquarters where he was charged with assault. "They also made Dr. King go with them," Dora sobbed, "and I know that he doesn't want to press charges against anyone. Can anything be done about it?"

I assured Dora that I would do everything I could. As soon as I had finished talking to her, I called police headquarters and spoke to Commissioner Eugene "Bull" Connor. "Dr. King isn't here," he told me. "He testified as to what happened and then left. James has already been convicted and sentenced to thirty days in prison and a fine of $25."

The incident was of more than passing interest to me.

James' attack had followed Dr. King's announcement that Sammy Davis, Jr., would appear in an SCLC benefit in White Plains, New York, on December 11.* Since my wife was general chairman of the benefit, I felt somewhat connected with the attack on King.

Monday, October 1, was my last appearance on the Gray show. The night before, a monstrous tragedy had taken place on the campus of the University of Mississippi at Oxford. Shortly after President Kennedy had informed the people of the United States that James Meredith had been successfully spirited into his dormitory, two men were killed as an infuriated mob battled federal marshals in the vicinity of the Lyceum, the university's administration building.

While I suffered from the same frustrations that plagued most Americans at the news from Oxford, for one night, at least, I did have an outlet. Convinced as I was that Governor Barnett and the men around him had set the stage for murder, I was determined to use my last night at a WMCA microphone to get a feeling of revulsion off my chest.

The program went on the air at 11:05 P.M. As soon as all of the routine announcements had been made, I spread my notes out in front of me and began what I hoped would be a burning indictment of wanton and unforgivable official irresponsibility.

"The governor of Mississippi," I said in part, "must bear the awesome responsibility for the deaths of two men and the shame of our republic. By offering himself as a prime example of public indifference to the judicial process, he encouraged others to take the law into their own hands. His finger may not have pulled the trigger, but his words and actions energized those that did. Morality cannot be a question of mere semantics."

---

* James was undoubtedly inflamed by the fact that Davis was married to white Mai Britt.

Even if Barnett had heard the broadcast, it wouldn't have made the slightest impression upon him. But I felt much better. As I left the studio, a warm congratulatory call from Fannie Hurst added to my sense of well-being.

"You put into words," she said, "what so many of us feel at this moment."

CHAPTER 18

A Cry for Help

In early December, Bill Higgs, the young Jackson attorney with whom I had worked so closely during the Freedom Rider litigation, came to see me.

"Bill," he said, "I have a plan to force the federal government to stop the reign of terror in Mississippi. Unless Washington shows a firmer hand, a lot of our friends are going to be maimed or killed."

Mississippi was fast becoming a police state where racial violence, with or without official blessing, was taking place on almost a regular basis. Since the Freedom Rides, it had been a rare week indeed that went by without some Negro who was attempting to exercise his civil rights being beaten or worse.

On August 22, 1961, Robert Moses, the leader of the voter registration drive in Mississippi, was slugged in Liberty by the sheriff's first cousin. Although it took eight stitches to close a wound in Moses' head, his attacker was acquitted of assault charges by an all-white jury.

Two weeks later, Travis Britt, an SNCC voter registration worker, was attacked by a crowd of angry whites on the

Liberty courthouse lawn. After striking Britt more than two dozen times, the group drove away in a truck. No arrests were made.

On September 7, in nearby Walthall County, John Hardy, another SNCC field worker, took two Negroes to the courthouse to register. Registrar John Q. Wood brusquely informed the group that he "wasn't registering voters" that day. When Hardy turned to leave, Wood took a pistol from his desk and struck him over the head. Hardy was then arrested and charged with disturbing the peace.

Herbert Lee, a Negro who had been very active in voter registration in Amite County, was shot to death in the streets of Liberty on September 25 by E. H. Hurst, a member of the Mississippi legislature. Hurst claimed self-defense and an Amite County grand jury refused to indict him.*

On October 11, two white sympathizers who were driving alongside a group of Negroes demonstrating against segregation in McComb, were dragged from their car by a heavy-set white man and severely beaten.

Two days later, in the same city, a Negro motorist who had been stopped for speeding, was shot and killed by a policeman. A coroner's jury promptly ruled that the officer had fired in self-defense.

At the beginning of November, five CORE workers were besieged by a large group of white men when they sought service at the McComb Greyhound bus terminal lunch counter. Jerome Smith, one of the victims, suffered head injuries when he was slugged with brass knuckles during the attack. According to Smith, FBI agents who were present did nothing but "take notes" while the mob assaulted him and his companions.

* Two and a half years later a Negro witness to Lee's killing who had agreed to reveal the full facts about the incident if he could be assured of FBI protection, was found dead in his front yard, all but decapitated by a shotgun blast.

The McComb bus terminal was the scene of another brutal attack on December 1 when a mob tried to drag three Freedom Riders from their parked automobile. Four men kicked at the windows of the locked car in a frenzied attempt to reach its occupants. Although the police succeeded in pulling the white men away from the vehicle, no arrests were made.

In early 1962, a Negro soldier en route to visit his sick wife in Laurel, was shot to death by a Taylorsville policeman when he insisted that he had a right to sit where he wanted on an interstate bus. No charges were ever brought against his killer.

A month later, the Negro editor of the Mississippi *Free Press*, a struggling liberal weekly which had been started shortly after the Freedom Rides, was stopped by police just outside of Jackson. After being beaten, he was held incommunicado overnight. The next day, he was tried on several unjustified charges and fined $150.

Higgs himself ran into trouble on June 21. Accompanied by four college students, he had gone to Clarksdale in connection with his duties as campaign manager for the first Negro candidate for Congress in Mississippi in the twentieth century. The lawyer and his companions were jailed and held for twenty hours without being able to communicate with the outside world. No charges were ever filed against them.

On July 5, Jesse Harris and Luvaghn Brown, two SNCC workers who were serving thirty-day sentences in the Hinds County jail for contempt of court, were slugged by guards. Both youths had been arrested when they refused to move from the "white only" section of the courtroom.

"Nigger, I'll kill you!" one guard roared as he savagely beat Harris across the back with a length of rubber hose.

Samuel Block, a young SNCC field secretary, was accosted and beaten by three white men in a Greenwood parking lot on August 16. The next day, Block and two fellow workers just managed to escape through the second-story window of their voter registration office when it was invaded by a band of armed white men.

During late summer and early fall, Negro homes in at least four Mississippi communities were fired into or damaged by bombs. On September 10, Marylene Burkes and Vivian Hillett, two young Ruleville girls, were severely injured when an unidentified assailant shot into the home of Miss Hillett's grandparents, who were active in voter registration work in that city.

A month later, in Harmony where Negroes had recently petitioned for the desegregation of the city's public schools, nightriders discharged shotguns into eight homes. One elderly man reported that he had been hit in the knee by squirrel shot while he was sleeping.

In early October, the Biloxi home of Dr. Gilbert Mason, a Negro physician who led integration activities in that Gulf Coast city, was set afire by a Molotov cocktail. The missile caused more than $4,000 in damage. A week later, in Columbus, a fire bomb was hurled from a speeding car into the home of Dr. James L. Allen, vice chairman of the controversial Mississippi Advisory Committee to the United States Commission on Civil Rights.

On Halloween, Reverend Thomas E. Johnson, one of Dr. Allen's colleagues, drove his car to a safe place because of anonymous threats to destroy it. When he returned to his Jackson home, he found a group of neighbors dumping garbage on his front lawn. After the leader of the garbage-dumping operation had been acquitted by a justice of the peace, Johnson and his wife were indicted for perjury because of their testimony at the trial.*

* The charges were subsequently dropped after the intervention of Arnold S. Trebach of the United States Commission on Civil Rights.

It was tragically obvious that almost everyone in Mississippi who was openly concerned with the attainment of equal civil rights had achieved an outlaw status and could expect no protection from the police. Under such circumstances, it seemed to be up to the federal government to step into the breach.

During the August meeting with Attorney General Kennedy, I had not been convinced that his hands were as tied as he said they were. There were a number of statutes which authorized federal marshals, FBI agents, and United States attorneys, all of whom were under his jurisdiction, to arrest and prosecute persons who willfully violated the civil rights of others.

In fact, one of these laws "required" federal officers "to institute prosecutions against all persons violating the provisions of civil rights criminal statutes and to cause such persons to be arrested and imprisoned or bailed for trial . . ."

This statute, which had been on the books since 1866, was specifically designed to protect Negroes. Senator Lyman Trumbull, one of its sponsors, had made this quite clear during the floor debate that preceded its passage.

"A law is good for nothing," he said, "without a penalty, without a sanction to it. That they [the ex-slaves] are entitled to be free, we know. Being entitled to be free under the Constitution, we have a right to enact such legislation as will make them free, we believe; and that can only be done by punishing those who undertake to deny them their freedom."

In explaining the proposed legislation to his colleagues, Trumbull emphasized its enforcement sections. "The various provisions of this bill make it the duty of the marshals and deputy marshals, the commissioners of the United States courts, the officers and agents of the Freedmen's Bureau, the district attorneys and others, to be vigilant in the enforcement of the act."

Even the bill's opponents acknowledged that it called for federal action to protect the civil rights of Negroes. "If, according to the letter of this act," observed Kentucky's Garrett Davis, "a free Negro's rights are infringed, the attorneys of the United States are required to institute civil and penal proceedings for the benefit of the Negro, to bring a criminal prosecution on behalf of the United States and also a suit in the name of the Negro."

In the House, Congressman James Wilson of Iowa, in opposing an amendment that would have eliminated the bill's penal provisions, put it somewhat more eloquently. "This bill proposes that the humblest citizen shall have full and ample protection at the cost of the government, whose duty it is to protect him. The amendment says that the citizen despoiled of his rights must press his own way through the courts and pay the bills attendant thereon. This may do for the rich, but to the poor it is a mockery. The highest obligation which the government owes to the citizen in return for the allegiance exacted of him is to secure him in the protection of his rights."

If there ever was any doubt that Congress was specifically ordering the Executive Branch to protect Negroes, it was dispelled in 1875 when a new section was added to the act. "Any district attorney who shall willfully fail to institute and prosecute the proceedings herein required shall, for every such offense forfeit and pay the sum of five hundred dollars to the person aggrieved thereby and shall, on conviction thereof, be deemed guilty of a misdemeanor."

According to Congressman Benjamin F. Butler, who reported the 1875 bill out of the House Judiciary Committee, "we make it the duty of the district attorneys to see that the penalties provided for in the statute are enforced."

There was more than ample legal basis to support federal intervention when any person's civil rights were threatened by state or private action. Simply stated, the question was how to get Bobby Kennedy to move in Mississippi.

Bill Higgs had been doing a great deal of thinking about this problem. When he came to see me, it was to propose that I join him in a lawsuit to force the federal government to lend a helping hand. I was happy to be a part of this effort.

On January 2, 1963, we brought suit in the federal court in Washington, D.C. With Higgs and seven Negro SNCC field workers as plaintiffs, the complaint asked the court to order Kennedy and FBI Director J. Edgar Hoover to "protect plaintiffs and their constitutional rights by investigation, arrest, and prosecution of offending law enforcement officers of the state of Mississippi and of its political subdivisions, and offending residents of the state of Mississippi acting individually or collectively and/or in concert and conspiracy with said law enforcement officers."

Hoover and Kennedy quickly responded by asking for the dismissal of the suit. In essence, they both claimed that no court could force them "to institute criminal investigations, arrests, or prosecutions." Moreover, they argued that "it is well settled that members of the general public cannot compel government officials to supply them with police or similar protection."

On April 3, 1963, we appeared in Washington before Judge Luther W. Youngdahl, the former Minnesota governor. The arguments were brief. Higgs and I insisted that federal courts had the necessary power to order Kennedy and Hoover to protect our clients. The young Department of Justice attorney who appeared for the defendants took a contrary position.

It took Youngdahl almost three months to decide the case. On July 2, he ruled that he had no power to do as we asked. "In the area of civil rights," he said in his eight-page opinion, "the Executive Department must be largely free to exercise its considered judgment on questions of whether to proceed by means of prosecution, injunction, varying forms of persuasion, or other types of action."

Although Youngdahl's decision was later affirmed by the appellate court, Judge J. Skelly Wright, one of its members, felt compelled to add a postscript.

"It seems more than passing strange, to me at least," he wrote, "that in some parts of this country citizens exercising their First Amendment rights of assembly, petition, and free speech are arrested and convicted by the hundreds, while perpetrators of innumerable church bombings and burnings, kidnappings, beatings, maimings, and murders of Negroes and civil rights workers are not prosecuted—or even apprehended. Perhaps, as appellants suggest, federal laws, or their enforcement, in this area are indeed inadequate. But I agree that an investigation as to the adequacy, or the execution of these laws is not a matter within the jurisdiction of the judicial branch of this government."

In the half-year that had elapsed since the filing of our complaint, violence in Mississippi had increased. On February 20, four Negro businesses on the same street as the SNCC voter registration office in Greenwood were mysteriously burned to the ground. When a SNCC field secretary suggested that there was some connection between the burnings and voter registration efforts, he was promptly arrested. The charge: circulating statements calculated to provoke a breach of the peace.

A month later, fire partially destroyed the voter registration office itself. Several witnesses claimed that, shortly before the blaze started, they saw two white men running away from the building.

During the spring, Negroes in Clarksdale were the targets of vicious racist attacks. In early April, a Molotov cocktail was hurled through the window of Dr. Aaron Henry's home.

Henry, a druggist and the NAACP state president, was entertaining Michigan Congressman Charles C. Diggs at the time. Three weeks later, a mysterious explosion tore a gaping hole in the roof of Henry's drugstore.

On June 8, three bullets were fired from a passing car into his home. Another ripped into the living room of Mrs. Vera Pigee, secretary of the Coahoma County chapter of the NAACP. At the time of the shooting, Mrs. Pigee was still recovering from a beating administered by a white mechanic when she had tried to use a service station rest room.

The day after the attack on Henry and Mrs. Pigee, Mrs. Fannie Lou Hamer, Miss Annelle Ponder, and four other registration workers tried to obtain service at the lunch counter of the Winona bus station. The six, who were en route to Greenwood from a registration workshop in Charleston, South Carolina, were arrested and held in jail for four days.

During their imprisonment, they were beaten by policemen with night sticks and whipped with leather straps by two Negro trusties who had been ordered to do so by the officers. Later, a federal jury, after being warned by the presiding judge not to forget that the assault victims were outsiders with a penchant for sowing discord, exonerated the policemen.

Jackson was no better than the hinterlands. On May 28, Memphis Norman, a Tougaloo student, was knocked off his stool at Woolworth's segregated lunch counter and stomped repeatedly by white youths. A Negro woman sitting alongside Norman also was dumped off her stool and kicked. Three days later, Willie Ludden, an NAACP youth organizer, was clubbed by police as he led a group of demonstrators out of a church.

But the state capital was to be the scene of the worst atrocity of all. Late on the evening of Tuesday, June 12,

Medgar Evers, the NAACP field secretary of Mississippi, was shot in the back as he returned home from directing the protest demonstrations that had erupted after the stomping of Memphis Norman. A bullet from a high-powered rifle so grievously wounded him that he died at University Medical Center fifty minutes later without ever regaining consciousness.

Two days earlier, I had called Medgar to discuss the situation with him. In April of 1963, I had begun a federal suit in Jackson to restrain the police from arresting peaceful pickets on the city's streets, and I wondered whether there was anything I could do in that suit which might help Medgar's demonstrations.

As we talked, I realized that I had caught him at a bad moment. "Bill," he said, "I'm too upset to even think about legal tactics or strategy. There's so much bad blood in this city that I just know someone's going to get hurt. I'm afraid for these kids who go out in the streets every day. Someone's going to run out of patience and we're going to have a real tragedy on our hands."

When I asked him whether he had demanded federal protection, he snorted. "The FBI men take our statements," he explained wearily, "but nothing is ever done about them. I guess we'll have to struggle along by ourselves. But I just wish I wasn't always afraid for my people."

In a little more than forty-eight hours, he was to become one more report in the burgeoning files of the Department of Justice.

"In the area of civil rights," Judge Youngdahl would soon say, "the Executive Department must be largely free to exercise its considered judgment on questions of whether to proceed by means of prosecution, injunction, varying forms of persuasion, or other types of action."

Or no action at all.

CHAPTER 19

Meredith v. Fair

On October 4, 1962, four days after James H. Meredith became the first Negro ever to enter the University of Mississippi, Dewey Roosevelt Greene, Jr., began the process by which he hoped to become the second. In a letter to Registrar Robert B. Ellis, he asked for the necessary application forms.

"I wish to apply to enter the University of Mississippi," Greene wrote, "as a transfer student or, if necessary, as a freshman for the second semester of the academic year 1962–1963, beginning in February, 1963."

Greene, who was twenty-one years old, had been born in Greenwood and attended Negro public schools in that city. After graduating from high school, he enlisted in the Navy where he was trained as a meteorologist. During his three years in service, he was stationed first at the Naval Air Station in Hawaii and then at Pearl Harbor. He was honorably discharged as an airman apprentice in December of 1961.

Returning to Greenwood, he enrolled at Mississippi Vocational College, a state-supported Negro institution some twelve miles west of the city. During his two quarters at the college, he completed a dozen courses, including business mathematics, grammar and composition, and a survey of biological sciences. He made both ends meet by working as a dishwasher in off-campus restaurants.

After Meredith's admission to Ole Miss, Greene wrote his letter. Registrar Ellis replied four days later, enclosing some application forms and stating that a University Bulletin had been mailed under separate cover. However, Ellis failed to include the required medical and character reference forms.

Immediately suspicious, Greene contacted a white friend and asked her to write the registrar for a full set of application forms. When these arrived, Greene completed them and, on October 25, mailed them back to the university. In preparing his papers, he was guided by the requirements of the University Bulletin.

It was not until November 16 that Greene heard again from Ellis. After acknowledging the receipt of his application, the registrar informed him that "the limited level of achievement indicated by your school records and the fact that applicants for transfer are accepted only from fully accredited colleges makes it necessary to deny the application at this time."

Ellis went on to state that he was sorry that so much publicity had been given to Greene's application. "There were two newspaper reporters inquiring about it at the very moment your first letter arrived in the office and I understand that there were announcements about it even earlier in the Jackson papers. It seems to me that this kind of activity would be avoided by an applicant who seriously wants an education at Ole Miss."

Since Ellis also indicated that the application was "not properly completed," Greene wrote and asked for an explanation of this statement. He did not receive a reply until December 10 when Ellis informed him that "your file was not complete for the reason that character recommendations are required from responsible citizens from your community. One of your recommendations apparently was signed by a resident of West Point and another fails to indicate place of residence."

On January 10, 1963, Greene forwarded two additional recommendations from local residents to Ellis. There was no response from the registrar. Two weeks later, Bill Higgs, Greene's lawyer, asked me whether the Gandhi Society would be interested in the case. I replied that it would.

Since registration for the spring term was scheduled to begin on January 31, I wrote to Ellis and told him that our client would apply in person that day.

As soon as he received my letter, the registrar sent a telegram to Greene. "You are not to appear at the University of Mississippi for registration," it read. "My letters dated November 16, 1962, and December 10, 1962, informed you that you are not eligible for admission."

Despite Ellis' telegram, Greene was determined to visit his office in the Lyceum Building, the scene of the bloody riot that had followed the admission of James Meredith four months earlier. On the evening of January 30, Dewey left Jackson for Memphis. The following morning, he took a bus to Holly Springs where he planned to have a friend drive him to the university. He arrived in Oxford at 10:45 A.M.

When he entered the Lyceum Building, he asked a student for directions to Ellis' first-floor office. The registrar was not in and Greene was advised by a secretary that he could wait for him. Some time later, Ellis, accompanied by Tom S. Hinds, the university's Director of Student Activities, entered the room.

"You are Greene?" he asked curtly. When Dewey nodded and held out his right hand, Ellis ignored it and walked behind his desk and sat down. Hines, who had followed Ellis into the room, avoided the Negro's outstretched palm by placing both hands behind his back.

The interview was brief. After Greene acknowledged that he had received the registrar's telegram, Ellis proceeded to read it aloud to him. When Greene asked why his application had been rejected, he was informed that "the denial had been based on provisions that had been established by our Committee on Admissions and by our Board of Trustees." Any exception to university policy, Ellis told him, had to be obtained by means of a petition to the Committee on Admissions.

Since Greene wanted desperately to become an accountant, it was patently impossible for him to obtain the requisite education at any of the three Negro colleges in the state. On the other hand, we did not want to involve him in the ordeal that had all but destroyed James Meredith. Higgs felt strongly that our best course would be to ask the federal court in Mississippi to order Ellis to comply with the injunction in the *Meredith* case and admit Greene for the spring term.

Since *Meredith v. Fair*, as the case was officially known, was a class action, it covered all colored applicants who were denied admission to any state supported college or university because of their race. Higgs, who had been Meredith's first lawyer,* was convinced that we fell under the aegis of the earlier suit. Moreover, there was a reasonable parallel between the careers of the two Negroes.

After graduating from high school at the age of seventeen, Meredith had enlisted in the United States Air Force. During his nine years in service, he earned thirty-four semester credits by taking night courses at the Far Eastern Division of the University of Maryland, the University of Kansas, and

---

* However, the NAACP Legal Defense and Educational Fund had handled *Meredith v. Fair* from its inception.

Washburn University. In addition, he completed numerous college level courses offered by the Armed Forces Institute.

In the summer of 1960, Meredith received his honorable discharge and returned to Mississippi where he enrolled in Jackson State College, a Negro institution. Because of the courses he had taken at the Armed Forces Institute, he was allowed fifty-seven quarter hours credit. By early 1961, he had earned some ninety credits.

Convinced that Jackson State was "substandard," Meredith decided to apply for admission to the University of Mississippi. On January 26, 1961, he mailed a formal application for admission to Registrar Ellis. In his letter of transmittal, he informed Ellis that he was a Negro and enclosed certificates from five Mississippi residents who stated that he was a person of good moral character.

Meredith was quick to point out that the certificates did not meet the requirements of the university regulations. "I will not be able to furnish you with the names of six University Alumni," he explained, "because I am a Negro and all graduates of the school are white. Further, I do not know any graduates personally."

Nine days later, the registrar sent Meredith a wire. It seemed that, because of overcrowding at the university, it had "been found necessary to discontinue consideration of all applications for admission or registration for the second semester which were received after January 25, 1961."

On February 20, Meredith requested that his application be considered as "a continuing application for the summer session beginning June 8, 1961." In addition, he asked whether the registrar needed any further information from him to make his application for admission complete. Ellis responded by returning Meredith's $10 room deposit.

During the next three months, Meredith wrote three letters to the university asking that his application "be considered a continuing one for the Summer Session and the Fall Session, 1961." In one letter he included five amended certificates from his character references reiterating their faith in his moral stability and specifically recommending him for admission. No answer to any of these letters was received.

On April 12, in desperation, he wrote directly to the Dean of the College of Liberal Arts. He asked the dean to review the case with the registrar and to advise him "what admission requirements, if any, I failed to meet and to give me some assurance that my race and color are not the basis for my failure to gain admission to the University."

It took almost four weeks for Meredith to receive a reply. On May 9, 1961, he was informed by the registrar that his application would "get proper attention." As for Meredith's ninety credits, Ellis stated that "under the standards of the University of Mississippi the maximum credit which could be allowed is forty-eight semester hours."

Three weeks later, the registrar closed his file on Meredith.

"The University cannot recognize the transfer of credits from the institution which you are now attending," he wrote, "since it is not a member of the Southern Association of Colleges and Secondary Schools. Our policy permits the transfer of credits only from member institutions of regional associations. Furthermore, students may not be accepted by the University from those institutions whose programs are not recognized."

In any event, Meredith's letters of recommendation were not sufficient "for either a resident or a nonresident applicant."

On May 31, Meredith lost patience.

Convinced that there was nothing to be gained by further correspondence with the university, he filed suit in federal court against Charles Dickson Fair, the president of the Board of Trustees of the State Institutions of Higher Learning, and several other officials. On behalf of himself and all other qualified Negro students, he asked for an injunction against the practice of limiting admissions to certain Mississippi colleges to white persons.

Shortly after his suit was filed, Meredith asked for a preliminary injunction enjoining the registrar from denying his admission solely on account of his race. Although the hearing on this motion was originally set for June 12, it took until August 16 to be finally concluded. By a series of unconscionable delays, the defendants, with the cooperation of Judge Sidney C. Mize, managed to avoid a decision until both summer sessions had ended and the fall term was almost over.

On December 12, Judge Mize denied Meredith's motion for a preliminary injunction. He gave three reasons for his decision. First, Meredith had not presented the six alumni certificates required for admission. Second, the denial of his admission in February had been based solely on overcrowded conditions at the university. Last, since Jackson State College was not an accredited institution, many of Meredith's credits were not acceptable.

"The overwhelming weight of the testimony," Mize concluded, "is that the plaintiff was not denied admission because of his color or race."

The Fifth Circuit promptly disposed of Mize's first reason. "We hold," it ruled, "that the University's requirement that each candidate for admission furnish alumni certificates is a denial of equal protection of the laws in its application to Negro candidates. It is a heavy burden on qualified Negro students because of their race. It is no burden on qualified white students."

Although it would not reverse Mize's refusal to issue a preliminary injunction, the three-judge court all but ordered him to try the case on the merits promptly.

"Within proper legal bounds," it stated, "the plaintiff

should be afforded a fair, unfettered, and unharassed opportunity to prove his case. A man should be able to find an education by taking the broad highway. He should not have to take by-roads through the woods and follow winding trails through sharp thickets, in constant tension because of pitfalls and traps and, after years of effort, perhaps attain the threshold of his goal when he is past caring about it."

Since the spring term would begin on February 6, 1962, it was "suggested" to Mize that he "proceed promptly with a full trial on the merits and that judgment be rendered promptly." For anyone who cared to read it, the handwriting was on the courthouse wall.

Things now moved much faster. On February 3, 1962, after a six-day trial, Mize again decided that Meredith had failed to show "that he was denied admission to the University of Mississippi solely because of his race." Five months later, however, the Fifth Circuit reversed Mize and ordered him to issue an injunction requiring the university to admit Meredith as a student.

"A full review of the record," its unanimous decision read, "leads the Court inescapably to the conclusion that from the moment the defendants discovered Meredith was a Negro they engaged in a carefully calculated campaign of delay, harassment, and masterly inactivity. It was a defense designed to discourage and to defeat by evasive tactics which would have been a credit to Quintus Fabius Maximus.* We see no valid, nondiscriminatory reason for the University's not accepting Meredith. Instead, we see a well-defined pattern of delays and frustrations, part of a Fabian policy of worrying the enemy into defeat while time worked for the defenders."

The rest is history. After a frantic summer-long rearguard

* The court was apparently referring to Roman General Quintus Fabius Maximus Verrucosus, who, during the Punic Wars, successfully out-maneuvered Hannibal by keeping his army out of the Carthaginian's reach.

action led by Governor Ross R. Barnett, Mississippi capitulated on September 30, 1962, when James Howard Meredith became the first of his race to enroll at the state's finest institution of higher learning. Although it took the direct intervention of the President of the United States and the deaths of two innocent men to secure Meredith's admission, it was clear that the law, despite some exasperating delays, had finally limped to triumph.

On January 31, as Meredith was registering for his second semester, Higgs and I filed a formal motion to intervene in the case on Greene's behalf. Not only did we ask for our client's immediate admission to the university, but we indicated that Ellis' refusal to register him amounted to contempt of court.

The matter was set down for a hearing before Judge Mize in Hattiesburg on Monday, February 4. The previous day, Clarence Jones of the Gandhi Society and I flew to Jackson where we were met by Higgs. That evening, we prepared our case around the young attorney's kitchen table.

Early the next morning, we drove to Hattiesburg, a sleepy town some eighty miles south of Jackson. The hearing was to take place in the small federal courthouse. Promptly at ten o'clock, Judge Mize mounted the bench.

Although Attorney General Joe T. Patterson was present, Charles Clark, one of his special assistants, represented the university. Clark's first move was to ask for permission to put Registrar Ellis on the stand to prove that Greene was "not qualified to attend the University of Mississippi any more than I am."*

Fearing another round of Meredith-type delays, we objected strenuously to the taking of any testimony. "We are not asking for registration," we told Mize. "We are only

---

* I have always wondered whether Clark realized the significance of this remark.

asking your Honor to admit him to effectuate your own injunction, to give it meaning. It will have very little meaning if another term goes by and this man reaches twenty-three years of age. We are trying to avoid what the Court of Appeals said should be avoided—delay beyond the opening of the school year."

When Mize overruled our objection, we put Greene on the stand. He testified simply that he wanted to go to the University of Mississippi because he "was interested in accounting."

> Q. Do you know of your own knowledge if a man can qualify as an accountant by attending any of the present so-called Negro colleges?
> A. I know he cannot become an accountant by attending any Negro college.

On direct questioning, Ellis insisted that Greene's color had absolutely nothing to do with the denial of his application. "Race has no bearing on the matter whatsoever," he said blandly. He also stated that he thought that there were at least two Negro colleges that offered some accountancy courses, but he readily admitted that they did not amount "to as broad a program as at the University."

When we questioned him, the registrar proved to be an adroit and suave witness who, with a remarkably straight face, reiterated that race had never been a consideration for admission to Ole Miss. In any event, he was certain that the fact that Greene was a Negro had not entered into the decision to reject him. The real reason was that Mississippi Vocational College was not an "accredited" institution.

Since he had told Clark that some one hundred other applicants had been rejected for the same reason, we decided to explore this with him. "The majority were from schools outside the State of Mississippi," he conceded.

Q. How many would you say were students from within
   the state of Mississippi?
A. Probably no more than fifteen.

And not one of these fifteen had come from any publicly
supported colleges "that are predominantly for white students."

Although he readily agreed that Greene would have been
eligible for admission if he had applied directly from high
school, Ellis maintained that this was no longer the case. "If
he had been enrolled in an institution of higher learning, he
would have to be considered a transfer student."

Q. If he has been enrolled in an accredited school you
   would admit him if he has maintained a D average in
   that school?
A. If he maintained a D average in the last semester or
   quarter and if he is eligible for readmission to that
   school.

Yes, Dewey Greene had "better than a D average" for his
last quarter at Mississippi Vocational College. Despite a failure in mathematics, he had three C's and two B's for his five
other courses. The division of the number of class hours into
his grade points showed an overall average of 2.8. Since 3.0
was a C, it was clear to me that Greene had attained a C-
minus rating.

Ellis disagreed. "The odds are that it would be called a D-
plus," he insisted.

Q. But it could be called a C-minus?
A. I think you are quibbling.
Q. But this could be a C-minus just as well as it could
   be a D-plus?
A. I call it a D-plus.

Q. If I call it a C-minus you won't fight me about it, will you?

A. You can call it anything you like.

But the registrar conceded that applicants from other colleges with similar averages would have been accepted.

Q. These grades would have been sufficient for a transfer student if he had come from an accredited institution?

A. Yes, if these were points from an accredited institution.

Q. So the only thing between us at this moment as far as his admission is concerned is whether he comes from an accredited institution according to your standards?

A. This is exactly what I told him.

In addition to his C-minus average, Greene boasted a composite score of 18 on the American College Test. According to Ellis, such a score "would rank him in the upper forty percentile of grades over the country."

Q. Do you now require a composite score?

A. Effective with the students who enter the University in the summer of 1963 and thereafter we will require a composite score.

For Mississippi residents, the requisite score would be "at least 15."

Before he left the stand, Mr. Ellis stated that Mississippi Vocational was the only four-year public college in the state that was not accredited.* This, he explained, meant that it had not been approved by the Council on Higher Education

---

* Jackson State and Alcorn Colleges, the other two state-supported Negro schools, had suddenly received their accreditation shortly after Meredith's case began.

of the Southern Association of Colleges and Secondary Schools. But it *was* on the approved list of the only official state accrediting body.

After all the lawyers had their say, Mize decided not to grant or deny our motion. He would take no action, he ruled, until Greene had appealed his turndown by Ellis to the university's Committee on Admissions. "So, without going further into it," he concluded, "the Court will abstain from passing on the question until the petitioner prosecutes his appeal to the Committee on Admissions."

Since Ellis was the committee's chairman and had conceded during the hearing that he would recommend that Greene's petition be denied, Higgs and I decided to appeal directly to the Fifth Circuit. On February 15, we urged the three-judge federal court to order the university to admit Greene for the spring term pending his full appeal.

Three days later, we were informed that our request had been denied. "Unless an appellant can demonstrate to the court on such an emergency motion as this that there is great likelihood, approaching near certainty, that he will prevail when his case finally comes to be heard on the merits," the court said, "he does not meet the standard which all courts recognize must be reached to warrant the entering of an emergency order of this kind."

On February 27, Greene followed Mize's recommendation and petitioned the Committee on Admissions for reconsideration of his application. Early in March, he received a curt letter from Ellis. "On the advice of our counsel," the registrar wrote, "your petition will not be presented to the Committee until such time as the Circuit Court of Appeals for the Fifth Circuit has ruled on your pending appeal from the decision made by the District Court."

Shortly before Greene had filed his petition, he had enrolled in fully accredited Jackson State College. In order to force the Committee on Admissions to reach a decision before the summer term, we withdrew our appeal to the Fifth Circuit. On May 8, Registrar Ellis informed Greene that "your petition could not be approved."

Greene made one last stab. On May 15, he mailed a new petition to Ellis, asking that his earlier application be considered a pending one for the summer session. Two days later, he received a letter from the registrar informing him that he was one day too late to apply for the new term.

"The deadline for the summer session," Ellis wrote, "was May 16."

Greene was not the only casualty of his ill-fated attempt to enter Ole Miss. Bill Higgs had long been the object of bitter hatred because of his liberal racial views. I cannot recall a single occasion when I visited him in Jackson that he did not receive at least one vitriolic or obscene telephone call.

The *Greene* case was destined to be his last. Shortly after the Hattiesburg hearing, he was arrested and accused of making sexual advances toward a white youth who had been working for him. A similar charge had also been made against Dr. Aaron Henry, the Clarksdale druggist, who was state president of the NAACP.*

Higgs had met the young man in question at a Jackson YMCA. Using the name of Tom Bono, he had approached the lawyer and asked for help. He was on his way to Texas, he said, and had run out of funds. Moreover, he was suffering from a severe eye infection.

Higgs saw to it that Bono's eyes were treated by a Negro physician. He then offered him a temporary job as a man of work at the small house that served both as his home and office. Bono accepted and for the next few weeks performed all of the chores assigned to him by Mrs. Syrella Van Buren, the lawyer's housekeeper.

Because Bono did not have an operator's license, he was

---

* Dr. Henry's conviction was later reversed by the United States Supreme Court.

not permitted to drive Higgs' car although he often asked for permission to do so. Shortly before Greene's hearing, however, he took advantage of his employer's absence from the city to commandeer the vehicle. When he collided with another car, he was taken into custody by the police under suspicion of auto thievery.

As soon as it was discovered that he was working for Higgs, he was questioned at great length by the authorities. After being held incommunicado for several days, he admitted that his real name was not Bono, that he was only sixteen and not nineteen as he had claimed, and that he was a runaway from his home in New Jersey. In addition, his captors gleefully announced, he had accused Higgs of making indecent advances toward him on several occasions.

That Bono had lied all along was readily apparent. Not only was Higgs' version of the fanciful stories the youth had told him confirmed by Mrs. Van Buren and others,* but Bono had contradicted them in a tape recording which was found in the house after his arrest. Moreover, when he returned to New Jersey, he executed an affidavit in which he recanted all of his charges against Higgs. The police, he swore, had frightened him into accusing the attorney.

But the damage had been done. Higgs was arrested, held on $500 bail, and ordered to stand trial. A sensitive man who was intimately familiar with the perverse workings of Mississippi justice insofar as "mixers" were concerned, he decided, after much soul-searching, to leave the state. He was convicted *in absentia* and subsequently disbarred.**

Today, he is working in Washington, D.C., where he directs the research activities of law students interested in

---

* Including Jerry Brown, a Yale law student and the son of California's governor, who had spent his Christmas holidays in Jackson doing legal research on the *Greene* case.

** It is significant, however, to note that he remains a member in good standing of the bar of the United States Supreme Court.

civil rights.* In this capacity, he has proved to be an invaluable asset to journeymen lawyers who, like myself, rarely have enough time to spend in the library. But no matter how productive his activities, his place was in Mississippi where, as the only white lawyer then willing to accept racial cases, he lived up to the highest traditions of the American bar.

* Higgs' group is now known as the Washington Human Rights Project.

PART **V**

BIRMINGHAM

CHAPTER **20**

Prelude

Toward the end of March, 1963, I received a call from Gloria Cantor, Harry Belafonte's secretary. "Dr. King and Reverend Shuttlesworth are meeting with some of their friends at Harry's apartment," she said. "They hope that you and your wife will be able to attend."

Curious, I tried to pump Gloria about the purpose of the meeting, but she divulged nothing more. "Come along," she said, "and you'll find out."

On the appointed evening, Lotte and I showed up at Belafonte's Manhattan apartment. Although we arrived early, the large living room was already jammed with people. In addition to King and Shuttlesworth, I saw Anthony Quinn, Ossie Davis, Ruby Dee, Fredric March, the New York *Post*'s James Wechsler, and Jimmy Hicks of the *Amsterdam News*. There were also a great many people whom I recognized as very active supporters of the Southern Christian Leadership Conference.

At nine-thirty, Belafonte called the gathering to order. He explained that King and Shuttlesworth had come to New

York to do what they had never done before—announce an impending protest campaign well in advance of its scheduled occurrence.

"When they have explained what they have in mind," the singer said, "we'll see how we can help them."

King spoke first. Birmingham, Alabama, which he characterized as the most segregated city in the United States, was the next target. On April 3, massive protest demonstrations were to start in the Steel City as a joint project of his Southern Christian Leadership Conference and Shuttlesworth's Alabama Christian Movement for Human Rights.

The goal—the formation of a biracial commission, the ending of segregation in such public accommodations as department stores and restaurants, increased public employment opportunities for Negroes, and a brake on police brutality.

The date, King explained, had been carefully chosen. On Tuesday, April 2, Birmingham, which had recently voted to change from the commission to the council type of government, would hold a run-off election to choose the city's first mayor under the new system. The major candidates were racist Police Commissioner Eugene "Bull" Connor and moderate Albert Boutwell, a former lieutenant governor.

Demonstrations prior to the election, the stocky minister warned, might well make underdog Connor the new mayor. Therefore, it had been decided to begin operations the day after the votes were counted. "If Boutwell is elected," he concluded, "we'll probably be criticized for not giving him a chance, but we feel that we must take advantage of the symbolic significance of the Easter season."

Shuttlesworth was far more emotional than King. The time was ripe, he said, to end segregation in Birmingham forever. His Alabama Christian Movement for Human Rights was fully mobilized and would march the moment the word was given. "Birmingham's Negroes have endured too much for too long," he warned. "If freedom doesn't come now, it may be too late for it ever to come. We hope that you will join us in the good fight. If you don't, we are prepared to go it alone."

When the two men had finished speaking, Belafonte announced that he hoped that we would all support the impending campaign. I saw Hicks and Wechsler wince when he insisted that no one reveal what had taken place that evening. For newspapermen to sit on a story of this magnitude is a torture that should not, in good conscience, be inflicted upon them. But to their credit, neither man leaked any news of the meeting.

CHAPTER **21**

The City of Churches

"Birmingham," one of its newspapers likes to trumpet proudly, "has more than seven hundred churches and temples whose weekly attendance is one of the highest in America."

It also has—and this community statistic is rarely heralded —the greatest number of unsolved bombings of, perhaps, any city in the world. To most of its Negro residents whose homes, churches, businesses, and bodies have often borne the brunt of these mysterious explosions, it is known simply as "Bombingham."

The Jefferson County seat, which its first families like to call the Magic City, is less than one hundred years old. Located in a mineral-rich valley in the heart of Alabama, it has been, from the very beginning, dominated by the wealth that could be wrested out of its red earth. As its iron, steel, and coal began to find a ready market throughout the United States, it emerged, despite periodic financial panics, as the economic pride of the postbellum South.

For most of its relatively short history, the city has been

dominated by Northern interests. First, it was the Tennessee Coal, Iron, and Railroad Company which, although it boasted a few Birmingham stockholders, was largely controlled from New York. Then, in 1907, its acquisition by the United States Steel Corporation virtually eliminated all local involvement in the conduct of its affairs.

The same metamorphosis also took place with most of the city's other large plants. As one writer puts it, "Birmingham became a Southern industrial stepchild to Northern financial interests." One result was the formation of the United Mine Workers and the great strike of 1908 which led to the widespread importation of scabs and convict labor.

By the time the strike ended, the future make-up of the city's population was clearly delineated. Birmingham was to become the repository for the poor and impoverished who worked in the mines from dawn to dusk and whose paychecks were drawn in New York or Pittsburgh. At the mercy of an economic system over which he had absolutely no control, and subjected to political forces that knew no other issue than that of white supremacy, the Birmingham worker was ripe for violence at any time.

By 1963, Birmingham had long been reconciled to the fact that most of its real wealth was controlled by Northerners. But it had never lost sight of its pioneer foundations of bigotry and hatred. Despite the many well-paid corporate executives who built charming suburban homes in the hills that looked down upon the city, its streets often echoed to the violence of racial strife.

"Nigger, nigger!" was, as it had been for generations, the rabble's most potent rallying cry.

On Tuesday, April 2, after twenty-three years as a city commissioner, Bull Connor was defeated in his bid to become Birmingham's first mayor under its new council system. Albert Boutwell, his successful opponent, together with a nine-member council, was swept into office by a significant plurality. But a court fight loomed over whether the new administration was entitled to take office on April 15 or in late 1965 when the commissioners' terms would have ended had there been no change in the city's form of government.

The next morning, twenty well-dressed Negroes who refused to leave a "white only" lunch counter in a downtown department store were arrested. The demonstrations had begun.

Dr. King arrived the following day. He was here to stay, he told a wildly cheering audience at the St. James African Methodist Episcopal Church, until "the battle is won." Informed of the Negro leader's words, Connor flew into a rage. "I will fill the jail if they violate the laws as long as I am at City Hall," he warned.

The Negroes' demands were widely publicized during the day. They were:

1. The desegregation of lunch counters and other public facilities in downtown department stores.

2. The establishment of fair hiring procedures in retail stores and city departments with Negroes being given an equal opportunity to qualify for other than menial jobs.

3. The dropping of all charges against arrested demonstrators.

4. The reopening of the parks and playgrounds which had been closed by the city rather than comply with a federal court order that they be operated on an integrated basis.

5. The appointment of a biracial commission to set up a timetable for the desegregation of the public schools.

On Friday, April 5, Boutwell was scheduled to address the Advertising Club. By the time he rose to talk, the number of demonstrators in jail had swelled to thirty-five. In his speech, the mayor-elect went to great lengths to make it quite clear that he attributed the recent arrests to "outside elements and agitators."

"We citizens of Birmingham," he said, "understand and respect each other. When these outsiders learn they are not going to get any more publicity out of this thing, they will move on to more profitable fields."

He proved a woefully poor prophet. Early the next day, a protest group assembled in a small park in the Negro area. Led by Fred Shuttlesworth, a column of Negroes, marching two abreast, started to walk along Fifth Avenue in the direction of City Hall. When they reached the Federal Building, three blocks from their objective, they found themselves surrounded by a small army of police. They were promptly arrested and charged with parading without a permit.

The first police dogs appeared on Sunday afternoon when Rev. A. D. King, Martin's younger brother, led twenty-six of his congregation downtown. When they neared City Hall, they found that the entire area had been blocked off by the police an hour before the march started. Like their predecessors, they were quickly taken into custody and lodged in South Side Jail.

At the request of the Gandhi Society I went to Birmingham on the evening of A. D. King's arrest. There I met with Orzell Billingsley and Arthur D. Shores, the two Negro lawyers with whom I had worked on the Shuttlesworth case a year earlier.

Our first move in Birmingham was to remove the cases of those who had been arrested over the weekend to the federal court. We relied on the same statute which Higgs and I had used during the Freedom Rider litigation in Jackson almost two years earlier. Although we were convinced that the cases would eventually be remanded to the state courts, we were also certain that the temporary halting of the prosecutions would give the movement a much needed respite.

Early on the morning of Monday, April 8, we filed the necessary removal petitions with the clerk of the federal court. We then saw to it that copies of the documents were served on the city attorney as well as the clerk of Recorder's Court. When these technicalities had been completed, Billingsley and I went to Recorder's Court where the trials of those who were covered by the removal petitions were about to begin.

When Recorder Charles Brown was informed that he no longer had jurisdiction over the cases, he appeared perplexed. As he studied the documents which we had handed up to the bench, Bull Connor appeared at a door behind the bench and signaled to him. Brown immediately left the courtroom. Almost two hours later he returned to the bench and announced that he recognized that the cases had been removed from his court.

Chief Judge Seybourn H. Lynne promptly ordered the defendants' release in $300 bail.

While we waited for the city's next legal move, it was apparent that the transfer of the cases to the federal court had buoyed up the movement. Even though there was almost no hope that they would not eventually be returned to state control,* for the moment at least we were on the offensive. "We've taken them by surprise," chortled Fred Shuttlesworth.

The demonstrations, which had been flagging, picked up momentum at once. On Tuesday, April 9, Al Hibbler, the blind blues singer, was arrested with a group of protesters at Nineteenth Street and Third Avenue North. Nicknamed Integration Corner, the intersection marked the dividing

---

* A few days later, Judge Clarence W. Allgood, as expected, sent all of the cases back to Recorder's Court.

line between the Negro community and the downtown shopping area.

Even though the police insisted that Hibbler's arrest had been in error, it had angered the Negroes of Birmingham. It was now fairly apparent that, unless something drastic happened, the city was in for protracted and bitter racial strife. A. G. Gaston, its wealthiest Negro, forecast a holocaust unless local leaders of both races were able to work together to ward it off.

CHAPTER **22**

The Struggle Deepens

Gaston's emphasis on "local leaders" underscored the
basic weakness of King's position. Unlike Montgomery,
where he had been a part of the local scene before the bus
boycott began, he was an outsider in Birmingham. Of even
more significance was the fact that the city had a sizable
number of wealthy and influential Negroes who did not take
kindly to absentee leadership.

To add to King's problems, some of Birmingham's most
liberal white clergymen had banded together to counsel
moderation on both sides. "We urge our own Negro community to withdraw support from these demonstrations and to
unite locally in working peacefully for a better Birmingham," they said. "When rights are consistently denied, a
cause should be pressed in the courts and in negotiations
among local leaders, not in the streets. We appeal to both our
white and Negro citizens to observe the principles of law and
order and common sense."

I had never quite understood how King enlisted the support of a community for extended protest demonstrations

and, when he invited me to accompany him to a meeting with Birmingham's Negro business and professional leaders, I was quick to accept. The meeting was held in a large room in the Gaston Building, an ultramodern, three-story structure on Fifth Avenue North. When we arrived, it was completely filled.

The session was a difficult one for King. Although he dominated it from beginning to end, he still had to cope with the views of many Birmingham Negroes who were hesitant about mass demonstrations.

"We ought to give Boutwell more of a chance," one man said.

"I think we should wait until we're better organized," another recommended.

"What we need is more community cooperation and fewer picket lines," a third volunteered.

For the first part of the meeting, King listened patiently to everyone who felt that he had something to say. When no more hands were raised, he began to speak. "This is the most segregated city in America," he said, "and we have to stick together if we ever hope to change its ways. I and my associates in the Southern Christian Leadership Conference have come to help you to break down the walls. With God's help, we cannot fail."

For the next thirty minutes, he outlined a comprehensive plan of peaceful picketing of downtown department stores and marches to City Hall, coupled with the expected arrival in Birmingham of such notables as Jackie Robinson, Sammy Davis, Jr., and Harry Belafonte. He had met with the city's Negro ministers and there would be mass meetings nightly at the various churches. "In short," he concluded, "we plan to use every nonviolent tactic we know to achieve our goals. We hope that you will help us in our task."

Although there was a brief flurry of questions after he had

finished talking, it was clear that he could now count on his audience. Those who hadn't been won over were at least neutralized and the rest seemed eager to help in the work that lay ahead. I didn't know quite when the turning point had been reached, but I was very much aware that it had.

The intensification of support for King was immediately apparent. Early the next morning, Wednesday, April 10, the day that the atomic submarine *Thresher* was lost in the Atlantic off Boston, eight Negroes began a sit-in at the city library. Although they were greeted by such comments as "It stinks in here" and "Why don't you go home?" they strolled around the building without incident.

At the same time, twenty-five pickets appeared in front of several downtown stores. Carrying such signs as "Don't Buy Segregation" and "Don't Shop Where You Can't Eat," they were quickly arrested by the waiting police who were under the direct command of Bull Connor. As they entered the paddy wagon, they were cheered by a large group of Negroes who had gathered shortly after the picketing started.

"We'll join you soon!" the bystanders shouted as the last of the pickets disappeared into the vehicle.

Freshly-bailed Al Hibbler, who had accompanied the pickets downtown, tried desperately to join them in the wagon.

"Get back against that wall!" Connor ordered the blind singer.

"Don't tell me to get back against that wall!" Hibbler retorted. "I'm a free man!"

"You can't work, and anyone who goes to jail has to earn his food," Connor replied cruelly. "You can't do anything, even entertain."

As Hibbler was being driven back to his motel in a police car, his shoulders shook with frustration. "They're trying to segregate me from my own people," he complained bitterly.

The city, sensing that Dr. King could now count on

widespread local support, retaliated at once. That afternoon, Connor and Police Chief Jamie Moore applied to Circuit Judge W. A. Jenkins for an injunction prohibiting such activities as boycotts, sit-ins, and picketing. They succeeded in convincing Jenkins that unless he issued such an order there would be "incidents of violence and bloodshed."

The injunction was served on King at 1:30 A.M. the next morning. As soon as he had read it, he announced that he intended to violate it on Good Friday. "I am prepared to go to jail and stay as long as necessary," he said. "I will be here until we get some good-faith demonstration of an intent to grant the things we are asking for."

Ralph Abernathy put it more biblically. "About two thousand years ago," he told reporters, "Christ died on the cross for us. Tomorrow we will take it up for our people and die if necessary."

Early the following afternoon, the two ministers left the Zion Hill Baptist Church on Fourteenth Street at the head of some fifty marchers. They were dressed in blue jeans and blue cotton shirts to dramatize the Easter boycott of the downtown stores. When they reached Seventeenth Street and Sixth Avenue, they found that the police had sealed off the entire block.

The marchers then turned south and walked to Fifth Avenue. As they started downtown again, they ran into the redeployed police who were waiting halfway down the block. "Stop them there!" Connor ordered as they passed a garage. King and Abernathy were immediately seized by four officers and dragged to a police van.

"Was King in that bunch?" Connor asked as the vehicle headed for the South Side Jail. Assured that he was, the burly commissioner laughed. "That's what he came down here for, to get arrested," he said. "Now he's got it!"

King's arrest caused a nationwide sensation. As he and

Abernathy were held incommunicado in the South Side Jail, President Kennedy, who was vacationing at Palm Beach, called Burke Marshall, chief of the Civil Rights Division of the Justice Department, to ask him what could be done. Marshall, a legal conservative, replied as he had so many times in the past that there was no grounds for federal intervention.

But the Negroes of Birmingham did not feel so constrained. The next morning, Rev. A. D. King led a line of marchers toward the South Side Jail. Although the police had blocked off Fifth Avenue, A. D. King eluded them temporarily by cutting across a vacant lot to Sixth Avenue. After he and his followers had finally been arrested and taken away in vans, angered Negro spectators began to hurl rocks at the remaining policemen.

Violence had begun.

Mayor-elect Boutwell was sworn in the next morning on the steps of City Hall. Although he made no direct reference to the demonstrations, he stressed the fact that Birmingham had to solve its own problems in its own way. "I am determined that we shall present the true and positive picture of both our city and people to the rest of the world," he said. "Whatever our shortcomings may be, they are our own local problems and we shall resolve them by local effort and local unity. We shall not submit to the intimidations of pressure or to the dictates of interference."

Shortly after Boutwell's inauguration, President Kennedy called Coretta King and told her that he had ordered the FBI to check on her husband's condition. "He said that if I had any anxiety or concern to feel free to call him or the Attorney General or Mr. Salinger," Mrs. King told reporters. The President's call was reminiscent of the celebrated one he had made to her during the 1960 campaign when King had been held in a Georgia jail on a traffic charge.

King was not idle in jail. While he waited for developments from the outside world, he came across a Birmingham newspaper which carried a statement by eight Alabama clergymen calling his activities "unwise and untimely." Depressed by their criticism, he answered every objection they raised in one of the most moving documents I have ever read.

His "Letter from the Birmingham Jail" was begun on the margin of the newspaper in which the clergymen's statement appeared, continued on scraps of writing paper supplied by a friendly Negro trusty, and completed on pads smuggled in by his attorneys. I read it sheet by sheet as I helped Wyatt Walker to collate it in the small office rented by SCLC a few blocks away from the Gaston Motel.

One of the longest letters Martin has ever written, it set the tone for the entire campaign. With the utmost patience and goodwill, he explained to his colleagues of the cloth that the demonstrations in Birmingham had been born out of long-standing injustice, deep-rooted frustration, and the suffering of more than three hundred years. "There comes a time," he wrote, "when the cup of endurance runs over and men are no longer willing to be plunged into the abyss of despair."

"I hope this letter finds you strong in the faith," he concluded. "I also hope that circumstances will soon make it possible for me to meet each of you, not as an integrationist or a civil rights leader but as a fellow clergyman and a Christian brother. Let us all hope that the dark clouds of racial prejudice will soon pass away and the deep fog of misunderstanding will be lifted from our fear-drenched communities, and in some not too distant tomorrow the radiant stars of love and brotherhood will shine over our great nation with all their scintillating beauty."

On Wednesday, April 17, fifteen more demonstrators were

arrested when they insisted on marching downtown to register to vote. In an unprecedented move, Police Chief Jamie Moore appeared at the Sixteenth Street Baptist Church and tried to stop the procession.

"I don't have anything against your registering to vote," he said. "But if you march out of here as a parade you will be in violation of a city ordinance, and we will take necessary action to keep you from violating the law."

Moore's words had no effect. Led by Reverend Henry Crawford, a group of demonstrators promptly marched out of the church and headed for City Hall. They had gone only one block before they were arrested.

On Saturday, April 20, Dr. King was released from jail after posting a $300 cash bond. Two days later, he was back in court, charged with violating Judge Jenkins' injunction. After a three-day hearing, he and six other Negro leaders were found guilty of contempt of court and sentenced to five days in jail and a fine of $50. The jail terms were stayed pending appeal.

By this time, the major legal work in Birmingham was being handled by the NAACP Legal Defense Fund. Dr. King, who had hoped that the Gandhi Society would provide the number of lawyers needed to service an on-going movement, had reluctantly come to the conclusion that it could not do so. The society continued to operate on a reduced scale for some six more months before passing into limbo. High hopes alone had not been enough to keep it going.

On the injunction hearing's last day, the country was shocked to learn that William Moore, a thirty-five-year-old ex-postman, had been shot and killed near Attalla, Alabama. Moore, who was carrying pro-integration signs, had hoped to walk to Jackson, Mississippi, and deliver a plea for racial understanding to Governor Barnett. Nobody was convicted for this senseless crime.

I was having a cup of coffee in the restaurant of the Gaston Motel when Judge Jenkins' decision was made public. Seated across the table from me was Billie Sol Estes, the bespectacled West Texas promoter who was awaiting a decision on his appeal from a mail fraud and conspiracy conviction. Estes, accompanied by a Negro family, was on the third lap of a strange goodwill tour in favor of racial understanding.

Jenkins' relatively mild sentences proved more a hindrance than a help to King's campaign. The demonstrations, which had begun to flag a week earlier, reached rock bottom. At a mass meeting a few nights later, I watched in dismay as both King and Ralph Abernathy exhorted a packed church for almost an hour in order to persuade a dozen people to volunteer to go to jail.

Significantly, the first one to come forward was a tiny girl in a pink party dress. Although she was obviously much too young to face police dogs and fire hoses, she was a portent of the wave of the future. If it was impossible to find enough adults to march downtown, why, I wondered, didn't the movement use more children. They had as much, if not a greater stake, in the ending of segregation in Birmingham as did their reluctant elders.

It was Jim Bevel, one of King's most effective direct action strategists and a former client of mine during the 1961 Freedom Rides, who brought the children into the struggle. Bevel, a small, intensely volatile man who uses his shaven head topped with an African-style, parti-colored *yarmulke* as his trademark, suggested that May 2 be scheduled as the day when the Negro students of Birmingham should go to jail in historic numbers. King readily agreed.

On the appointed day, hundreds of teen-agers met in the Sixteenth Street Baptist Church. As fast as they arrived, they were sent downtown in successive waves, each larger than the last. Before nightfall more than a thousand were behind bars.

No obstacle deterred the Negro children of Birmingham. When one principal locked the schoolyard gates to keep his pupils from demonstrating, they swarmed over them. A threat of expulsion from the Assistant Superintendent of Schools went unheeded. Frightened parents who saw the old order shaking before their eyes could not deter their sons and daughters.

In his book, *Why We Can't Wait,* Dr. King repeated the remarks of one boy when his father forbade him to leave school. "Daddy," the boy explained, "I don't want to disobey you, but I have made my pledge. If you try to keep me home, I will sneak off. If you think I deserve to be punished for that, I'll just have to take the punishment. For, you see, I'm not doing this only because I want to be free. I'm doing it also because I want freedom for you and Mama and I want it to come before you die."

With more than twenty-five hundred children in jail and more arriving every day, Bull Connor, who had been strangely restrained since the first weeks of the campaign, reverted to type. Out came the billy clubs, the police dogs, and the fire hoses, and the country watched in horror as young boys and girls, in the best tradition of nonviolence, countered brutality with peace and love. History was being written in the streets of Birmingham.

Until Birmingham, I was not certain that I really believed that good could triumph over evil. Like Herman Melville, I had always looked upon the two extremes of human behavior as competing forces which, at best, held each other in check.

One incident helped to change my mind. On Sunday, May 5, several hundred Negroes decided to hold a public prayer session for the imprisoned children. As they marched toward the City Jail, they were met by Connor and his men.

"I'm asking you to turn back," the police commissioner told Reverend Charles Billups who was heading the march.

"I'm sorry, Mr. Connor," Billups replied, "we're going down to pray for our children."

Connor, his neck bristling, spun on his heel.

"Dammit, turn on the hoses," he ordered.

For a moment, it looked as if the Negroes, most of whom had fallen to their knees at Connor's approach, would be washed down the street by the high pressure nozzles. Then, in one of those rare moments in human affairs, morality proved irresistible. The policemen did not turn on their hoses.

Instinctively, Billups sensed that they could not bring themselves to obey Connor's command. His face still mirroring his disbelief, he rose to his feet.

"Let us proceed," he said quietly. Silently, his kneeling followers stood up and walked by the immobile policemen. A few minutes later, the Negroes were praying in front of the jail.

The end was almost near. With Burke Marshall, the Chief of the Civil Rights Division of the Justice Department as a catalyst, King and his aides met with members of the Senior Citizens Committee representing Birmingham's business community. After thirty-six hours of negotiations, the following agreement was reached:

1. All department store lunch counters, restrooms, fitting rooms, and drinking fountains would be desegregated in planned stages within ninety days after signing.

2. Negroes would be upgraded and employed on a non-discriminatory basis throughout the city with some hired as clerks and salesmen within sixty days after signing. A committee of business, industrial, and professional leaders would be formed at once to implement an area-wide program for the upgrading and employment of Negroes in job categories previously denied to them.

3. Appropriate city officials would cooperate with the movement's lawyers in accomplishing the release of all persons in jail.

4. Communication between the Negro and white communities through the Senior Citizens Committee or the Chamber of Commerce was to be publicly established within two weeks after signing.

The negotiations almost ended before they began. Late on Wednesday, May 8, King and Abernathy were unexpectedly jailed. It was apparent that there were people in Birmingham who did not want an honorable peace. Their last resort was to keep King from the bargaining table by fair means or foul.

Bail was set at an exorbitant $2,500 each. If the two men had to remain in jail all night, the negotiations might have broken off for good. In New York, I contacted Harry Belafonte who had been instrumental in raising much of the bail fund for the demonstrations.

"Harry," I said, "we simply have to get the money and fly it down to Birmingham tonight."

We both agreed that we would raise whatever cash we could and meet at his apartment at midnight. In the interim, I made a reservation on a 2 A.M. flight from Newark.

To my surprise, I found that there was a lot of available cash around New York late at night. When I arrived at Belafonte's apartment, I had picked up several thousand dollars from friends. The singer met me at his front door with the balance of the $5,000 which had been donated by Mike Quill, the President of the Transport Workers Union, and other neighbors.

I was about to leave for the airport when the telephone rang. It was Wyatt Walker who reported that A. G. Gaston had just posted the necessary cash bonds and that King and

Abernathy were on their way back to the conference table. Belafonte and I spent the rest of the night returning the money to the people who had lent it to us.

The pact could not, of course, solve Birmingham's racial problems. The day after it was signed, bombs severely damaged the Gaston Motel and the home of Dr. King's brother. The news of these outrages caused a major riot in the Negro section of town which lasted well into Mother's Day.

The next day, President Kennedy, determined to save the Birmingham agreement, sent three thousand Army troops into the area. At the same time, he ordered all "necessary preliminary steps" to be taken to call the Alabama National Guard into federal service.

The next move was up to Birmingham. If the city could keep the peace, federal intervention would be avoided. If not, the troops were ready.

With state patrolmen imposing virtual martial law throughout the Negro community, relative quiet was restored. On Monday, May 13, King made a pilgrimage to the pool halls to urge Negroes to avoid violence. Two days later, the tension broke when sixty business leaders gave implied support to the desegregation plans and agreed to publicize the names of the members of the Senior Citizens Committee who had helped to carve out the agreement.

But the die-hards had one more arrow in their quiver. On May 20, the Birmingham Board of Education suspended more than a thousand students who had participated in the demonstrations. It took only two days for the federal courts to order them reinstated.

Chief Judge Tuttle, his voice taut with anger, castigated the Birmingham school authorities:

It appears shocking that a board of education interested in the education of children committed to its care should thus, in effect, destroy the value of one term of school for so many children at a time when any persons professionally interested in the educational process and the welfare of young children are bending their efforts toward minimizing school drop-outs and emphasizing the need for continuing education.

The next morning, the Alabama Supreme Court, in an appropriate postscript, ruled Connor and his fellow commissioners out of office.

Birmingham had begun to shake its past.

CHAPTER **23**

A Lasting Victory

The Battle of Birmingham had an effect far beyond the city's smoke-filled perimeter. One after another, it spawned similar demonstrations across the South. In quick succession, Negroes went into the streets in Jackson, Mississippi, Danville, Virginia, Savannah, Georgia, Selma, Alabama, Cambridge, Maryland, Williamston, North Carolina, and scores of other segregation strongholds.

But the six-week struggle was destined to have even a more profound result. On June 19, 1963, the Kennedy Administration sent the most comprehensive civil rights bill since Reconstruction to the Congress. Introduced as H.R. 7152, it would, if passed and enforced, lay the legal foundations for ending most segregation throughout the United States.

It is indisputable that this bill was the direct result of Birmingham and its progeny. The President's State of the Union message in January had not included any mention of new civil rights legislation. But the events of April and May had convinced the Administration that if it wanted to avoid another long, hot summer of racial discord, it had to act—and fast.

When I heard of the bill's introduction, I realized that the direct action movement had scored one of its most impressive triumphs. The thousands who had gone to jail in Birmingham and other Southern cities had forced their national government to respond in a meaningful fashion. The police dogs, billy clubs, cattle prods, fire hoses, overcrowded cells all suddenly seemed worth enduring.

It is indeed ironic that Kennedy, like Lincoln before him, will be remembered best for those steps he could not avoid taking. In the civil rights field, he reacted only to the dictates of dire emergencies and, in many instances, almost too late. Political considerations often outweighed moral ones, and the result was often near chaos.

Not that President Kennedy was a malicious or hypocritical man. He was merely the product of a political system grounded on the tyranny of its own built-in checks and balances. The passage of a sorely needed appropriations measure may well depend on the Administration's hands-off attitude in an Alabama racial dispute or the appointment of a racist federal judge in Mississippi.

We are, I am afraid, too much the prisoners of the ingenious constitutional structure created in 1788. It is workable only to the extent that it accommodates all of its component parts. Unfortunately, the diverse and often sharply conflicting nature of our sectional interests conspire to force the federal government, no matter how well intentioned, into positions which can be justified only if one is able to equate expediency with morality.

Lincoln signed the Emancipation Proclamation only when it became critically apparent to him that it was necessary as a war measure. That it did not free the slaves in territories under his control while purporting to do so in those that were not, indicates that strategy rather than sensibility dictated its issuance. Much the same could be said of the Civil Rights Act of 1964 which permitted Mrs. Murphy* to continue her segregated boarding house while prohibiting the hotel across town from doing likewise.

There were some of us who saw in the proposed bill a chance to make the civil rights removal statute which we had used in Mississippi, Alabama, and Virginia much more workable. Although the Reconstruction Congress had provided for the removal of cases to the federal courts when it was impossible for a defendant to get a fair trial in the state court or when the issue was his reliance on a "law providing for equal rights," very few successful removals had taken place. One of the prime reasons for the statute's lack of use was the fact that the federal court's remand order sending a case back to its state counterpart was believed to be nonappealable.

Congressional hearings on H.R. 7152 began in late June. By that time, I was deeply involved in Danville, Virginia, where we had used the removal statute to good advantage. In addition, some law students who were working with Bill Higgs' Washington Human Rights Project had discovered that there was good reason to believe that remand orders might be appealable. When Congress had ended appealability for other types of remands in 1887, it had, it seems, excluded civil rights cases.

Although H.R. 7152 did not contain any reference to civil rights removals, Higgs was exploring the possibility of including a provision making the denial of such removals expressly appealable. The day before I appeared in Washington to testify before the subcommittee considering the new bill, he had recommended to several of its members that it do just that.

* A fictitious name given to the owners of small boarding houses during the Congressional hearings on the bill.

At the conclusion of my testimony on July 18, I heartily endorsed Higgs' suggestion. The following colloquy then took place between Chairman Emanuel Celler and myself:

The Chairman: I think the idea you suggest about courts is a good idea, but I wonder whether or not it would be wise to put it, since it is so highly controversial, into a bill of this character? It might be the reason why we would have to pull an awful load if we had it in a bill.

Mr. Kunstler: You mean the removal aspect?

The Chairman: It is extremely difficult because that would give rise to tremendous controversy. We have enough controversy.

Mr. Kunstler: I would agree with you on that, and I would say this: If it isn't in the bill, it ought to be considered at least separately. I think it is an extremely important point.

When the subcommittee counsel stated that he agreed with Celler, Representative Robert W. Kastenmeier of Wisconsin dissented. "I still have hopes that at least this committee will consider it," he said, "and that we can do something about it, and I appreciate the discussion on it of this witness."

The Chairman: I want to say that we undoubtedly would consider this proposal. I did not make the statement that I would not consider it. I certainly would consider it.

Mr. Kastenmeier: My dissent goes procedurally to the motion that it should be introduced separately and keep separate civil rights matters. It is only if it gets into a civil rights bill that it has any chance of survival, I am convinced. Of course, I am talking about tactics. For this reason, I hope the committee hasn't given up on this.

The next day, a representative of the American Veterans Committee reiterated Kastenmeier's sentiments. "Another vital area in the civil rights struggle is not covered in the bill at all," he testified, "the question of removal of criminal prosecutions or civil actions of a discriminatory nature from the state to the federal courts."

On July 31, Dr. King gave his blessing to Higgs' recommendation. Reverend Walter E. Fauntroy, testifying on King's behalf, urged the subcommittee to make remand orders appealable. "The approach is to amend the existing civil rights removal statute, which has a ninety-seven-year history of nonuse," Fauntroy said. "The remand order has not been reviewable by appeal since 1887. Thus, the early, narrow Supreme Court interpretation was frozen into the statute, and Southern district judges are given *carte blanche* control."

As a result of such testimony, Kastenmeier introduced a proposal that appealability be expressly restored. Despite a great deal of opposition from Southern congressmen, it remained in the Civil Rights Bill throughout the debates. On October 3, 1963, Attorney General Kennedy appeared before the full House Judiciary Committee and refused to recommend the deletion of the provision. On July 2, 1964, it was signed into law by President Johnson.

When Judge Allgood remanded the removed Birmingham cases back to the state court just after the demonstrations had begun, we did not appeal because we were convinced that his order was not reviewable. Had it been so, perhaps a great deal of the human misery caused by the struggle could have been avoided. As we had discovered by hard experience, a significant weapon of racist power structures is their control of state judges.

The ready availability of federal courts is a vital factor in ending this threat. Even with prejudiced local federal judges, it is possible now to appeal swiftly to fair appellate courts where relief can be obtained. The proof is that during the summer of 1964 thousands of civil rights cases were removed throughout the deep South, thus stopping local authorities dead in their tracks.

Birmingham may have been just one of the factors in the enactment of the Civil Rights Act of 1964, but it surely played an important role in bringing it into being. As Dr. King put it, "The sound of the explosion in Birmingham reached all the way to Washington where the Administration, which had firmly declared that civil rights legislation would have to be shelved for 1963, hastily reorganized its priorities and placed a strong civil rights bill at the top of the Congressional calendar."

But it will not be for this bill alone that the spring of 1963 will be remembered. The dream which King so eloquently expounded during the March on Washington was framed when, as he said, "the City of Birmingham discovered a conscience." If one city could be moved by the force of nonviolence, then possibly all cities could be moved.

PART VI

DANVILLE

CHAPTER **24**

Another Summer Begins

Medgar Evers was shot to death in his driveway near midnight on Tuesday, June 12, 1963.

For more than three weeks, Jackson's Negroes, inspired by recent events in Birmingham, had been demonstrating throughout the city. These protests had resulted in a wave of police brutality ranging from the wresting of American flags out of the hands of marching children to the brutal clubbing of demonstrators. The Mississippi capital was fast becoming a major civil rights battlefield.

Recognizing the importance of the rapidly developing situation, the NAACP decided to concentrate on the area. For the first time in his long career Roy Wilkins, its executive secretary, found himself in jail for demonstrating. Gloster Current and Ruby Hurley, two of the association's key organizers, were on hand to coordinate plans for a massive non-violent attack on racial segregation.

The Jackson demonstrations had been a long time coming. The Mississippi brand of oppression, combining violence and terror with across-the-board legalized segregation, had kept the state's Negro population severely in check since the end of Reconstruction. Only the painstaking preparatory work of such men as Tougaloo instructor John Salter, Rev. R. Edwin King, the college's white chaplain, and Evers himself had created a viable movement in the capital.

But it was much too young to survive one blast from a high-powered rifle. The bullet that tore into Medgar's back killed more than a man. It destroyed the Jackson movement.

I left for Jackson the day after Medgar's death. At a mass meeting the next evening, I indicated that Dr. King, who expected to attend Medgar's funeral on Saturday morning, was ready to put himself at the movement's disposal in any way it could use his presence. But as I spoke, I realized that the will to resist had died with Medgar. In the audience there was fear, hatred and bitterness—but no spirit to continue the fight.

The funeral took place in the auditorium of the Masonic Temple on Lynch Street. An hour before it began, I met Dr. King and Wyatt Walker at Municipal Airport. As we drove into the city, I gave both men my impressions of the situation in Jackson. "The movement is dead here," I said. "Only Salter and his youth groups are prepared to keep going."

The services were an ordeal. Not only was the crowded auditorium stifling, but the many eulogies somehow did not catch the essence of the man whose body lay in a flag-draped coffin in front of the stage. As the seemingly endless voices droned on, I tried to recall Medgar Evers as I had known him. Somehow, it made the morning bearable.

Medgar was a direct but hardly simple man. A strapping six-footer with a strong, purposeful face, he did not easily reveal himself to others. Outside of his immediate family, only a few people knew him well. To everyone else, he appeared pleasant but somewhat removed and aloof. A remarkably efficient person with boundless energy, he inspired respect rather than reverence.

As its field secretary in Mississippi, Medgar was intensely loyal to the NAACP. But he often complained that its national office did not take kindly to the development of local leadership. "I don't think that all decisions about this state should be made from New York," he once told me. "Nothing's going to be right down here until our own people are in the driver's seat."

He also disliked the NAACP's hostility to other civil rights organizations in Mississippi. "We must all work together," he often said, "or we'll never get anywhere. Our goals are identical—why can't we join hands to get there?"

This was why he was so concerned with the idea of a confederation of all civil rights groups in the state. Today, the NAACP takes credit for the origin of the Council of Federated Organizations (COFO) because Medgar was instrumental in planning it. It is indeed ironic that he was interested in the concept because he feared that his home office's reluctance to cooperate with SNCC, SCLC, and CORE was not in the best interests of the Negroes of Mississippi.

Unfortunately, I cannot say that I was one of Medgar's intimates. Our paths crossed frequently but, as so often happens in the civil rights movement, our relationship was on one plane only. When we met, we talked about demonstrations, boycotts, and lawsuits rather than of wives, children, and college days. I shall always bitterly regret that a sniper's bullet has made it forever impossible for me to bridge the gap.

The last time I saw him alive was just before Christmas. I had come to say goodbye after a hearing in federal court on the constitutionality of the arrests of a few Tougaloo College students who had picketed Woolworth's. When I arrived at his office on the second floor of the Masonic Building, Medgar was on the telephone.

As I listened to his part of the conversation, I realized at once that he was dealing with a hate call. "If you feel that way," he said earnestly to whomever was on the other end of the line, "why don't you come up here and tell it to my face?"

There was an excited crackle in the receiver. Medgar looked moderately shocked. "That's no way for a Christian to talk," he retorted. A sharp click indicated that his caller had hung up.

Medgar put the receiver down. "If I live to be a hundred," he said, "I'll never understand what satisfaction there is for one man to get on a telephone and, without telling who he is, give another man holy hell just because he doesn't agree with him."

My reverie was interrupted by the end of the funeral. As soon as the pallbearers had carried the coffin out of the auditorium, the mourners assembled on the sidewalk for the long march to the Collins Funeral Home on North Farish Street, several miles away. The Jackson police had agreed to permit us to walk together in columns of threes behind an escort of eight motorcycles.

My place in the line of march was directly behind Dr. King. I was flanked on the right by Reverend George Lawrence of Brooklyn's Antioch Baptist Church and on my left, by Dick Gregory. It was only while we were walking that I learned that Gregory's infant son had died after a brief illness just two weeks earlier.

As we headed toward Farish Street, the sidewalks were lined with solemn Negroes. Every street and railroad overpass contained small groups of grim-faced young men and boys who watched silently as the long procession passed underneath. Even the children seemed unnaturally subdued.

"Man," Gregory muttered to Lawrence and me, "it wouldn't take much to set things off in this town today."

We all knew that there was a possibility of real trouble. At a meeting of the Executive Committee of the Jackson Movement on Friday night, its more militant younger members had urged that the funeral march deviate from its planned route and turn up Capitol Street, a move that was sure to precipitate a clash with the police. Although the recommendation had been defeated by an eight-to-four vote, it was by no means certain that everyone would adhere to this ruling.

Dr. King was close to the head of the six-thousand-man line, and he reached the funeral home long before the last marchers had left Lynch Street. Since he had to make an early plane back to Atlanta, I borrowed John Salter's car to take him to the airport.

As I dropped King's party off at Municipal Airport, Wyatt asked me to call him before I left Jackson. "There's big trouble brewing in Danville, Virginia," he said, "and I'd like you to go there with me tomorrow night." I nodded my assent.

As I drove back into town, I soon realized that something had happened in the forty minutes it had taken to make the round trip. Salter's youth groups, which brought up the rear of the funeral march, had begun to sing "We Shall Overcome" as they approached the intersection of South Farish and Capitol Streets, the dividing line between the white and Negro business communities. Suddenly, some two hundred boys and girls turned right onto Capitol Street, and surged up the broad avenue.

The wary police reacted at once. At a signal from the ever-present Captain Ray, some fifty or sixty helmeted patrolmen, detectives, and auxiliaries, heavily armed and accompanied by snarling dogs, quickly surrounded the marchers and began to push them back toward Farish Street.

"Head them off!" Ray shouted excitedly.

When the marchers showed no inclination to return to the intersection, Ray lashed out at them. "Your leaders said you wanted to have a private, mournful march and we agreed under those circumstances," he roared through his bull horn.

"We want the killer! We want the killer! We want the killer!" the young people roared back. "Freedom! Freedom! Freedom!"

Ray was not prepared for this outburst. "You came here to honor a dead man," he remonstrated, "and you have brought dishonor, you have brought dishonor." He turned to his men. "Push 'em all the way back!" he ordered.

In the face of shotguns, rifles, and drawn pistols, the young people grudgingly gave way. Just as it looked as if the incident had ended, a bottle crashed to the pavement in front of the advancing police. Seconds later, the street was littered with broken glass, beer cans, and assorted pieces of metal and wood.

A moment of truth had come to Jackson.

A few minutes earlier, I had parked Salter's car near the Collins Funeral Home. Out of sheer curiosity, I ran around the block so that I could get as close to Capitol Street as possible. When I arrived back on Farish Street, I found that I was behind the police line.

Because of the bottles which were being thrown from buildings on the west side of Farish Street, I thought that it would be a little safer if I could get under their eaves. As I started across the street, I passed a paddy wagon which was parked in the middle of the intersection.

Suddenly, I heard a whispered "Bill!" Startled, I looked around. A second later, there was a more insistent "Bill!" It was only then that I realized that the voice was coming from the paddy wagon.

I peered into the small barred window at the rear of the truck. As my eyes became accustomed to the darkness, I recognized Salter and Tougaloo chaplain Ed King. It seemed that they had been arrested in Jack Young's office shortly after the bottle barrage had started.

Completely forgetting that I was in the middle of a Jackson street, I started to question the two men. But I was soon brought back to reality by the business end of a double-barreled shotgun shoved into my midriff by a bulky auxiliary patrolman. It was to take two weeks before the two circular bruises on my stomach disappeared.

"If you don't want to get in there with them," the policeman warned, "you'd better get the hell out of here!"

I took the hint and headed back down Farish Street where the situation had grown even more tense. As the distance between the advancing police and the main body of mourners decreased, a bloody clash seemed imminent. One well-directed missile, one itchy trigger finger, and there would be a major tragedy.

It was at this moment that one man's quick thinking saved the day. Shirt-sleeved John Doar,* a Justice Department attorney who had attended the funeral, sprang into the narrowing gap between the police and the Negroes. He held his hands up.

"Hold it!" he pleaded. "Is there someone here who can speak for you people?"

Because of the noise of the crowd, few people heard him. But one Negro youth sprang to his side. "This man is right!" he shouted. The sight of the black and white man standing together succeeded in bringing a degree of quiet to Farish Street.

"My name is John Doar, D-O-A-R," the lawyer said. "I'm from the Justice Department, and anybody around here knows I stand for what is right. Go home before someone is killed or badly hurt. You can do no good here."

* On January 15, 1965, Doar replaced Burke Marshall as Chief of the Civil Rights Division of the Justice Department.

Miraculously, the crowd began to disperse. As it broke up, I watched with relief as Ray's men uncocked their guns. In a matter of minutes, Farish Street had returned to normal.

As I flew to Danville with Walker the next evening, I realized that, but for Doar's intervention, a bloody massacre might have taken place. Would we always be this lucky, I wondered, as our plane began its descent into Greensboro, North Carolina.

Only time and patience would tell.

CHAPTER 25

A Successful Skirmish

Danville, a city of some fifty thousand inhabitants in southwest Virginia, is located on the Dan River some ten miles from the North Carolina border. Its largest industry is the mammoth Dan River Mills, which employs almost twelve thousand people. In addition, there are numerous tobacco processing plants and factories of the Corning Glass Works and the H. K. Porter Disston Company.

Until 1959, the city was totally segregated. However, as a result of student sit-ins at the library, the last capitol of the Confederacy, the building was closed to the public. It took a federal court order to reopen it on a stand-up integrated basis. Shortly after the conclusion of the library suit, the public park was desegregated.

Subsequent sit-ins succeeded in desegregating lunch counters in the five-and-ten-cent stores and the largest chain drugstore. But by the spring of 1963, all hotels, motels, restaurants, motion picture theaters, hospitals, golf courses, bowling alleys, most churches, and almost all public schools remained rigidly segregated. This included the all-white Stratford

Junior College and Averett College, the two local institutions of higher learning.

For almost thirty years, Danville's Negroes had been trying to lift some of these color bars. In addition to instituting several federal lawsuits, they had time and time again asked the City Council for help. But outside of the legal actions and a conference in 1962 between City Manager T. Edward Temple and several Negro leaders which had resulted in the hiring of one Negro social worker, no appreciable progress in ending or alleviating segregation had taken place.

During 1962 and part of 1963, the Danville branch of the NAACP and the Danville Christian Progressive Association (DCPA), an SCLC affiliate, submitted scores of petitions to the City Council. None was ever acted upon and, in fact, the council, by the passage of a restrictive ordinance, made it virtually impossible for Negro leaders to get on the agenda of its meetings by requiring the submission in advance of detailed requests in writing for permission to address it.

On May 31, 1963, the first protest march was held. It was peaceful and orderly, and no arrests were made. Subsequent marches, all of which were to the steps of the Municipal Building, were conducted up to June 5, when the first arrests took place during a sit-in at the City Manager's office.

After leaving Temple's office, those demonstrators who had not been arrested previously marched up Main Street to Chestnut where they were addressed by Judge A. M. Aiken of the Danville Corporation Court. Aiken ordered Reverend Lawrence G. Campbell, one of the Negro leaders, to "disperse the meeting and break up the crowds."

When Campbell refused to do so, the judge told Police Chief Eugene McCain "to arrest the leaders." Five Negroes were immediately taken into custody by McCain and charged with riotous and disorderly conduct in a public place and contributing to the delinquency of a minor.

On June 6, the Danville *Bee,* the city's evening newspaper, proclaimed that Danville would resist direct action protest movements. The city "has too many peaceful-minded Negroes in the upper-age brackets," it editorialized, "to see that the record of racial homogeneity shall not be broken down, even if the lawless elements are fortified in their action by the support of the federal courts and the Kennedy Administration which now seeks to achieve its ends by new and sharper teeth in civil rights legislation."

Earlier that day, at the instigation of moderate Councilman Charles R. Womack, a two-and-a-half hour biracial conference was held by Mayor Julian R. Stinson at the Municipal Building. The meeting resulted in some limited understanding and an agreement to meet again the next day.

"I didn't go in there expecting much," Stinson later said. "I felt a little better about it when I came out."

As the conference broke up, City Attorney James Ferguson announced that Judge Aiken had just issued a sweeping temporary injunction against further demonstrations. In addition, he disclosed that a special grand jury was then meeting to consider whether any Negro leaders had violated an old antebellum statute that made it a crime punishable by five to ten years in the penitentiary to incite Negroes to revolt.*

On June 7, when the biracial meeting resumed in the conference room at the Municipal Building, the grand jury on the floor above was busy indicting Reverend A. I. Dunlap, Reverend Lawrence G. Campbell, and Julius E. Adams, three movement leaders. The next morning, the indicted men surrendered and were held in $5,000 bail. At the same time, Womack was threatened by a censure resolution introduced by Councilman John W. Carter, a rabid segregationist.**

Although the censure resolution did not pass, the biracial

---

* This statute was the same one used to send John Brown to the gallows more than a hundred years earlier.

** Two years later, Carter was named by the Conservative Party of Virginia as its candidate for attorney general. He was soundly defeated.

group never met again and street demonstrations were resumed. On the night of June 10, forty-eight out of fifty Negroes who were praying in the alley between the City Jail and the Municipal Building were savagely and brutally attacked by Chief McCain and his officers. While the Negroes were kneeling on the pavement, the mayor ordered McCain to "give them all you've got!"

High pressure hoses were trained on the demonstrators, smashing them to the asphalt. As they lay there bewildered and helpless, they were viciously beaten by police. As the Danville *Register* gleefully reported next morning, "Several sought refuge from the flailing nightsticks by crawling under the cars; others ran and fell into the parking lot but were promptly dragged into the street by policemen and sent running down the street with still more licks from the nightsticks."

The result; broken heads, fractured noses and wrists, contusions, bruises, lacerations, and in some instances lasting injuries to sight and hearing. It took the night-long efforts of three doctors and a number of nurses to treat the wounded at the all-Negro Winslow Hospital. It was not until early morning that the last victim received treatment.

Of the four dozen who were wounded that night, only one was arrested by the police. He was charged with resisting arrest because he had sought refuge from the nightsticks by crawling under a parked car.

Othia Davis, a Negro insurance agent, armed with a motion picture camera, arrived at the hospital shortly after the attack. The color film which he took that night is vivid proof of the carnage that occurred. The damage that a nightstick can do to the thin skin of a man's skull or to the bridge of a young girl's nose is horrible to witness. In twentieth-century America, it is difficult to believe that such wanton brutality can take place within the sanction of the law.

Chief McCain later testified that none of his policemen had reported to him that they had injured any people that night. But City Manager Temple, he admitted, had told him "that twelve people were treated at Winslow Hospital for various injuries."

Q. Did you check the report at Winslow Hospital your-self?
A. I did not.

But he readily admitted to a reporter for the Greensboro *Daily News* that his men "were tired and their nerves were on edge. They were not acting in their best capacities."

The next morning, thirty state troopers moved into Dan-ville and promptly joined forces with the police in harassing and arresting demonstrators. On June 12, the mayor an-nounced that he would name an advisory committee, com-posed of three prominent white citizens, to counsel him on racial problems. In addition, it would seek to negotiate with Negro spokesmen who had not been arrested for demon-strating.

Two days later, the City Council, spurred by John Carter, adopted a stringent antipicketing ordinance. According to that evening's *Bee* it was a "Get-Tough Law." Before the day ended, Len W. Holt, the lawyer who had worked with me in Monroe, North Carolina, just two years earlier,* was arrested and charged with violating Judge Aiken's injunction.

He did not long want for company. By the time I arrived in town on Sunday, June 16, at least 105 other persons had been arrested on the same charge. The hearings that would determine whether they were going to be punished for con-tempt were scheduled to begin the next afternoon.

After landing at Greensboro, Wyatt and I were driven the sixty miles to Danville. Shortly after we arrived, I met with

* See Chapter 8.

the local lawyers at the office of Ruth Harvey, a diminutive graduate of the Howard University Law School, and her husband, Harry I. Wood. There was Jerry Williams, a dark, stocky man with an amazing mind for retaining facts; bright and energetic A. C. Muse, who is the only man I have ever met who travels with stereophonic portable radios; and finally Sam Tucker, one of the finest constitutional lawyers in the state of Virginia—or anywhere else.

Before the evening ended, we had decided to remove all of the contempt cases to the federal court. Early the next morning, we filed the necessary papers. All that remained was to notify Judge Aiken of our action when Corporation Court opened that afternoon.

The first contempt trial, which was scheduled for 2:30 P.M., was that of Ezell Barksdale, a teen-ager who had been arrested on the steps of the City Jail shortly after Aiken's injunction had been issued. As we walked up to the Municipal Building, we were surprised to find that our pictures were being taken by police photographers who lined the entrance way. When we entered the courtroom, which had been closed to the general public, all of the Negro lawyers, including Ruth Harvey, were searched by attendants.

The courtroom itself was ringed with at least forty state troopers, city policemen, and sheriff's deputies.

As soon as Aiken, a heavily jowled man in his early seventies with a dour, humorless face, had mounted the bench, Holt informed him that he no longer had jurisdiction over the case. The judge, who had been escorted into the Municipal Building by armed guards, was not one to be dissuaded by the law from a course he was determined to follow. Without even permitting Holt to read the removal statute to him, he insisted on trying the case.

The three-hour trial was a farce. Not only did Aiken refuse to permit me to participate because he would not take my word that I was a lawyer, but he did not allow defense attorneys to raise any constitutional questions or to pursue pertinent cross-examination of prosecution witnesses. At one point, he threatened to throw me into jail when I objected to the action of City Manager Temple in wresting a document from Holt's hand.

"One more disturbance like this," he barked, "and I will put you where you will be quiet."

The crowning injustice of the afternoon took place as the trial ended. As soon as the defense had rested, Aiken began to read his opinion finding Barksdale guilty of violating the injunction from a typewritten sheet which had obviously been prepared before the trial.

"I don't know just when I wrote it," he told a federal court later. "I wrote it after considerable study because I thought that a question like that might come up, and I gave it careful study."

Q. Was it before the trials?
A. Yes.

Barksdale was immediately sentenced to forty-five days in jail. There was to be no bail because, as Aiken explained, "that would result in an almost complete disruption of any effectiveness or any deterring effect of the injunction and rendering it almost meaningless." Before we knew what had happened, the defendant was on his way to the County Farm.

I left Danville that night. The next day Aiken sentenced Ernest Smith, another demonstrator, to sixty days in jail. On June 20, he ordered all of the remaining defendants to be in court with their lawyers every day until the trials were finished. As next day's *Register* put it, "A 'day in court' that could extend into weeks has been assured the multitude of defendants still awaiting trial on contempt charges from

Judge A. M. Aiken's injunction against disorderly demonstrations.''

Two days later, ten more persons, including Len Holt, were indicted by the Corporation Court grand jury for violating the "John Brown statute." Three of the defendants were arrested by police who invaded the High Street Baptist Church and forced open the door of an upstairs sanctuary to apprehend them. Bail was set by Judge Aiken at $5,000 apiece.

Danville's Negroes were in the grip of a reign of judicial terror.

When I returned to Danville on June 23, I was accompanied by Arthur Kinoy, a Columbia Law School classmate who had been forced out of active practice in 1959 by an attack of spinal meningitis. Several months earlier, I had been asked by Dr. King to appeal two convictions for rape of a seventeen-year-old Negro youth in Lynchburg, Virginia, and Arthur, who had fully recovered his health, had consented to work with me on the case.* This association quickly ripened into a deep friendship and it seemed only natural that we go to Danville together.

A small, fragile-looking man whose chief physical characteristics are a jutting chin, flaring nostrils, and a perpetually wrinkled brow, Arthur is one of the most unusual persons I have ever met. Not only is he a fine lawyer, but he has so many personal mannerisms that he is a writer's dream. Among other things, he chews constantly on pencils and paper clips, possesses a pair of hands that move as incessantly as a hummingbird's wings, and has a way of cocking his head

---

* The collaboration was a successful one. Both convictions were later reversed by Virginia's highest court. The cases are now pending in the Lynchburg Corporation Court where, on November 16, 1965, after a two-day trial in which Alexandria attorney Philip Hirschkop and I represented the defendant, an all-white jury could not agree on a verdict on a related charge of the robbery of $1.37 from one of the alleged rape victims.

to emphasize a point that reminds one of a hungry puppy at dinner time.

We returned to Danville because Judge Thomas J. Michie, the local federal judge, had set a hearing on the removals for Monday morning. Since the city had filed a motion to remand the contempt cases back to the Corporation Court, we would be given an opportunity to convince Michie that they ought to remain in his court. To do so, we had to establish that the demonstrators couldn't get a fair trial before Judge Aiken and that their prosecutions violated federal law.

The hearing lasted two days. Unlike Aiken, Judge Michie, an amiable and courteous man, did not raise any issue about out-of-state attorneys practicing in his court. By this time, we had allied with us Dean Robb of Detroit, Shelley Bowers of Washington, D.C., and Professor Chester Antieau of the Georgetown Law School. Michie welcomed us all.

"I am happy to have you here," he said, "and the clerk will give you your certificates of admission as soon as they have been prepared."

As the hearing progressed, we were convinced we had clearly shown that our clients could not get fair trials in Aiken's court. Not only did the latter admit that he had prepared the Barksdale opinion in advance of the hearing, but he stated that he had worn a gun into the courtroom. "I didn't wear any revolver on the bench," he said. "I wore it in a holster going home at night and coming to work in the morning."

Despite the fact that he had never received any threats, he said that he wore the weapon for "protection."

The United States government, which later submitted a powerful brief on our behalf, put it even more bluntly:

Indeed, there is much more involved here than the mere denial of a fair trial. The trial itself is being conducted in a most unjudicial atmosphere. The Judge conceded that he has been armed with a pistol which he removes only when reaching his office. One witness testified that Judge Aiken was armed on the bench. However that may be, the fact remains that it is common knowledge that the trial judge is armed and this alone is bound to intimidate Negro citizens of Danville, to reduce their expectations of obtaining a fair trial in the Corporation Court, and thus to interfere with their campaign for equal rights.

Moreover, the evidence reveals that Negro counsel, male and female, have been searched upon entering the courtroom; that the courtroom has been closed to the public (except to the press); that perhaps 40-odd armed police officers were stationed throughout the courtroom during the two contempt trials which have already taken place; that the Judge had prepared in advance of the trial, a written memorandum of his decision finding the first two defendants guilty of contempt; and that Judge Aiken refused to examine into the contention made upon motion of the defendants just prior to the first trial, that the Corporation Court had no jurisdiction to proceed because filing of the removal petitions transferred the cases to this court and ousted the Corporation Court of any power to act upon them. This conduct of Judge Aiken surely suggests that he will be somewhat unreceptive to arguments grounded upon controlling federal law.

Furthermore, Judge Aiken refused to release on bail, pending appeal, the two defendants convicted of contempt. Since the sentences imposed are relatively short, this ruling—which Judge Aiken apparently intends to apply to all the pending contempt cases—effectively denies appellate review of his judgments of guilt. And, finally, the practice of imposing 45 and 60-day jail terms in contested cases, while imposing either no confinement as in one case, or only a two-day term, as in the second case, upon the two defendants who pleaded guilty, simply exacerbates the situation by suggesting that those who choose to assert their rights will suffer the consequences.

The combination of the trier of the fact who has apparently prejudged the issues and was a participant in the events culminating in the very charges to be tried, considered together with the general atmosphere of the proceedings and its inevitable result, make it quite clear, it seems to us, that a fair trial cannot be had in the Corporation Court. But that is not all. It is not simply that whatever rights defendants have to demonstrate for the equal protection of the laws will be disregarded in the contempt trials. The situation is further aggravated by the fact that racial antagonism lies at the root of this denial. The entire controversy now before this Court stems from the conflict over Negro equality, and the proceedings in the Corporation Court which are here challenged are a direct result of this conflict. We do not suggest that Judge Aiken is racially prejudiced against the defendants; but a Court would have to close its eyes to the realities not to notice that the peculiar proceedings in the Corporation Court are the direct result of this racial conflict. Judges, and especially federal judges, are not "forbidden to know as judges what [they] see as men." The denial of a fair trial in these circumstances, then, is in the most fundamental sense, grounded upon race.

The remainder of our evidence had to do with the peaceful nature of the Negro demonstrations as contrasted with the brutality of Chief McCain's police department. The most dramatic moment of the hearing occurred when nineteen-year-old Mary Shirley Thomas testified that her nose had been broken by a policeman on the night of June 19. When I asked her if the man who had struck her was in the courtroom, she was too frightened to answer. I then walked over to Chief McCain.

"Is this the man who struck you?" I asked her. She hesitated for a moment as she fought to control her trembling body.

"Yes, he is the man," she replied in such a low voice that she had to repeat her answer for the court stenographer.

When the hearing ended, Michie announced that he would reserve his decision until he had a chance to read all the briefs. Then we took up the cases of Barksdale and Smith who had been tried and convicted by Aiken after their cases had been removed to the federal court. "Under federal law," Kinoy insisted, "these defendants are entitled to a writ of *habeas corpus* transferring them to the United States Marshal."

Michie, who was totally unfamiliar with the removal procedure, appeared bewildered as Kinoy completed his explanation of the law. Finally, in desperation, Arthur opened the statute book and placed it in front of the judge. With his finger, he pointed to the applicable law.

"Why, I believe you're right, Mr. Kinoy," Michie finally said. "I'll sign your writs of *habeas corpus.*"

As soon as the judge had put his signature on the documents, Arthur and I delivered them to Marshal C. N. Bordwine. Ten minutes later, the latter was on his way to the County Farm. We followed in the car of New York *Times* reporter Ben Franklin and pulled up in front of the Administration Building just as Bordwine was serving Michie's orders on the warden.

Barksdale and Smith were working in the fields and it took almost a half-hour before they arrived in a pick-up truck. They disappeared into the Administration Building where they bathed and changed from overalls into their street clothes. Bordwine then drove them back to the Federal Building where Mrs. Ola Haynes, the deputy court clerk, accepted bonds of $500 each. After the brief formalities had been completed, both men were released.

"We feel fine to be out," Smith said gleefully as he left the building. "It's okay," echoed young Barksdale.

CHAPTER 26

Of Stays and Sieges

The release of Barksdale and Smith had a significant effect on movement morale. Not only did it end the threat of imprisonment without bail of hundreds of demonstrators, but it clearly marked the supremacy of federal law. From now on, Judge Aiken could no longer try cases that had been removed to Michie's court until they had been returned to him by federal order.

But the Danville story was far from over.

Judge Aiken's injunction and the city ordinance curtailing demonstrations were still in effect. To add to the misery of the Negroes of Danville, the Virginia Employment Commission had begun to cut off the unemployment benefits of persons who participated in picketing and protest marches. This last move was particularly onerous since many Danville Negroes existed on seasonal employment in the area's tobacco-processing plants.

We decided on a direct attack against the injunction, the ordinance, and the action of the employment commission. In quick succession, we filed federal lawsuits in which we claimed that all three violated the constitutional rights of the demonstrators. In short, we alleged that they were part of a massive effort "to prevent the just grievances of the Negro community from being stated to their elected officials."

In each suit, we asked for a temporary restraining order until the cases could be fully tried. While we waited for Michie's decisions, the movement, which had been slowed down by the city's legal maneuvers, showed definite signs of revival. On June 28, Dr. Milton Reid, the regional director of the Southern Christian Leadership Conference, announced that a protest pilgrimage to Danville would take place on July 3.

Next morning's *Register* was aghast at the prospect. "Not within the memory of living Virginians, if ever," it raged, "has any organized group of people before chosen deliberately to pressure a judge of the U.S. District Court and a judge of the Corporation Court of Danville into doing as they would have them do, rather than as the learned judges find the law and the facts may lead them to do."

The city reacted at once. It filed a petition with Michie asking for an order forbidding further demonstrations. At the same time, it instructed the owner of Peters Park, where Dr. King was to speak on July 3, "to discontinue use of the grandstand until such time as the structure is repaired to a safe condition or removed."

Kinoy and I had returned to New York after the release of Barksdale and Smith. When Ruth Harvey informed us that Michie had been asked by the city's lawyers to restrain demonstrations, I called the judge at his chambers in Charlottesville. I had never argued a case over the telephone before, but I did my best to convince him that an injunction of the type sought by the city would violate both the Constitution and the Civil Rights Acts.

My words did no good. On July 2, Michie granted Danville's request. His order restrained Dr. King, Dr. Reid, and local Danville Christian Progressive Association (DCPA) leaders from, among other things, "inciting any person to, or participating in, any riot or violating of the laws of the Commonwealth of Virginia or City of Danville designed to maintain the public peace within the City of Danville."

The injunction, which would last for ten days, was almost as broad as the one granted by Aiken one month earlier.

Since the rally itself was not banned, it was held the next day on the Langston High School athletic field. Because King had to remain in Atlanta, his place was taken by Fred Shuttlesworth who bitterly attacked Michie's order. "I thought federal courts supported people's freedom," he said. "I assume that this court does, too, but if he doesn't, there are some boys higher than this federal judge."

He read aloud a portion of Michie's order that prohibited "unnecessarily loud, objectionable, offensive, and insulting noises which are designed to upset the peace and tranquility of the community."

Shuttlesworth's voice hardened. "If singing 'We Shall Overcome' is upsetting, let's upset the hell out of the community! It needs to be upset when it keeps people down."

On July 9, Michie returned to Danville. The purpose of his visit was to listen to testimony on the advisability of extending his restraining order. We seized the opportunity to file a motion asking him to dissolve it at once.

The city relied on some police officers who claimed that they had been fired on while patrolling Negro areas. One policeman said that one of his hub caps had been perforated by a bullet which had then mysteriously disappeared. Another stated that a shell had smacked into the interior roof of his patrol car without causing any other damage to the vehicle. A third had been able to spot bullets passing through the leaves of a tall tree a considerable distance away.

In attempting to dissolve Michie's injunction, I called his attention to the fate of a similar order issued by Judge Elliot in Albany the preceding summer. In that case, I argued, Judge Tuttle had invalidated Elliot's restraining order as an unlawful exercise of judicial power.* Michie countered by declaring that Tuttle's action was that of a single appellate judge and therefore not binding on the lower federal courts.

Then Arthur Kinoy took over. Insisting that the city had not shown any of the elements necessary to justify the granting of an injunction, he claimed that Michie had no alternative but to reconsider his decision. "We urge you to dissolve this temporary restraining order," he concluded with a flourish, "or else we will be living in an Alice-in-Wonderland world."

Carter, who had supplanted City Attorney James Ferguson as the city's main spokesman, was "amused by these impassioned pleas." As he was to do so many times in the days that lay ahead, he maintained that blood would flow in the streets if the Negro demonstrators were not prevented from asserting their rights.

"Only a permanent injunction, your Honor," he argued, "will save the peace of our city."

When the five-hour hearing ended, it was obvious that Michie was not going to dissolve the injunction. At an emergency meeting of all the lawyers that evening, it was decided that I would fly to Baltimore the next morning to see whether I could persuade Chief Judge Simon E. Sobeloff of the Fourth Circuit to grant us a special hearing. Sobeloff, a former Solicitor General, was regarded as a fair man who could be expected to see the invalidity of the federal injunction.

I arrived in Baltimore at eleven o'clock and went directly to Sobeloff's chambers. The judge, whose air of perpetual

* See Chapter 14.

distraction is highly misleading, listened patiently as I explained what was happening in Danville. When I finished, he directed me to contact the city's attorneys and ask them to come to his office at two o'clock that afternoon.

"I'll see if I can get one of the other judges to sit with me," he said.

I called Ruth Harvey and told her to notify Carter and Ferguson of Soberoff's instructions. After lunch, I went back to the judge's chambers where I was introduced to Judge Albert Bryan of Alexandria, Virginia, who had rushed to Baltimore at Soberoff's request. "We've heard from your adversaries," the Chief Judge said, "and they will not be able to be here. However, if you will wait outside, we will try to talk to Judge Michie."

As I waited in the anteroom, I would have given my eyeteeth to hear what was going on inside. After what seemed an eternity, the door to Soberoff's chambers opened, and I was asked to enter. "We've spoken to Michie," Soberoff said, "and I think that you can go back to Danville with the assurance that the restraining order will be dissolved."

Without knowing exactly what had happened, I sped back to Danville. When I arrived that evening, I learned that Michie had indeed ended the injunction. At the same time, he had also decided to remand all the removed cases back to the Corporation Court. I had often read of Pyrrhic victories— now it seemed that we had just won one.

Dr. King came to town the next day. Just before he arrived at the High Street Church, I had talked to Judge Soberoff about the possibility of an immediate hearing on Michie's denial of our request for an order restraining the enforcement of the antipicketing ordinance and Aiken's injunction. After some discussion, Soberoff said that he and Judge Albert Bryan would hear both sides at 2 P.M. on Tuesday, July 16.

In honor of King's visit, some sixty Negroes tried to march

to City Hall and were arrested during the day. At a luncheon talk, the Atlanta minister scoffed at Aiken's injunction against demonstrations. "I have so many injunctions," he said resignedly, "that I don't ever look at them anymore. I was enjoined January 15, 1929, when I was born in the United States a Negro. These injunctions are not going to stop our movement."

During the two days King remained in Danville, ninety-one arrests were made. Fourteen more persons went to jail on July 13 for picketing in front of downtown stores. The following evening, six Negroes were arrested for demonstrating in front of the mayor's house. One defendant was Private First Class Buford Holt, a soldier on furlough from Fort Bragg, North Carolina.

Arthur and I met Ruth Harvey, Jerry Williams and A. C. Muse in Baltimore on Tuesday morning. When the hearing began, it was obvious that Judge Soboloff hoped to act as a mediator. But the city, speaking through Carter, would not give an inch. Even a direct plea by Soboloff did no good.

When the hearing ended, Soboloff said that we would hear from the court when it had reached a decision. Six days later, we were informed that it had decided to do nothing. "The court has decided to pass no order at this time," the clerk wrote to all counsel on July 22, "but the various appeals already taken or which may be taken will be heard during the special term of this court which begins September 23."

To say that we were profoundly depressed by the court's action would be the understatement of the summer. We simply did not understand how the court could not see what to us was so painfully clear—that Danville's Negro citizens were being ground into the dust by the city's white power structure and there seemed no place to turn. If the federal courts would not help, where were they to go?

The city was jubilant over the Fourth Circuit's failure to

act. City Manager Temple said that he "couldn't believe the good news at first." The mayor gloated that the two-month period until September 23 "ought to just about give us time to clean house." City Attorney Ferguson said that the Corporation Court was now free to try all of the violators of the injunction and the ordinance.

At the same time, Chief McCain warned that anyone violating Aiken's injunction would be immediately arrested and that out-of-towners would be the first to be apprehended. A battery of movie and still cameras would be used to identify participants in demonstrations for future arrest and prosecution.

Those who depended for their livelihood on the tobacco-processing plants were reminded by the chief that, if they joined the movement, they would probably not be able to report for work when the plants reopened in a few weeks.

For a week, Danville was quiet as its Negroes reacted to the bad news from Baltimore. Then on Sunday, July 28, some eighty people left High Street Baptist Church and marched two abreast in 100° heat toward City Hall. They were all arrested at the intersection of Main and Union Streets, one block short of their goal. The same multiple charges that had characterized previous arrests were lodged against them.

It was clear that the movement had come back strong.

The next day, a hearing began in Corporation Court to determine whether the temporary injunction issued by Aiken in early June should be made permanent. It was highlighted by the dramatic appearance of Reverend Lendell W. Chase, the DCPA president, who had been arrested at his home at 4:55 A.M. on Sunday for contributing to the delinquency of his children who had participated in the demonstration. Chase entered the courtroom barefooted and dressed in the bathrobe he had been wearing when he was taken to jail.

After a week of hearings which indicated that there had

been no violence on the part of any demonstrator since the issuance of the temporary injunction, Judge Aiken not only made it permanent but greatly enlarged it in scope and effect. Throughout the hearings, the city's attorneys were permitted to introduce pamphlets and clippings which supposedly proved that the demonstrators were Communist led and inspired.

With the exception of sporadic picketing, the permanent injunction completely paralyzed the protest movement. Because of the injunction's broad terms and the knowledge that Aiken would not grant bail in the contempt cases, persons sympathetic to the DCPA were inhibited from participating in any activity even remotely related to the protest movement. According to an Associated Press headline on August 3, "Racial Incidents Subside in Danville."

On August 6, the first of the forty-seven contempt cases were set for hearing. Shortly after the cases were called, the city filed an unexpected motion for a change of venue. The motion was immediately granted by Aiken and, the following morning, forty-one of the cases were transferred to five counties, from 80 to 250 miles away.

We promptly called Judge Sobeloff once more and informed him of what the city had done. "In view of this new situation," he said, "I think that I have no alternative but to grant you another hearing. We will hear you and your adversaries the day after tomorrow."

On August 8, we were back in Baltimore again. In addition to Sobeloff, the panel consisted of Judges Clement F. Haynsworth, Jr., and J. Spencer Bell. After two hours of argument, the three judges retired to consider whether to issue a stay of all of the Danville cases.

The wait was intolerable. If the court did nothing, then the Danville movement might reach a dead end. It was a foregone conclusion that, coupled with all the other deterrents dreamed up by the city, the prospect of having to travel hundreds of miles to be tried would keep most of Danville's Negro citizens from daring to violate the injunction or the ordinance.

But this time the city had gone too far. When the court filed back it announced that it had granted a stay. Danville was "hereby restrained and enjoined from bringing to trial any person for the alleged violation of said ordinance and the injunctive orders of the Corporation Court until the determination of the appeals which have been set for hearing at the term of this court beginning on the 23rd day of September next."

As soon as Soberoff had announced the stay, the three judges, pursuant to a charming custom of the court, left the bench to shake hands with all the lawyers. I have since appeared before the Fourth Circuit on numerous other occasions, but I have never failed to appreciate this courteous recognition of the attorneys who appear before it.

Before we left the courtroom, Judge Soberoff recommended that "the interval between now and September 23rd be utilized by persons of good will of both races to seek eventually acceptable solutions to these problems out of which these cases arise."

The next day, three Negro ministers asked Mayor Stinson to arrange for a meeting with the full City Council at which areas of possible settlement could be explored.

Although the mayor scheduled such a meeting for August 10, six of the nine councilmen, headed by John Carter, informed him that they would not attend the conference because it was "untimely."

With all channels of communication between the white and Negro communities effectively blocked, Danville settled down to a state of perpetual siege that ended only with the passage of the Civil Rights Act a year later.

On August 11, the New York *Times* reported that the "Danville Method" was being studied throughout the South. "Officials of other Virginia cities have traveled here to observe and learn," it said, "in an unspoken compliment to a defense strategy that is the most unyielding, ingenious, legalistic, and effective of any city in the South."

PART **VII**

BETWEEN
SUMMERS

CHAPTER **27**

New Orleans and Jackson

The full appeal in the Danville cases was argued on September 23.*

Within two weeks, Kinoy and I found ourselves deeply involved on two more Southern fronts. On October 4, Ben Smith and Bruce Waltzer, two white New Orleans law partners who had been very active in civil rights cases, and Dr. James A. Dombrowski, the executive director of the integrationist Southern Conference Educational Fund (SCEF), were arrested and charged with violating Louisiana's anti-subversive law. The real reason for the arrests, as announced by Chairman James W. Pfister of the Louisiana Joint Legislative Committee on Un-American Activities was "racial agitation" by the defendants.

A week later, I received a frantic midnight call from Ed King, the chaplain of Tougaloo College. On October 6,

* Nine months later, the court, by a three-to-two vote, decided, because of what it considered changed circumstances in Danville, to affirm Michie's refusal to halt the state prosecutions. On June 1, 1965, the Supreme Court declined to review this decision.

World Wide Communion Sunday, three of his women students, one white and two Negro, had been arrested for attempting to worship together at Jackson's Capitol Street Methodist Church. Charged with trespass and disturbing divine worship, they had been quickly tried without a lawyer and sentenced to one year in jail. Bail had been set at $1,000 each.

Before we realized it, we had been retained to defend Dombrowski and the three girls. In the latter case, the Commission on Race and Religion of the National Council of Churches agreed to support our concept that it was a violation of the Constitution to use the police power of the state to prevent integrated worship.

The arrests of Smith and Waltzer took place almost before our eyes.

Arthur Kinoy and I had accepted an invitation to participate in the first open interracial lawyers' meeting ever held in New Orleans. Conducted at the Hilton Inn adjacent to Moisant Airport, one of the few desegregated hotels in Louisiana, it was sponsored by virtually every civil rights organization in the city. The only fly in the ointment was the fact that our conferences took place in the Confederate Room.

During one workshop, Waltzer and Smith were called to the telephone. A near-hysterical secretary informed them that a battery of city and state policemen had just finished ransacking their office. They had taken table lamps apart, removed the frames from pictures, searched through library books page by page, and looked through every individual client's private papers. When they left they took several files with them.

The same outlandish scene had taken place at SCEF headquarters on Perdido Street. Before the police finished, they had carted away a truckload of the organization's files, membership lists, and books. As a federal judge later sarcastically put it, "Among the dangerous articles removed was Thoreau's *Journal.*"

At the same time, similar raids had taken place at the homes of Dombrowski and the two lawyers. The three men were then arrested and taken to a district police station where they were booked. Some five hours later, after being mugged and fingerprinted, they were paroled in their own recognizance and allowed to return home.

Significantly, the SCEF records mysteriously disappeared shortly after their seizure. Late one evening they were spirited across the border to Woodville, Mississippi. There they were turned over to a representative of Senator James O. Eastland, the chairman of the Senate Internal Security Subcommittee, and taken to Washington. This disgraceful piracy revealed the true purpose of the raids.

With the help of Milton E. Brener,* Leon Hubert, Edwin Baldwin and Robert Zibilich, white New Orleans attorneys, we moved for a dismissal of the charges. On October 25, 1963, Judge J. Bernard Cocke, a veteran member of the Criminal Court for the Parish of Orleans, granted our motion.

"There are no facts whatsoever," he ruled, "to justify this court binding these three defendants over for trial."

There was still one more avenue open to Pfister. Since Dombrowski, Smith, and Waltzer had been arrested on the strength of affidavits alone, he could try to persuade a grand jury to indict them. Because of this possibility, we decided to ask the local federal court to declare the antisubversive law unconstitutional. No sooner had we filed our complaint, the theory of which had been conceived by Arthur, than the Orleans Parish Grand Jury was convened to consider returning indictments against the three men.

To safeguard them, we applied to United States Circuit

* Throughout the ensuing litigation Hubert, Baldwin, and Zibilich represented Smith and Waltzer, while Brener, Kinoy, and I appeared for Dombrowski.

Judge John Minor Wisdom for a stay of any indictments until the federal suit had been decided. On November 18, 1963, the stay was granted.

Three weeks later, we appeared in New Orleans prepared to offer evidence as to the history and objectives of SCEF. Because we had challenged the constitutionality of state statutes, Chief Judge Tuttle, as required by law, had convened a three-judge court composed of Wisdom and District Judges E. Gordon West and Frank Ellis. Over Wisdom's strenuous objection, his two colleagues, who are widely regarded as segregationists, decided to hear only oral argument on the constitutionality of the antisubversive law.

In early January, after another equally frustrating hearing, Ellis and West dismissed our suit and set aside Wisdom's stay. Louisiana was now free to indict Dombrowski, Smith, and Waltzer.

On the day of the dismissal, I was in Washington, North Carolina, where I had gone to argue a *habeas corpus* application for Golden Frinks, an SCLC field secretary who had been jailed for picketing in front of the segregated drugstore of Edenton Mayor John A. Mitchener, Jr. (Three months later, we defended Mitchener's son who had been charged with much the same offense by the authorities of St. Augustine, Florida.)*

After Frinks' hearing, I had gone to nearby Williamston to see a basketball game at the Negro high school. Between quarters, a note was passed to me in the stands. It was a telephone message from my wife who, with great ingenuity, had managed to locate me.

"Dombrowski's stay has been vacated," it read. "Arthur wants you to meet him at the Supreme Court tomorrow morning at 9 A.M."

With the aid of Jack Pratt of the National Council of

* See Chapter 29.

Churches, who must surely qualify as one of the country's fastest back-road drivers, I got to Norfolk in time to catch the early morning plane to Washington. At exactly nine o'clock, I arrived at the Supreme Court where I found Arthur and Milton Brener waiting for me. The two lawyers had prepared an application to Chief Justice Earl Warren for a stay of the expected indictments, and we submitted it to Deputy Clerk Michael Rodak, Jr.

After we had cooled our heels for the remainder of the day, Rodak advised us to return on Monday. Before leaving Washington, we telephoned Judge Wisdom and asked him whether he intended to file a dissenting opinion. When he said that he did, we urged him to send it to us as soon as he had finished it so that we could submit it to Warren. He replied that he would work on it all weekend and, if we could send a courier to his office on Sunday afternoon, it would be ready.

Shirley Fingerhood, a New York attorney, happened to be in New Orleans at the time and we asked her to pick up the Wisdom opinion. I met her at Kennedy Airport in a driving snowstorm and, after taking her home, joined Arthur on the sleeper to Washington. There we pored over the twenty-five page dissent, one of the most remarkable legal treatises either of us had ever read.

An Eisenhower appointee, Wisdom is a warm and sympathetic man of enormous sensibilities. Among other things, he had written the opinion that had invalidated most of Louisiana's discriminatory voting laws which were aimed at disfranchising Negroes. Urbane and charming, he is deeply interested in the world around him, and he and I have had many stimulating conversations about everything under the sun.

"The distinguishing feature of this case," he wrote, "is the contention that the State, under the guise of combatting subversion, is in fact using and abusing its laws to punish the plaintiffs for their advocacy of civil rights for Negroes. If those contentions are sound, unquestionably the plaintiffs have a right to relief in the federal court."

Ellis and West had insisted that federal judges were powerless to act until the state courts had done so. Wisdom disposed of this contention in glowing language:

The crowning glory of American federalism is not States' Rights. It is the protection the United States Constitution gives to the private citizen against *all* wrongful governmental invasion of fundamental rights and freedoms. When the wrongful invasion comes from the state, and especially when the unlawful state action is locally popular or where there is local disapproval of the requirements of federal law, federal courts must expect to bear the primary responsibility for protecting the individual.

It took the Chief Justice two days to make up his mind not to stay the indictments. An Orleans Parish Grand Jury promptly indicted the three men. Smith was charged with belonging to the National Lawyers Guild and SCEF, as well as being the latter's treasurer. Dombrowski's accusation stemmed from his position as SCEF's executive director. Waltzer was cited because of his National Lawyers Guild membership.

The indictments of Smith and Waltzer pointed up the dangers inherent in representing integrationists in the deep South. According to a survey conducted by the United States Commission on Civil Rights in 1963, only a minute segment of the Southern bar is willing to handle such cases. Many of the lawyers who did so reported to the Commission that they later suffered threats of physical violence, loss of clients, or social ostracism.

Smith and Waltzer were not the only attorneys who had been punished for their civil rights activities. In 1959, disbarment proceedings were begun against Sam Tucker, who had been so helpful in Danville during the Summer of 1963. The charge: Tucker had appeared in three cases in 1950 and 1952 at the request of the NAACP. Only after a year of intensive litigation was the proceeding dismissed.

Four years later, federal disciplinary proceedings before Judge Cox were begun against R. Jess Brown, one of the four Negro attorneys in Mississippi, on the ground that, in a school desegregation case, he had appeared for one of thirteen plaintiffs without authority. After a hearing which proved conclusively that Brown's appearance was authorized, the charges were dismissed, but heavy costs were assessed against him by Cox on the preposterous grounds that he had not demonstrated his innocence before the hearing.[*]

Len Holt's firm, which consistently accepted racial cases, was kept under constant and annoying surveillance by various state investigative agencies. It had to get a federal court order to prevent its records from falling into the hands of one of these committees. But long before this ruling, the firm had closed its doors. Even the most devoted clients will not risk public disclosure of their private transactions.

But Virginia did not stop at a single assault. Holt and E. A. Dawley, Jr., one of his partners, were also fined by a state judge whom they had accused of bias in a contempt prosecution instituted by him against Dawley. In reversing both convictions, the United States Supreme Court stated that "our conclusion is that these petitioners have been punished by Virginia for doing nothing more than exercising the

[*] On June 3, 1965, the Fifth Circuit held: "All of the testimony in this matter was taken, not at the instance of Brown, but at the instance of the court itself, and it completely exonerates Brown from any improper conduct. There was, therefore, no justification for assessing him with the costs of this proceeding, and the District Judge abused his discretion in doing so."

constitutional right of an accused and his counsel in contempt cases such as this to defend against the charges made."

In Georgia, Don Hollowell and Howard Moore, one of his partners, two Negro lawyers who have been most active in racial cases in that state, were recently cited for contempt because they moved to disqualify Atlanta Judge Durwood T. Pye on the grounds of bias and prejudice in racial cases. The contempt citation followed the denial of the motion by Judge Pye who described its very presentation as an insult to the court.

The caning of C. B. King by a county sheriff during the hectic summer of 1962 has already been described. A year later, acid was poured on the front seat of King's car while the lawyer was visiting jailed demonstrators in nearby Americus.

In Birmingham, the home of Arthur D. Shores, who had worked with me in the *Shuttlesworth* case, has been severely bombed on three separate occasions. After the 1963 demonstrations in that city so many threats were made against the lives of all its Negro lawyers that, for a time, voluntary guards were stationed at night around their residences.

But, as the Smith-Waltzer indictments indicate, the most severe sanctions are reserved for white lawyers. Clifford J. Durr, a former member of the Federal Communications Commission, speaking of his own experience in racial cases in Montgomery, Alabama, says: "Certainly in the present climate of opinion a white Southern lawyer cannot handle cases of this kind without serious consequences to his law practice and, for that matter, his social position as well."

In Maryville, Tennessee, Edward Lynch, a well-intentioned lawyer who had lived in rural Blount County all his life, defended an interracial group whose members had been charged with a variety of petty crimes. The result: the total destruction of his practice and his own banishment. Charles

Morgan, Jr., a successful Birmingham practitioner, was forced to leave Alabama after speaking out against the fatal bombing of the Sixteenth Street Baptist Church.* The expulsion and disbarment of Bill Higgs by Mississippi have already been discussed.

In Miami, Tobias Simon, who was responsible for the first ruling by the Supreme Court sustaining the right of all Americans to unsegregated travel, was cited for contempt of court on the completely unfounded charge that he had failed to show up for the trial of a young Negro girl arrested in a civil rights demonstration in Tallahassee. To his great credit, Fuller Warren, a former Governor of Florida, represented Simon at his trial, and the charge was dismissed. Simon was later threatened with disciplinary proceedings because of his involvement in the St. Augustine cases.**

It was with some of these examples in mind that the NAACP Legal Defense Fund asked the Supreme Court to reverse Ellis and West. "While we have no connection with Smith and Waltzer and have not worked with them in the past," its brief read, "if the files of our legal staff and our cooperating attorneys may be subjected to the same lawless invasion as is here alleged to have occurred, without relief being available in the federal courts, our activities and, indeed, the cause of civil rights will be most severely prejudiced."

On June 15, 1964, the Supreme Court consented to hear

* Morgan now heads the Southern Regional Office of the American Civil Liberties Union in Atlanta, Ga.

** Recently, the Florida State Bar Association's Board of Governors found "no probable cause" that Simon had acted improperly in representing the St. Augustine demonstrators. During the disciplinary proceedings, Dade County Attorney John L. Britton informed the association that "there is no lawyer in this state who has fulfilled more completely the responsibilities each of us undertook to assume when we entered the practice of law. [His] determination to represent those who most require representation . . . should receive the active support of every lawyer in this state, rather than the opposition of our organized bar."

our appeal. Shortly after our brief was filed, we were joined by the American Civil Liberties Union and other civil rights organizations. In his usual eloquent fashion, Arthur argued our side of the case the morning after President Johnson's inauguration.

We couldn't have been more successful. On April 26, 1965, we received a call from Mr. Rodak of the Supreme Court. "Mr. Justice Brennan is reading the Dombrowski decision now," he said. "It looks like a complete victory for you."

We were ecstatic over the Court's opinion, which voided the significant sections of the Louisiana statute. "Appellants' allegations and offers of proof," Brennan wrote, "outline the chilling effect on free expression of prosecutions initiated and threatened in this case. So long as the statute remains available to the State, the threat of prosecutions of protected expressions is a real and substantial one."

The decision is probably one of the most important Supreme Court pronouncements in recent years. In the first place, it sets forth the ingredients necessary to justify federal interference with state prosecutions. Overly broad criminal statutes, whose enforcement would have irreparable adverse effects on constitutional freedoms, could now be enjoined by federal courts.

Secondly, United States judges could no longer refrain from looking into the constitutionality of such statutes pending a similar investigation by the state courts. In other words, faced with statutes like the Louisiana one, federal courts had to decide whether they were valid or not without waiting for the outcome of a state trial. "In these circumstances," the opinion read, "to abstain is to subject those affected to the uncertainties and vagaries of criminal prosecution. . . ."

Lastly, the Court held that statutes which made membership in or association with "a subversive organization" a criminal offense were "unduly vague, uncertain and broad."

The existence of such a statute makes "the threat of prosecutions of protected expression . . . a real and substantial one. Even the prospect of ultimate failure of such prosecutions by no means dispels its chilling effect on protected expression."

The lower court was directed to issue a prompt order "restraining prosecution of the pending indictments against the individual appellants, ordering immediate return of all papers and documents seized, and prohibiting further acts enforcing the sections of Subversive Activities and Communist Control Acts here found void on their face."*

Judge Wisdom had been right, after all.

The Jackson church pray-ins started two days after the New Orleans arrests. On October 6, 1963, Bette Anne Poole, Ida Hannah, and Julie Zaugg decided to worship together at the Capitol Street Methodist Church. They were followed by a police car from the moment they left the Tougaloo campus, eight miles north of the city. When they arrived at the church, they were met at the bottom of the steps by a white man who told them that they were not welcome.

At this moment, a policeman who had been standing at the side of the church joined the quartet. He advised the three girls to go to one of Jackson's "nigger churches" and gave them several minutes to leave the area. As they turned to depart, he accused them of taking too long and arrested them.

Because they were unable to obtain the services of an attorney to represent them in court, the girls pleaded *nolo*

* Shortly after this decision, Louisiana reenacted these statutes in an attempt to meet the Supreme Court's objections. On June 29, Judge Wisdom, now joined by Judge West, ordered the state not to enforce the new statutes until "a hearing by this Court on the motion for temporary injunction previously filed in these proceedings."

contendere to charges of trespass and disturbing divine worship. They were then sentenced to one year in jail. They were also fined $1,000 each.

After four days in jail, they were released in $1,000 bail. On October 12, I arrived in Jackson to file a federal complaint which I had put together with Arthur and Professor Louis Lusky of the Columbia Law School. In addition to seeking a permanent injunction against the arrests of persons who wished to worship God in an integrated fashion, we asked for a temporary restraining order covering the same ground.

A hearing on the latter motion was set by Judge Cox for October 21. The day before, Arthur and I landed in Jackson only to find that our original three clients were back in jail charged with a repetition of the same offense. But this time they were not alone. Four white Methodist ministers from Chicago, a white physics instructor at Tougaloo, and a handful of Negro students who had tried to enter two other Jackson churches were with them.

Ed King picked us up at the airport and drove us to the City Jail. There we met Leland Rayson, a Chicago attorney who had accompanied the four white ministers to Jackson. Rayson, who is now a member of the Illinois legislature, quickly brought us up to date. He was delighted to accept our invitation to join us at the counsel table the next morning.

We worked all night preparing petitions to remove all of the prosecutions to the federal court. We filed them just before the hearing on our motion for a temporary restraining order on Monday. Although the hearing had been scheduled for 10 A.M., Judge Cox adjourned it until that afternoon in order to give the state time in which to prepare motions to remand all of the cases back to the state court.

The testimony clearly revealed that the city had cooperated fully with those churches which wished to maintain segregated congregations. Bette Poole testified that, after the usher at Capitol Street had told her that she could not worship at the church, she had tried to give him a copy of Dr. King's Letter from the Birmingham Jail. "As the usher was fixing to say no, the policeman said no, we don't want none of that."

Her cross-examination emphasized the policeman's role in maintaining segregation.

Q. And it was not until after you had your conversation with the usher that the police came into play, is that correct?

A. The police was always interrupting when the usher wanted to say something to us and he gave us two and a half minutes. I had my watch on, and we left before two and a half minutes. The policeman was emotional and excited and angry until he called us back and said we were under arrest.

No arresting officer was able to say that he had ever been asked by any member of the three churches to force anyone to leave. Deputy Chief J. L. Ray, of Freedom Rider fame, who had made the arrests on October 20 at Capitol Street and Trinity Lutheran candidly admitted that the arrests had been his idea.

Q. But no word was ever said to you about arresting anybody, was it?

A. No, that's correct.

It was the "operation of his own mind as to the arrests."

Officer Joseph D. Griffith, who had arrested an integrated group at Galloway Memorial, was equally frank.

Q. Did the usher tell you to arrest them?

A. No, sir, he didn't tell me.

The ministers of two of the churches specifically denied that they had asked for either police protection or the arrests of any prospective worshiper. Dr. W. Cunningham of Galloway Memorial couldn't have been more definite on this score.

> Q. Did you ask Mayor Thompson for any police help with reference to maintaining any policy of racial segregation in your church?
> A. No, I did not.
> Q. Have you ever made any request of the police of Jackson to arrest anybody for attending worship at your church because of any racial difference?
> A. I have not.

The testimony of Reverend Wade Koons of Trinity Lutheran revealed that he had no objection to anybody worshiping at his church. His own desires became crystal clear when he was questioned by Cox.

> Q. Was their arrest in violation of your wishes in this connection?
> A. In my personal opinion.
> Q. I didn't ask you for an opinion. I asked you if it was violative of your wishes as the minister of this church that they be arrested?
> A. I certainly would not order, Judge, the arrest of anyone unless they were disturbing.

He commented that he had not heard that any of the people who had been arrested at his church had disturbed the other worshipers.

Mayor Allen Thompson startled us with his frank admission that city policemen would be used "to enforce segregation."

> Q. If anybody in the city decided that their policy shall be in their establishment whatever it be, church,

> business, what have you, to keep the races strictly
> separate, not to serve Negroes, and told you of his
> policy, would you then utilize whatever means you
> had officially at your disposal?
>
> *A.* That's right.
>
> *Q.* To perpetuate or adhere to that policy?
>
> *A.* That's right.

Any remaining doubt as to the city's determination to keep
its churches segregated was dispelled in a letter addressed by
one of its commissioners to his fellow parishioners at Trinity
Lutheran. He bluntly warned them on official city stationery
that anyone interfering with the segregation of the church
would be "handled according to law."

He went on to add that the method of using breach of
peace statutes to prevent desegregation in Jackson had been
used "for a number of years and the lawyers for the NAACP
have tested it in every court of the land including the
Supreme Court of the United States, and we have not had a
vote aginst it."

Our clients were superb in articulating why they had
attempted to go to church on the morning of October 20.
Bette Poole felt that it was "part of my religious belief that a
church shouldn't segregate or discriminate and the churches
are open to all people." Ruth Moore, who had been arrested
at Trinity Lutheran, believed "that there is one church and
that's God's Church and if we are all Christians then we can
worship together."

John Garner, a white physics instructor at Tougaloo, was a
member of Galloway Memorial. He testified that he had
taken a Negro girl and two white Chicago ministers with him
to church that Sunday because "I feel that if anybody wants
to come and worship in my church this is wonderful and I

would accept anyone who wanted. He wouldn't even need to be a Christian."

At the conclusion of the first day's testimony, we asked Judge Cox to sign writs of *habeas corpus* to place our clients in the custody of the United States Marshal. Although the removal statute contains an express provision for such a writ, Cox refused to sign any. Three days later, the Fifth Circuit, sitting in Atlanta, ordered him to "forthwith issue the writ of *habeas corpus* directing the custody of the petitioners be given to the United States Marshal."

When we returned to Jackson with the *habeas corpus* order, Cox still refused to issue one. However, he finally permitted us to have a bail hearing before the United States Commissioner and, by eight-thirty that evening, all of our clients had been processed and released. After five days in jail, they were a mighty happy crowd as we drove back to Tougaloo.

Lotte had come to Atlanta with me for the hearing on Cox's refusal to authorize writs of *habeas corpus*. She had continued on to Jackson and, after bail had been posted for the twelve defendants, we were invited for dinner at the Beittels. As the meal came to an end, we heard the tolling of the Woodworth Chapel bell.

"I understand that there's to be a campus rally for the released students," Dr. Beittel told us.

The chapel, where, some two years earlier I had addressed the Freedom Riders, was completely filled when we entered. When Lotte and I tried to find empty seats in the rear of the room, a group of students seized my arms and rushed me up to the platform where camp chairs had been placed in a semicircle around the pulpit. They were occupied by all of the defendants and by Lee Rayson who had been of inestimable aid during the hearing.

Despite the fact that it was highly unorganized, the meeting was one of the most moving I have ever attended. As each of the defendants finished describing his or her experiences in jail, the entire audience broke into a freedom song. By the time it was my turn to say a few words, I had become so caught up in the emotion of the evening that it was difficult to speak.

"I can't tell you how much meaning you have given to my life," I blurted out. "Without you as my clients and my friends, I would never have known how deeply I could feel about people and ideals. It makes much more sense for me to thank you than for you to thank me. No matter what becomes of all of us, I shall never forget the magic and the wonder of this night. It has made everything worthwhile."

When I had finished, Joyce Ladner, one of the jailed Tougaloo students, stepped to the center of the platform. Joyce, a thin, intense young lady in overalls, held up her hand for silence. As soon as the audience had become quiet, she began to sing in a voice that, despite its low range, could be heard in every corner of the chapel.

> We've been 'buked and we've been scorned,
> We've been talked about sure's you're born.
> But we'll never turn back,
> No, we'll never turn back,
> Until we've all been freed
> And we have equality,
> And we have equality, and we have equality.

As she finished the first chorus, other voices had joined hers.

> We have served our time in jail,
> With no money for to go our bail,
> But we'll never turn back,
> No, we'll never turn back,
> Until we've all been freed
> And we have equality, and we have equality.

By this time, everyone in the chapel was on his feet. I could see Lotte standing near the back wall, her eyes glowing and her cheeks flushed as she joined in the moving song.

> We've had to walk through the shadow of death,
> We've had to walk all by ourselves,
> But we'll never turn back
> Until we've all been freed,
> And we have equality, and we have equality.

When Joyce started the last stanza, I suddenly realized that my eyes were wet. I was completely carried away, and I sensed that I was experiencing one of those rare occasions in a man's life when he yields completely to the inspiration of a moment.

> We have hung our heads and cried,
> Cried for those like Lee* who died,
> Died for you and died for me,
> Died for the cause of equality.
> But we'll never turn back,
> No, we'll never turn back,
> Until we've all been freed
> And we have equality, and we have equality.

* Herbert Lee, whose murder by a member of the Mississippi state legislature is described in Chapter 18.

CHAPTER 28

State v. Lowry

No sooner had Kinoy and I returned to New York to await Judge Cox's ruling in the church case,* than I received a call from Dick Scupi, a Washington attorney who was co-counsel with me in defending John Lowry against a charge of kidnapping a white couple during the August, 1961, Freedom Rider riots in Monroe, North Carolina.

"Bill," Scupi said, "it looks as if the *Lowry* case will soon be called to trial. I think that we ought to get together soon to prepare for it."

Although Lowry had been indicted more than two years earlier, he had not been tried because the prosecution had been involved in extraditing Mrs. Willie Mae Mallory, one of his co-defendants, from Ohio. Since the Ohio courts had just ordered Mrs. Mallory's return to North Carolina, the long delayed trial was sure to take place shortly.

* It eventually took the threat of an appellate court order to force him to decide our motion for a temporary injunction. His denial was later affirmed by the Fifth Circuit and the case will soon be tried on its merits.

Scupi was right. In late January, we were informed that it would start on Monday, February 17.

I landed at Charlotte's Municipal Airport on the afternoon of February 19.* As my taxi began the twenty-mile drive to Monroe, I could hardly believe that more than two-and-a-half years had passed since I had first come to this south-central portion of North Carolina. It didn't make sense that we were going to try a case in 1964 that had been born in the turbulent summer of 1961.

As we left the outskirts of Charlotte, I caught a glimpse of a roadside steak house where I had taken John Lowry on October 31, 1961, for his first meal after his release on bail. After almost two months in the Union County Jail he had reveled in his unexpected freedom. "I'm free! I'm free!" he had shouted as we left Monroe that bright fall day.

Just before my cab turned off Highway 74 toward the Monroe business district, I could see the distinctive red-brick tower of the Union County Courthouse with its neon cross. The selection of the jurors had started the day before my arrival, so I asked the driver to take me directly to the courthouse. As we drove through the almost deserted streets I was amazed that I was able to recall so vividly the sights and sounds of this sleepy Southern town.

Monroe, the Union County seat, lies almost as far south as one can get on the Piedmont Plateau and still be in North Carolina. The center of an agricultural region devoted mainly to dairy products and cotton, the city offers the usual retail and service facilities that one would expect. Its normal population of some eleven thousand more than doubles on weekends when the outlying farmers come to town.

While it has few distinguishing features, it is not an un-

* I had remained in New York to prepare the necessary papers to remove the case to the federal court while Scupi held the fort in Monroe. When the federal judge finally refused to hear us, I left for North Carolina.

attractive place. Its main streets are wide and tree-lined, and many of its stores and offices are quite modern in decor.

But despite the up-to-date trimmings, it gives the impression of having changed little since the Civil War. From the shirt-sleeved, tobacco-chewing oldsters who spend most of their waking time lounging around the courthouse to the farmer families which flock into town on Friday nights, everyone seems to have stepped right out of yesterday.

Union County, like most of North Carolina, can boast of a largely homogenous white population. I was very conscious during the jury selection of the Scotch-Irish origins of its prospective members. I was also aware of the fact that extensive inbreeding had resulted in a remarkable number of people with the same last names. Almost everybody seemed to be a Griffin, a Baucom, a Helms, or a McCollum.

Although Negroes made up only seventeen percent of the county's population, they had, under the dynamic leadership of Robert Williams, the erstwhile NAACP president, made their presence felt. A militant and energetic man, Williams had made Newtown, Monroe's Negro section, a hotbed of discontent with the existing order. It was only when he urged his followers to meet force with force that the NAACP national office had disowned him.

Williams' fall from grace had not diminished his influence among Monroe's Negroes. He grew more militant and, with the acquisition of a charter from the National Rifle Association, began to train his followers in marksmanship and close order drill. His home at 410 Boyte Street in the heart of Newtown became the command post of what had all the earmarks of a semimilitary organization.

It was Williams who, in the late summer of 1961, asked the Freedom Riders who were returning home from their arraignments in Jackson to stop off at Monroe. Lowry, a white youth from New York City, and sixteen of his companions had accepted the invitation. The newcomers had joined local Negroes in week-long picketing of the Union County Courthouse, culminating in an attack by enraged whites.

During the melee at the courthouse, Mr. and Mrs. G. Bruce Stegall, a middle-aged white couple from neighboring Marshville, had driven into Boyte Street. According to the Stegalls, they had been surrounded by armed Negroes, forced to leave their car, and taken to Williams' home. As they later testified, the object of their capture had been to force the Monroe police to release the picketers who had been arrested at the courthouse.

Although the Stegalls had been released unharmed, Williams and his family had left town one step ahead of a kidnapping charge. Eventually, they found their way to Cuba where they now live. Williams spends much of his time working on shortwave broadcasts of racial issues which are beamed toward the United States.

Four other people, however, were indicted for kidnapping the Stegalls. Two of them, Harold Reap and Richard Crowder, were local youths who had been ardent followers of Williams. The third was Mrs. Mallory, a short, squat Brooklyn woman who had come to Monroe in the middle of the summer to serve as a movement cook.

The last, and the only white, was Lowry, a good-looking young man with an ardent devotion to the cause of human liberty.

When I walked into the fan-shaped, second-floor courtroom, Dick Scupi and Walter E. Hafner, a Cleveland attorney who represented the three Negro defendants, were busy examining prospective jurors. I quickly became aware of the quality of the panel when Scupi asked one of its members if he thought Lowry was guilty of kidnapping.

"I don't think he's guilty," the man answered. "I know he is."

When the laughter in the courtroom had subsided, Judge Walter E. Brock, a handsome man in his early forties who had been specially selected for the trial by Chief Justice Emery B. Denny, immediately excused the candid witness.

By the end of the day, eleven jurors had been seated. That evening, the Charlotte *News,* the largest afternoon daily in the state, blared: "Communists in Monroe as Kidnap Trial Opens." The article claimed that leading members of the Communist Party of the United States had arrived in Monroe for the trial. The source of the report was Monroe Police Chief A. A. Mauney who told the *News* that he had been informed that high-ranking American Communists were covering the trial.

The next morning, the Monroe *Inquirer,* a widely read biweekly, ran an inflammatory feature story which implied that the Communists had "adopted" the case. Quoting the Winston-Salem *Twin City Sentinel,* the newspaper stated that "Communist leaders have served notice they intend to use the trial for propaganda purposes throughout the world."

Scupi and I were shocked by such a blatant disregard of the rights of all four defendants. In white heat, we prepared a motion for the transfer of the case to another county.

"Under these circumstances," we said, "it is absolutely impossible for John Lowry to get a fair trial in Monroe, and it will not alleviate his situation for the passed jurors to state that they would not be influenced by the articles referred to. The cry of 'red' or 'Communist' is too powerful and too compelling to be eradicated from the mind of any juror who has been subjected to it."

Before denying our motion, Judge Brock went through the formality of asking whether any juror had read either article. Several indicated that they had read the Charlotte *News* story and one had read that in the Monroe *Inquirer.* The entire panel, however, assured his Honor that, despite the newspaper reports, they "could enter into the trial of this case with completely open and unbiased minds."

The jury was finally completed on Friday morning. Composed of five women and seven men, it was as good a panel as we could hope for in Union County. At least none of its members had admitted publicly that he thought the defendants were guilty. But neither Scupi nor I had much faith in their impartiality.

Prior to the selection of the last juror, we were permitted to offer evidence to support our contention that Negroes had been systematically excluded from Union County juries. The county officials we called testified that whenever Negroes appeared on the jury rolls the designation "Col." followed their names. Scupi, who conducted this phase of the case, clearly showed that the percentage of Negro grand and petit jurors was far less than their proportion of the population and that few, if any, Negroes had ever been permitted to serve in criminal cases.

Brock promptly found that there had been no exclusion of Negroes from jury service. Not only was the Grand Jury which had indicted the defendants properly selected, but he could find no fault with the composition of the regular jury panel for the current session of court. There was no surprise at the defense table when he announced his decision.

The trial proper began on Monday, February 24. Because of the hospitality of Dr. and Mrs. Albert E. Perry, Scupi and I had a place to stay each night. We quickly converted the Perrys' spacious basement where, some thirty months earlier, I held my first strategy session with Lowry's companions, into a legal headquarters. Every evening after supper we would meet there with Walter Hafner to plan the next day's activities.

The first two witnesses for the state were the Stegalls. With some minor exceptions, their stories jibed. At approximately 5 P.M. on August 27, 1961, they had driven into Monroe from their home outside of Marshville. After a brief stop in front of the courthouse, they had headed toward Morgan Hill Road to visit Mrs. Stegall's mother.

For some inexplicable reason, Stegall, who was driving, turned into Boyte Street which runs in the opposite direction from Morgan Hill Road. There, the car was surrounded by armed Negroes who demanded that Stegall get out. A timid, easily dominated man, he obeyed at once.

As soon as her husband had left the vehicle, Mrs. Stegall heard someone ask, "Lady, can you drive this car?" She had just started to slide over to the driver's seat when the right-hand door opened and Mrs. Mallory ordered her to get out of the car.

As she hurried to obey Mrs. Mallory's command, a male voice said, "Well, I'll just drive the car out of the street." When she looked around to see who was talking, she noticed Lowry entering the vehicle.

"I was moving out of the car at the time Lowry was getting in," she said.

She had seen him for "only a second." Several days later, she had picked him out of a police line-up. "When I identified him, he had on a white shirt, the others had on colored shirts. I think he was wearing a tie, he was the only one with a tie on. None of the other two bore any resemblance to the person I saw in the car."

According to the couple, it had been Mae Mallory who had engineered their capture. They had then been taken to Robert Williams' house where Stegall had been forced to talk to Police Chief Mauney on the telephone.

"Well, they have got us held here at Robert Williams'," he had told the officer, "and they're going to hold us until you release their folks uptown that you captured this evening. I'd appreciate it if you would release them if it would help them to turn us loose."

After the call had been completed, the Stegalls were tied

back to back with venetian blind tape by Mrs. Mallory. Then they were taken from Williams' house to an empty one a hundred or so yards away. "My wife was walking forward and I was walking backward," Stegall recalled. "Our hands were tied at that time."

When they arrived at the second house, they were guarded by Mrs. Mallory who was armed with a rifle. "We asked her to let us go," Stegall said, "that we were not involved in what was going on, and she said, 'The quieter we could be the longer we'd live,' and 'Don't make me get itchy fingers.' "

According to Mrs. Stegall, both Reap and Crowder had been present in Williams' house. "Those two colored boys were helping along with the others," she swore. "I saw Harold Reap there, but as far as just exactly the very thing he did, I don't know. I saw Richard Crowder there; he was helping to tie me up."

After the Stegalls had been moved, Crowder had joined Mrs. Mallory in guarding them. "Then he helped take turns keeping the gun at the door behind us," Mrs. Stegall said. "I don't know what kind of a gun they had. It was one of the funniest looking guns I have ever seen. I don't know how long Richard Crowder was there, there were different boys."

At one point, Mr. Stegall had asked Mrs. Mallory for permission to urinate. "My husband needed to go to the bathroom," Mrs. Stegall put it, primly, "and asked if she had a bathroom he could use, and she said, 'No, there wasn't.' So I said, 'Can he use the window over there,' and she said, 'I guess he can.' "

The fact that both of Mr. Stegall's hands were tied posed some technical problems. "Well, how can he manage with both hands tied?" Mrs. Stegall asked. Mrs. Mallory ordered one of the boys in the room to untie one of Stegall's hands and indicated that he was free to use the open window. Dragging his wife behind him, he lurched across the room and relieved himself.

At approximately 9 P.M., the couple's hands were untied, and they were told that they could go home. As they left the house, someone handed Stegall the keys to his car which he found parked at the curb in front of Williams' house. They then drove to their son's where they were first interviewed by the police.

When M. G. Boyette, the imperturbable State Solicitor, had finished questioning the Stegalls, we couldn't understand why they had gone to Boyte Street. Not only was it out of their way, but they had been warned earlier that afternoon that there had been trouble in town. A taxi driver at City Hall had told Mr. Stegall that "there had been a war about two hours ago."

Moreover, the two versions contradicted each other on one important point. According to Mrs. Stegall, the reason for stopping in Monroe before continuing on to her sister's house was because "we thought we'd get a Coca-Cola." But Mr. Stegall maintained that he "was not thirsty."

The Stegalls were followed on the witness stand by H. C. Dutton, a burly Union County deputy sheriff who had interviewed them shortly after their release. Over our strenuous objections, he testified that Lowry had admitted to him and several other officers that he had moved the couple's car from the middle of Boyte Street to the curb.

On cross-examination, he admitted that he had a criminal record himself. Among other things, in 1937 he had been convicted of simple assault in Richmond County. A year later, he had been sentenced to eighteen months in federal prison for conspiracy in connection with the operation of an illegal still.

After two State Bureau of Investigation (SBI) agents had echoed Dutton's story, Brock adjourned for lunch. Scupi and I, who had been eating our lunch at Dr. Perry's every day, decided to try the Oasis, a restaurant across the street from the courthouse. Accompanied by Berta Green, a prema-

turely gray young woman who directed the affairs of the
Committee to Aid the Monroe Defendants, we walked into
the restaurant.

As soon as we entered, I knew that we were not going to be
served. The waitress took one look·at us and busied herself at
the far end of the counter. When I asked her if we could
order, she said that she would have to speak to the manager.
In a moment, she had her answer. "He says that you can't eat
here."

When court resumed, I related the incident to Judge
Brock. "Well, you understand, of course," he began, "that
whether or not there is integration of facilities in Monroe is
not a question before the court at this time, and I would not
undertake, in any event, to try to desegregate by edict any of
the businesses of Monroe." However, he assured us that he
would take "some steps" to make certain we did not go
hungry during future lunch hours.*

One of the SBI agents testified that Crowder had admitted
to him that after the release of the Stegalls he and Reap had
moved ten rifles and a large suitcase filled with ammunition
to his grandmother's attic. Because Boyette wanted to insure
his almost certain victory, he asked Chief Mauney to bring
in the rifles and ammunition he had in his evidence room.

Mauney, a fussy little man eager to please the judge and
the solicitor, obeyed at once. At a nod of his head, several of
his officers dumped a number of army rifles and more than
twelve hundred rounds of ammunition directly in front of
the jury box. Its occupants craned their necks to look at the
arsenal on the courtroom floor.

Boyette's maneuver backfired, however, when we counted
the guns. In his eagerness, Mauney had brought in every
weapon in his evidence room and there were four more rifles

* These steps consisted of ascertaining that we could be fed at the local
hotel.

than had apparently been found in Crowder's possession. When I asked him whether he could tell us which of the guns had been seized from Crowder, he insisted that he would have no trouble in so doing if he could locate his list.

Brock, who had been growing visibly worried at the chief's inability to identify the guns, promptly took an early noon recess.

After lunch, Mauney was back on view. It seemed that he could not locate his list. The official transcript records the extent of his discomfiture.

Court: Where did you have the list yesterday, Chief?
Witness: I had it in my office.
Court: Well, is it still in your office?
Witness: I wouldn't say.
Court: Did you throw it away?
Witness: I may have.

Brock finally excluded both the guns and the ammunition. Unfortunately, the members of the jury had seen them all, and it would take more than the judge's order to disregard them to erase the effect from their minds.

Although I did not call any witnesses, Hafner offered Harry Boyte, Dr. King's special assistant, and James Forman, the executive secretary of SNCC. Both men had been present in Monroe during the summer of 1961 and, although Brock cut them short, they did manage to show the tense nature of Negro-white relations in the city.

Forman gave a graphic description of the attack by whites that had ended the peaceful picketing of the courthouse on August 27, 1961, just before the Stegalls had driven into Boyte Street. A city truck had circled the square during the afternoon spraying insecticide on the demonstrators. At the same time, a car bearing a sign reading "Open Season on Coons" had appeared at 2:30 P.M.

"It kept circling the courthouse and the square," Forman said.

Forman himself had been arrested that day. The officer who apprehended him had given a police rifle to a pedestrian on the street and asked him to guard his captive. "I do not know who the pedestrian was," Forman said, "but he gave him the gun, and he held it on me. It was not six inches away."

Suddenly, the man with the rifle struck Forman over the head with it. The latter implored a policeman sitting in a nearby car to help him, but the officer ignored his pleas. "Later, when we got to the police station, a man came after me with a knife, and this knife was pointed at my genitals. I insisted that Officer Helms stop this man from coming at me with the knife. I was bleeding profusely from the head. Blood was flowing down and it was in my shirt."

Before resting, Hafner read into the record depositions of Robert Williams and his wife, Mabel, taken in Cuba. According to Williams, he had escorted the Stegalls into his home to protect them from a huge crowd of enraged Negroes in Boyte Street. "You have to take us out of this block!" Mrs. Stegall had insisted. "You can protect us and keep them from bothering us!"

Mrs. Williams had met the Stegalls as they entered the house. "I asked the white man and woman if they wanted to sit down, and the woman said yes. They sat in chairs in my front bedroom and I sat on the bed and talked with them. The woman thanked me for allowing them to remain in my home and praised my husband for saving their lives and protecting them from the angry crowd."

In what the Charlotte *Observer* characterized as "an impassioned summation," I tried to convince the jury that no kidnapping had taken place. At the most, there had been a great deal of confusion both at the square and in Boyte Street that day and it was impossible to say, some three years later, exactly what had happened. At any rate, it didn't seem fair that the defendants should now have to answer with twenty years of their lives for the events of that tumultuous day.

As I drew to a close, I almost believed that I could persuade twelve Union County jurors to acquit Lowry. If my client was guilty of anything, I pointed out, he was guilty of kidnapping a 1961 Ford sedan. Assuming the Stegalls' testimony to be true, Lowry had done nothing more than drive an empty car a few feet.

"If he did this," I concluded, "it was a foolish, stupid act done in a moment of excitement, but it was not a kidnapping."

The jury retired at 4:03 P.M. on Thursday, February 27. While we waited, we formed a pool as to how many minutes it would take for them to decide the four cases, each of which had two counts. The slip of paper which I drew bore the number "10."

I was destined not to win the pool. The jury took all of thirty-two minutes to grind out its eight verdicts. Precisely at 4:35 P.M., Foreman F. C. Black led his eleven charges back into the courtroom. When none of them would look in the direction of the four defendants, I knew that acquittals were out of the question.

"Ladies and gentlemen of the jury," Brock asked, "have you agreed upon a verdict?"

Black rose. "We have," he replied.

"How do you find as to the defendant Mae Mallory, upon the charge of kidnapping G. Bruce Stegall? Guilty as charged, or not guilty?"

Black stared straight ahead. "She's guilty!" he blurted out.

In quick succession, all of the defendants were found guilty on each count. As Lowry's verdict was announced, tears welled up in the eyes of his wife, Marcia, a pretty, dark-haired girl who had sat alongside him at each court session. Wanting to be by herself for a few moments, she jumped up and hurried from the courtroom.

Bond in the sum of $4,000 was set for Lowry. Although Dr. Perry had agreed to lend us the necessary money, he was now no longer in a position to do so. Several days earlier, when we had arrived at his house for lunch, we had found George L. Weissman, a reporter for the *Nation*, tied up in the basement and Perry's closet safe broken open. The cash which he had allocated for bail purposes was missing.

According to Weissman, who was finishing an article on the trial, he had been working in the basement when the front bell rang. As soon as he opened the door, a Negro with a drawn revolver forced him back into the basement where he was blindfolded and tied. He then heard another person enter the house and the sounds of hammering coming from upstairs. When the intruders apparently found what they wanted, they departed.

The next morning, Brock sentenced Lowry to confinement "in the State Prison for not less than three nor more than five years in the Youthful Offenders Division." The penalties for the three Negroes were considerably—and unaccountably— stiffer. Mrs. Mallory received sixteen to twenty years; Crowder, seven to ten; and Reap, five to seven.

By this time, we had managed to scrape up the necessary cash for Lowry's bond, and he was able to leave town that evening. Before doing so, however, we stated in open court that we intended to appeal to the Supreme Court of North Carolina.

The appeal was argued by Hafner and myself on the morning after Election Day, 1964. Three months later, the seven-judge court reversed all of the convictions. It found that there had been a systematic exclusion of Negroes from both the grand and petit juries in Union County, and it voided the convictions on that ground alone. But it indicated that once the jury rolls had been reformed, the solicitor was free to ask for new indictments and try the defendants again.*

* Within months, Lowry and his co-defendants were reindicted by another Union County Grand Jury. Since Reap and Crowder no longer reside in North Carolina, all four have decided to remain out of the state and resist extradition.

PART **VIII**

ST. AUGUSTINE

CHAPTER 29

The Beginning

In June of 1942, as a brand new second lieutenant fresh out of officer candidate school, I was sent to join the II Army Corps at Jacksonville, Florida. When I arrived I found, to my dismay, that the unit had just left for England and the eventual invasion of North Africa. While I awaited further orders, I decided to visit the historic city of St. Augustine, some thirty miles to the southeast.

I didn't know it then but that one-time Spanish settlement was to become, some twenty-two years later, a bitter battlefield in the struggle for Negro equality. In the wartime spring of 1942, it was, as the country's oldest city, a glamorous and romantic spot. Like thousands of tourists before me, I visited the Fountain of Youth, the Old Slave Market, and the Castillo de San Marco.

As I strolled from one sight to another, I don't think that I was consciously aware that the city was rigidly segregated. Like so many white Americans, I was mildly uncomfortable about racial discrimination but remarkably adroit in disregarding it. It was a fact of American life that one accepted,

271

however distastefully, because it had always been and seemed destined to endure.

But two decades later—March 31, 1964, to be exact—a frail, seventy-two-year-old white woman set out to do something about it. Because she insisted on having lunch in a public restaurant with four Negro women, she was arrested and charged with violating Florida's undesirable guest and trespass laws. By that simple act, Mary Elizabeth Peabody, the wife of an Episcopalian bishop and the mother of a governor of Massachusetts, made her own personal witness for morality.

In late 1963, I had represented a group of ministers who, under the auspices of the Boston affiliate of the Southern Christian Leadership Conference, had demonstrated in Williamston, North Carolina. Upon their return home, they had decided to concentrate on St. Augustine during the Easter season of 1964. Deeply concerned that the Florida city, which was preparing to celebrate its quadricentennial, was a stronghold of segregation, they were determined to dramatize their protest.

After assembling a task force of college students and fellow clergymen, they descended on St. Augustine during the last week in March. With the aid of local Negroes under the leadership of Dr. Robert B. Hayling, a young dentist, they formed integrated groups which visited various public accommodations in the old city. They were promptly arrested and confined in the St. Johns County Jail.

At midnight on Tuesday, March 31, my telephone rang.

"Are you attorney William M. Kunstler?" drawled the long distance operator. "I have a call for you from St. Augustine, Florida." My caller was a Boston minister who told me that Mrs. Peabody and several hundred others were in jail. Could I come at once?

I replied that I would get there as soon as I could. I immediately put in a call to Tobias Simon, the Miami attorney with whom I had worked during the Worthy passport trial in 1962, and asked him to go to St. Augustine the next morning. We agreed that our first step would be to remove the pending cases to the federal court in Jacksonville.

Although this maneuver had failed in Jackson and Birmingham, we had learned during the summer of 1963 that orders remanding removed civil rights cases back to state courts might be appealable. Moreover, the Fifth Circuit, which included Florida, had already granted a stay of such remand orders in a Louisiana case which Kinoy and I had briefed and argued for CORE five months earlier. It was reasonable to expect that we would get the same treatment in the St. Augustine cases.

At least it was worth trying.

Simon moved with lightning speed. Within minutes of my call, he had started to prepare the necessary removal papers. He flew to Jacksonville the next morning and filed them with the federal court. By late afternoon, he was able to inform me that Chief Judge Bryan Simpson had set a hearing for two o'clock the next afternoon.

I arrived in Jacksonville late Thursday morning. Since Simon was still in St. Augustine where he had spent the night, I went directly to the courthouse. I thought that it might not be a bad idea to introduce myself to Judge Simpson.

The judge, who had been appointed by President Eisenhower, was a tall, white-haired man with a gentle smile. He received me courteously and said that he was intrigued by the removal proceedings we had instituted. "I've had no experience with them at all," he said, "and I look forward to hearing your arguments as to why I should retain jurisdiction of all these state prosecutions."

After listening patiently to an entire afternoon of them, Simpson was far from convinced that the St. Augustine cases belonged in his court. But he did grant us permission to call witnesses to prove our contentions that we couldn't get a fair trial in St. Augustine and that our clients were being prosecuted for doing acts which were permitted by federal law. "Hope springs eternal," I muttered to Toby Simon as the judge left the bench.

We had supper at the George Washington Hotel and then drove to St. Augustine. Our first stop was the County Jail on the outskirts of the city where we began to interview many of the jailed demonstrators. We had agreed to call only five witnesses the next day, and we wanted those who would be the most representative. We finally settled on Mrs. Peabody, Dr. Hayling, Yale chaplains William Sloane Coffin, Jr., and David Robinson, and Annie Ruth Evans, a fifteen-year-old local Negro girl.

It took several hours to interview each of our five selections. They were brought to a little room on the first floor of the totally segregated jail where Toby, Jack Pratt of the National Council of Churches, and I questioned them. By the time we had finished, we were convinced that they would present a compelling story to Judge Simpson when court resumed in the morning.

Mrs. Peabody, an angular woman with wispy white hair, seemed none the worse for her two days in jail. She quickly grasped the rationale of our legal position and eagerly awaited all our questions. "I hope that I'll do all right," she said when we had finished. "I've never done this before."

Our interviews concluded, we met with L. O. Davis, the St. Johns County Sheriff. A dour, obstinate man in his early fifties, Davis was rumored to be extremely friendly with Klansmen and other racist vigilantes who kept the county's Negroes in a perpetual state of terror. In fact, it was a rare day indeed when some of these worthies could not be found lounging around the jail compound.

Davis insisted that he would accept only cash bonds for the release of the demonstrators. Since this was clearly a discriminatory ruling, we arranged for a midnight *habeas corpus* hearing before the local state judge in his chambers. It was only then that Davis capitulated and agreed to accept bail bonds issued by the Allegheny Mutual Casualty Company.

As we prepared to go back to the jail, the sheriff, who had become increasingly irascible as the evening wore on, insisted that he saw no point in bailing out our clients. "These bums will all be back here for holding hands with niggers," he snapped as we left the judge's office.

It was 1 A.M. when we arrived back at the jail. A representative of the surety company had already flown up from Orlando and was prepared to start writing the necessary bonds. The sheriff, whose temper was now at the boiling point, ordered the deputy on duty to cooperate with us.

"All right, release them!" he snarled. "It's okay for you to go ahead and release them. I'm going to go on to bed."

As soon as he had left the building, we readily agreed with the deputy's suggestion that the prisoners be released at eight the next morning. "They're all asleep anyway, and I'm sure that you're good and tired yourselves," he said. "Come back at eight, and we'll start processing your people."

But, with a night's sleep under his belt, the sheriff suddenly reversed his field. When we entered the jail the next morning, we were informed by Deputy James Wylie that Davis had rescinded his order of the night before. No prisoners, Wylie told us, were to be released until the sheriff had personally approved their bonds. When we asked to see the sheriff, we were informed that he could not be located.

Since we had to be in court in Jacksonville at ten, we decided to subpoena Wylie. His testimony about the sheriff's change of heart would, we thought, support our contention that we couldn't get a fair trial in St. Augustine. Toby, who had a blank subpoena in his briefcase, promptly served it on Wylie.

This maneuver had unexpected results. The deputy immediately ordered three Florida highway patrolmen who were in the room to bar the outside door so that we could not leave. We were to stay, he explained, until he could reach the missing sheriff and learn whether he was to honor the subpoena.

As the minutes dragged by, I was increasingly aware that we had to be in Judge Simpson's court at ten. A few minutes after nine, I attempted to push my way past the highway patrolmen who were blocking the front door. One of them retaliated by ramming both of his hands into my chest with all the force he could muster. Before I knew what had hit me, I was propelled backward across the entire length of the room until I crashed into Toby Simon who had been standing near the rear wall.

"Don't say that I never back you up," he whispered hoarsely as soon as he had recovered his breath.

Twenty minutes later, we were released. After telephoning Judge Simpson's office to say that we would be a little late, we raced to Jacksonville. No sooner had we arrived in the courtroom than Simon proceeded to read into the record the events of the last twelve hours. "We felt that this activity on Wylie's part and that of the sheriff constituted further evidence of our allegation that a fair trial cannot be secured in St. John's County," he explained to Simpson.

William Sloane Coffin, Jr., the Yale chaplain, was our first witness. He had been arrested in the dining room of the Ponce de Leon Motor Lodge where he, three whites, and four Negroes had gone for lunch. The biracial group had arrived at 1:15 P.M.

Q. What happened after that?

A. We were seated. The manager came to us and told us that he could not serve us, that we were undesirable guests, and requested us to leave.

Q. Will you describe your conduct at that time?

A. I believe it very closely resembled the rest of the people in the dining room.

Q. In what respect?

A. We were well dressed, mannerly, seated quietly at the tables, and simply wished to have lunch as they did.

A short time later, two armed St. Augustine policemen had entered the dining room.

Q. What did you do when they requested that you leave?

A. I requested the officer to read us the law which made it impossible for us to stay. He said it wasn't necessary, we were just undesirable guests and we should get going.

The group was then driven in two police cars to the County Jail.

Coffin, who had been one of the first Freedom Riders arrested in 1961, was at his best when he explained why he had come to St. Augustine. "I believe that segregation is the Number One problem facing the entire nation," he said earnestly, "and as a Christian I'm deeply committed to integration. And when the Negroes started a demonstration in St. Augustine, Florida, I simply wanted to be a part of this demonstration, feeling that it was both necessary and right."

At this point, Simpson, who had been following the clergyman's testimony with obvious interest, broke in. "As a means of social protest or something of that sort?" he asked.

"Right, yes, sir," Coffin replied. "I believe that these injustices need to be dramatized."

The judge continued. "Moral protest might describe your state of mind a little better?" he asked.

"As well as a legal one, sir," Coffin answered. "These are constitutional rights guaranteed all citizens."

"I understand," Simpson said simply.

Coffin was followed on the stand by Dr. Hayling. The tall, handsome dentist, who had been all but murdered when he stumbled into a Klan meeting in the fall of 1963, was a strong witness. In no uncertain terms, he described how he also had been arrested at the Ponce de Leon Motor Lodge where he had gone for dinner with Mrs. Peabody and several other Boston ladies.

"We had hoped," he concluded, "having such distinguished visitors in our midst, that possibly the management would have a change of heart and agree to serve a mixed party."

Annie Ruth Evans can best be described as a typical American teen-ager. She was one of almost a hundred St. Augustine high school students who had been arrested the day before for marching downtown "to have a meeting about segregation." She had participated in the march "because, as a citizen of the United States, I think that we all should be created equal and have the same privileges that the white people have, too."

Annie gave a graphic description of the conditions existing in Sheriff Davis' jail. At first, fifty-seven children had been crowded into a cell which contained only four bunks. During the night, a turnkey took pity an Annie and her companions and escorted eleven to another cell.

Q. Where did you sleep last night?
A. It was two in the beds and the rest had to sleep on the floor.

The beginning of Annie's cross-examination provided one of those rare and inspiring moments that all too infrequently illuminate the dignity of man. James E. Holton, the Ancient City's attorney, launched into his interrogation as he had for hundreds of Negro witnesses in the past. "Now, Annie . . . ," he began.

In an instant, every lawyer at the defense table was on his feet.

"Your Honor, we object," I interjected. "The Supreme Court has just ruled . . ." Simpson interrupted at once. "Last Monday," he said. He had reference to a recent decision of the United States Supreme Court holding that Negroes addressed by their first names did not have to answer lawyers' questions.

The judge turned to Holton. "You will address the witness as Miss, please," he admonished sternly. "She's entitled to be addressed as Miss."

The perspiration glistened on the lawyer's brow. "Oh, I understand," he stammered. "Excuse me. I was just getting the name itself in my mind. I missed it; I didn't hear it over there."

After fumbling with the papers in his hand for a long, tortured moment, he turned back to Annie who had listened to the interchange with a bemused expression on her face. Holton swallowed twice. "Miss Evans," he finally blurted out, "what time does school start?"

Annie's fleeting smile turned into one of the most expressive grins I have ever seen. For the first time in her experience and that of everyone in the courtroom, a federal judge, speaking for an outraged country, had ordered a Southern attorney to afford a Negro witness that measure of respect and dignity to which every American is entitled. Annie's crinkled face mirrored that triumph.

The courtroom, which was filled to overflowing with the

Negroes of St. Augustine, had suddenly become a warm and
hospitable place. Just as Annie had, by one simple act,
become a person and not a cipher, so had every black man
and woman seated on the hard benches been given a brief
and rewarding glimpse at what the future might hold. Emancipation had at long last begun in St. Augustine.

Annie was a cool witness under fire. When Holton, his
voice heavy with disapproval, asked her why she had joined
the marchers on a school day, she replied crisply that "we all
are fighting for the same thing, so I just joined in."

Q. What do you mean, you "wanted the same thing?"
A. We all, freedom together.

Mrs. Peabody was next.

She had not, she testified, come to St. Augustine with the
intention of getting arrested. In fact, on Monday, March 30,
she had left the dining room of the Ponce de Leon Motor
Lodge when asked to do so by the manager. But first she had
made Sheriff Davis read the Florida undesirable guest statute
to her.

"It's a very long law with a great many words in it," she
recalled, "and I realized that I couldn't fit some of those parts
of it that described why I should leave."

The following day, however, she had decided not to leave.
"We began to feel that we were pretty cowardly to leave our
friends taking the brunt of this," she said. "At first we
thought that we could make our witness without breaking
this particular ordinance which we do not have in Massachusetts and which we therefore do not think is in accordance
with the Constitution; but finally we decided we would
rather stand up for the Constitution than we would for the
ordinances of the City of St. Augustine."

Our last important witness was Earl M. Johnson, an
NAACP Negro attorney who practiced law throughout north

Florida. He was convinced that defendants in racial cases in
St. Johns County could not get a fair trial. "Given a challenge of a policy or a practice or custom of racial discrimination, no defense will avail any defendant of an acquittal, in
my opinion."

In the afternoon, the city called its police chief, Virgil
Stuart, whose soft voice and ingratiating attitude combined
to make him a formidable witness. When he described a sit-in
that some Negro children had conducted in the Ponce de
Leon Hotel, he was at his ingenuous best. "It puzzled us
because we couldn't figure out why small children, in their
innocent way, would go in a place like that when the price of
food would be so high."

But his kindliness did not keep him from using police dogs
and electrified cattle prods in breaking up demonstrations.

> *Q.* You have been using the police dogs and cattle prods?
> *A.* I wouldn't exactly call them cattle prods. They are—
> we call them persuasive sticks.
> *Q.* And you use these in connection with breaking up
> demonstrations?
> *A.* Only about once or twice.

The only arrests in which Stuart himself had been involved took place at the Monson Motor Lodge. He had not
wanted to put anyone in jail, he maintained, but circumstances had forced his hand. "We tried to figure out some way
to serve them—we were trying to keep down the adverse
publicity for the community."

> *Q.* Did you feel personally that it would be a good idea
> if they were served?
> *A.* Well, the manager told them this. He said that he
> offered to serve them himself if they would sepa-
> rate, if the colored group would get over to one side.

The manager had insisted that his business would suffer if he served mixed groups.

> *Q.* So that his only reason for refusing to serve was that he felt that there would be some economic loss?
>
> *A.* Boycott to his business, that's the impression I got.
>
> *Q.* Do you believe that the economic pressures of any individual persons would lift if all restaurants were required to serve all people provided they were peaceful and orderly, just like these people?
>
> *A.* Not in St. Augustine at the present time.

It was late in the afternoon when the hearing drew to a close. Judge Simpson, who had indicated from the beginning that he intended to follow the old precedents that foreclosed the transfer of civil rights cases to the federal courts, had not been swayed by either our arguments or our witnesses. "I conclude," he said, "that the state prosecutions were improvidently removed to this court and that remand should be ordered by me."

However, he kept our hopes alive by forcing the prosecution to agree that no cases would be tried before May 5. "This lapse of time," he observed, "provides ample opportunity for the petitioners to attempt an appeal to the United States Court of Appeals for the Fifth Circuit and, as an incident thereto, to seek from that court a stay of the pending state prosecutions sought to be removed here."

A few weeks later, the Fifth Circuit granted such a stay.*

We drove back to St. Augustine that evening. While we had been in court, the process of bonding out our clients had begun and we stopped at the County Jail to see how things were going. As I watched a group of Yale students completing their bonds, I heard one answer to the name of Mitchener.

---

* On May 11, 1965, it unanimously reversed Judge Simpson's order of remand and, in effect, directed him to dismiss all of the prosecutions.

"I know that this is crazy," I said, "but are you related to Mayor Mitchener of Edenton, North Carolina?"

The boy looked at me quizzically. "I'm his son," he replied.

Two years earlier, I had defended a group of demonstrators who had been arrested for picketing the mayor's drugstore in Edenton. Yet it didn't seem at all strange to me that I was now representing his son who had been arrested for the very same type of social protest in another segregated town.

"I'm very happy to meet you," I told young Mitchener. "It is a pleasure to be one of your attorneys."

He smiled broadly. "I'm happy to be one of your clients," he drawled, "but don't tell my daddy right away."

There was a joyous mass meeting that night in the First Baptist Church. The tiny building was so packed with people that it was impossible to see where the seats ended and the aisles began. There were many speakers, but I remember Mrs. Peabody most vividly. I don't know whether she had ever attended such a meeting before, but it was obvious that she was deeply moved.

"I am so glad that I came down to St. Augustine," she said. "I couldn't stay safe in Boston while you were suffering here. But I know in my heart that I didn't do anything for you—you did everything for me. You helped to give my life purpose and meaning and when I go back tomorrow I want to leave behind my most heartfelt gratitude. Thank you all so very much."

I flew home the next morning. Through the intervention of Governor Peabody, we had been able to get last minute reservations on National's nonstop flight to Newark. Although we had not succeeded in keeping the St. Augustine cases in federal court, we were hopeful that the Fifth Circuit would stay the state prosecutions and that the delay itself would prove helpful. I felt in my heart that the old city would never be the same again.

Just before we landed, Mrs. Peabody came down the aisle. "I understand that you have written a book about the old Hall-Mills murder case in New Jersey," she said. "I wanted you to know that Judge Parker who presided at that trial was my uncle."

Concentric circles are sometimes more than geometric phenomena.

CHAPTER 30

The Middle

With the departure of the New Englanders, St. Augustine quickly and quietly returned to its segregated ways. The Monson Motor Lodge, the Ponce de Leon Hotel, and the other places where so many arrests had taken place were just as lily white as they had ever been. It almost seemed as if the Easter Week demonstrations had all been for naught and that Negroes in the old city would never break out of the black world into which they had been forced since the first Jim Crow laws in the 1880's.

But things were not quite the same. Beginning in early May, staff members from the Southern Christian Leadership Conference had begun to move into St. Augustine. Although Dr. King had had almost nothing to do with the Easter Week demonstrations, he was quick to see that they had softened up the city for a frontal assault. A major triumph now, he thought, might well force the passage of the Civil Rights Bill which had been pending in Congress for almost a year.

Reverend Andrew Young, one of King's chief aides, arrived in St. Augustine in the middle of May. A handsome young man with amazing organizational ability, he decided that the best way to dramatize the city's racial imbalance was to stage a series of night marches to the Plaza, a narrow two-block-long public square in the center of St. Augustine. The marches, which would emanate in the city's Negro section, were to be peaceful and orderly.

The first one took place on Tuesday, May 26. Some four hundred marchers, in columns of two abreast, left the First Baptist Church at 10 P.M. It was a warm, balmy night and the Negroes, in rollicking good spirits, sang freedom songs as they walked down Cordoba Street, turned east on King Street, and proceeded to the Plaza. When the reached the Old Slave Market they joined in a prayer and sang several hymns.

St. Augustine's Old Slave Market, a covered pavilion with benches and tables, is used by both tourists and local residents as a place in which to sit and rest. It is lighted by overhead lamps which can be turned on by an easily accessible switch. It forms the easterly boundary of the Plaza which consists mainly of shrubbery, lawn, and shade trees.

Although the police were present in substantial numbers, no attempt was made to interfere with the march. After the ceremony at the Old Slave Market, the Negroes returned to the First Baptist Church where they disbanded. "It was a quiet and dignified demonstration," Young said.

The next evening, some eight hundred Negroes left St. Mary's Baptist Church. In contrast with the night before, this was to be a silent march with no singing, talking, or hand-clapping. When the marchers neared the intersection of King and Cordoba streets, they were met by Sheriff Davis and Chief Stuart who advised them not to go downtown because another group was meeting in the Slave Market.

As Stuart later put it, "The town was full of Klan types, armed with sticks, metal rods, chains, and knives."

Young, who was leading the procession, ordered elderly

people and small children to leave the ranks. The remainder then continued their orderly, silent march around the Plaza. When they reached the Slave Market, they found it in darkness but occupied by almost one hundred white men. Although many of these men were armed, they confined their activities to heckling as the Negroes circled the Plaza and headed back toward Cordoba Street.

On Thursday night, another march formed in St. Paul's A.M.E. Church. As previously, the demonstrators left about 10 P.M. and headed for the downtown section. When they reached the Slave Market, they found that the darkened structure was again filled with jeering whites. Just as the Negro column was passing the market, the lights from several television and still cameras flashed into the night. At that moment, the white men poured out into the Plaza and began to attack the marchers.

Instead of trying to defend themselves, the Negroes sank to their knees on the pavement and started to pray. "Niggers ain't got no God!" screamed one enraged white man as he ran toward them, a raised stick in hand.

At least one marcher was struck on the head by a club wielded by an assailant hidden behind a hedge bordering the sidewalk. Several stitches were required to close the gaping wound. Some photographers were roughed up and their cameras damaged or stolen. Irving Gans, an NBC cameraman, was beaten so severely by a chain-wielding tough that he had to be hospitalized.

Harry Boyte, one of Dr. King's white assistants, was appalled as he watched the carnage. When he tried to photograph it, Deputy Sheriff W. E. Haynie, accompanied by a snarling police dog, ran toward him. "There's that nigger lover!" he shouted as he wrestled the fifty-two-year-old Boyte to the pavement.

After the police finally succeeded in breaking up the

attack, the Negroes returned to St. Paul's. Shortly after they had entered the church, Reverend Young and several other leaders were called out by Sheriff Davis and Chief Stuart. "We are declaring martial law," Stuart informed them. "You had no permit for the earlier marches, and no permits will be given for other marches."

When Young said that he would like an appointment with Stuart the next morning to apply for a permit, the police chief said that he would not be available. "I can't see you in the morning or the afternoon," he said.

But the violence was far from over. Later that evening, Harry Boyte, after picking up his son at the bus station, drove him to the Holiday Inn where they planned to spend the night. As Boyte parked his car in front of the room which had been assigned to him, a shotgun blast shattered the vehicle's rear window.

At the same time an empty beach cottage, some eight miles south of St. Augustine, that had been rented for Dr. King was struck by rifle and shotgun fire from three sides. More than twenty bullet marks were later found on the walls of the small house, while inside furniture was shattered and china was broken. Although Sheriff Davis knew of the incident by nine the next morning, he made no effort to investigate it until it was formally reported to him by an SCLC staff worker several hours later.

On Friday morning the *St. Augustine Record* had nothing but scorn for the Negro demonstrators. "Most solid citizens who believe in strong law enforcement and general adherence and respect by the public," it proclaimed, "are rapidly becoming 'fed up' with minority groups that flaunt the law and then cry 'police brutality.' Both the city and county law enforcement officers have done an excellent job in prohibiting serious violent actions during the latest period of unrest."

At nine-thirty that evening, some three hundred marchers

started downtown from the Trinity Methodist Church. Near King Street, they were met by a small army of police officers, some with police dogs. Chief Stuart told them that they would have to return to their homes. "You can't go downtown tonight or any other night," he said.

When the Negroes asked for permission to pray silently for a few minutes, Stuart permitted them to do so. After a brief prayer session, they returned to the Negro quarter of the city.

Earlier that day, Toby Simon had called Judge Simpson and told him that we would like to apply for an injunction against the stopping of night marches. Simpson promptly notified Harris Ditmar, a member of a well-known Jacksonville law firm which now represented St. Augustine, that he would hold a hearing at 2 P.M. on Monday, June 1.

In conjunction with our application, we had brought a suit in the name of Andrew Young against Chief Stuart, Sheriff Davis, and Mayor Joseph A. Shelley. In the main, we claimed that the stopping of the night marches violated the rights of the Negroes of St. Augustine to free speech and assembly as guaranteed by the federal Constitution.

I flew to Jacksonville on Monday morning and met Toby and our witnesses in Earl Johnson's office. When I arrived, the room was filled with people who had been involved in the night marches, including Andy Young and Harry Boyte. After two hours of interviews, we selected a number of persons we thought would most adequately present our side of the case.

Precisely at two o'clock, Judge Simpson entered the courtroom from a little door behind the bench. Without further ado, he asked us to call our witnesses. We relied mainly on Young and Boyte, who gave graphic and moving descriptions of the night marches of May 26, 27, 28, and 29.

When we finally rested our case on Tuesday morning, we

were convinced that we had shown that the night marches had been conducted peacefully and that any violence that had occurred had been caused by white toughs. Now it was up to the city to prove that its ban on demonstrations had been justified. To do so, it was absolutely necessary to convince Judge Simpson that such action was required to prevent bloodshed.

Accordingly, we were dumbfounded when, instead of trying to show that St. Augustine had become a major racial battlefield, the city's lawyers did everything in their power to demonstrate how peaceful things were. All of their witnesses —Mayor Shelley, Chief Stuart, Sheriff Davis, and numerous police officers—outdid themselves in pointing out that, with the exception of some minor disorders caused by high-spirited white youths, nothing very much out of the ordinary had taken place at the Slave Market during the week of May 25.

During the testimony, Judge Simpson, who amused himself by carving wooden blocks which were piled on the bench in front of him, kept asking defense witnesses if they had identified or arrested the white hoodlums. In every case, the answer was no.

"They were just a bunch of kids," insisted Chief Stuart. "We were happy enough to see them leave the area."

Sheriff Davis was the city's last witness. A deeply tanned man in his sixteenth year as the chief law enforcement officer of St. Johns County, he testified that he had eight full-time deputies, fourteen auxiliary deputies, and a number of "special" deputies. Judge Simpson's ears perked up at this last statistic.

Court: What is the number of these special deputies?
Witness: Well, I had around forty for fifteen days in Easter,

I have a total now of about, I'd say, thirty—thirty-five special deputies.

To our surprise, Simpson was suddenly intensely interested. He wanted to know where Davis obtained his "special" deputies. Eight or ten, the sheriff stated, came from a local factory, while others were recruited from "around town."

Court: Do you recruit them from the Ku Klux Klan there in St. Augustine, Sheriff Davis?
Witness: No, sir.
Court: Are some of them Klansmen, some of the special deputies?
Witness: No, sir, not to my knowledge, if they are.
Court: Are you a Klansman?
Witness: No, sir.

The judge intensified his attack: "What is the Ancient City Gun Club?" he demanded. The sheriff looked flustered. "That was formed by a man there that's a—he has a forestry outfit there . . ."

Court: I ask you this, isn't the Ancient City Gun Club just the local name for the Klan down there?
Witness: I—I don't think it is, Your Honor. I've questioned everyone that I've had contact with. In fact, I've—

Simpson interrupted the now thoroughly flabbergasted witness. "When you go to recruit these special deputies or somebody tells you to put on a special deputy, how carefully do you look into the background of the people that you put on?"

Davis thought for a moment. "At that time, I couldn't look into it when I put them on."

When Davis insisted that he had between thirty-five and forty special deputies, the judge exploded. "I suggest you have around a hundred special deputies," he insisted, "men that you have deputized and told you may call upon them!"

> *Witness:* I don't know, Judge, I really don't—
> *Court:* Don't you know how many you've got?
> *Witness:* No, sir, I don't.

Before the all-day session ended, the sheriff was ordered to bring in a complete list of his special deputies. On Wednesday morning, he read into the record more than a hundred names of men whom he had deputized. When he came to the name of Holsted Manucy, Simpson sat bolt upright.

"Why, that man's a convicted felon in this court!" he exclaimed.

Known as "Hoss" to everyone in St. Johns County, Manucy, a short, barrel-bodied man who always wore a black cowboy hat, was the leader of an armed band of toughs which had terrorized the Negro community of St. Augustine for years. His followers, who patrolled the county in specially equipped radio cars whose aerials sported Confederate flags, had been very much in evidence during the attacks at the Slave Market.

When Davis had finished his stint, I asked Simpson's permission to put Dr. Hayling on the stand. The young dentist had been severely beaten at a Ku Klux Klan meeting in September of 1963. Because he had seen Sheriff Davis at this meeting, I thought that it might serve some purpose to describe the incident.

Shortly after the bombing of the Sixteenth Street Baptist Church in Birmingham, a crowd of 250 Klansmen, some robed and masked, had assembled in a field just outside of St. Augustine to listen to an inflammatory harangue by an itinerant preacher. When Hayling and three friends arrived, the clergyman was berating the FBI.

"They came by and said, 'Now, you don't really advocate violence, do you?' And I said, 'The hell you say. The niggers has declared all-out war on the plan of God and on God's family, the white man, and in the war you shoot.' Then they said to me, 'Do you know who bombed the church in Birmingham?' And I said, 'No, and if I did, I wouldn't tell you.'

"But I'll tell you here tonight, if they can find those fellows they ought to pin medals on them. Someone said, 'Ain't it a shame that them little children was killed?' Well, they don't know what they're talking about. In the first place, they ain't little. They're fourteen or fifteen years old—old enough to have venereal disease, and I'll be surprised if all of them didn't have one or more.

"In the second place, they weren't children. Children are little people, little human beings, and that means white people. There's little monkeys, but you don't call them children. There's little dogs and cats and apes and baboons and skunks and there's also little niggers. But they ain't children!

"And in the third place, it wasn't no shame they were killed. Why? Because when I go out to kill rattlesnakes I don't make no difference between little rattlesnakes and big rattlesnakes. So I kill 'em all and if there's four less niggers tonight, then I say, 'Good for whoever planted the bomb!' "

Hayling and his friends had attended the meeting in order to find out more about the Klan's plans. When their presence was discovered, they were seized and carried before the crowd. The stunned silence which greeted their audacity was broken finally by a woman's scream: "Kill 'em! Castrate 'em."

The four Negroes were then beaten senseless. Before he lost consciousness, Hayling heard someone say: "Work on his right hand—he's a right-handed dentist!"

When he came to, he found himself piled upon the bodies of his three friends "like firewood." A small group of Klansmen hovered nearby. "Did you ever smell a nigger burn?"

one of them asked. "Just wait until Klan brother so-and-so gets back with five gallons of gasoline and then you can. It's a mighty sweet smell."

It was at this moment that Sheriff Davis arrived on the scene. After a lengthy conference with the unperturbed Klansmen, the sheriff arrested four of them on assault charges. It was only then that he made arrangements for transporting the stricken Negroes to the hospital.

A St. Augustine justice of the peace promptly acquitted the white men. At the same time, Dr. Hayling and his unfortunate companions, despite the fact that they had been beaten within an inch of their lives, were themselves charged with assaulting their assailants. They were subsequently convicted solely because a revolver was found in their car.

When Dr. Hayling had finished his harrowing tale, Judge Simpson gaveled the three-day hearing to a close. But before he adjourned, he requested that all demonstrations cease until he had decided whether to end the ban on night marches. Before giving him an answer, I asked for a few moments in which to consult with our clients.

In the corridor outside the courtroom, I conferred with Dr. Hayling and Andy Young. While all of my instincts rebelled against ending the demonstrations, even temporarily, I felt that we were on the threshold of a great victory and should not jeopardize it. "This is a very important thing," I said. "It will show the nation that we are responsible."

When the two Negro leaders agreed with me, I returned to the courtroom.

"Your Honor," I told Simpson, "I have consulted with the plaintiff, Reverend Andrew Young and Dr. Hayling, and they will give your Honor the assurance, that while this is residing with the court, they will not utilize any methods of protest in the City of St. Augustine that will bring them in conflict with the sheriff's order or the two ordinances."

The judge looked greatly relieved. "I appreciate this very much," he said, "and I appreciate it on their part and give them this assurance, that there will be no disposition, as far as I'm concerned, to hold up a decree. I'm going to study it and get out a decree as fast as can be accomplished."

That evening I returned to St. Augustine. The nightly mass meeting at the First Baptist Church was already in progress when I arrived. As I walked down the side aisle, my old friend C. T. Vivian, who was now SCLC's director of affiliates, was describing in vivid tones Sheriff Davis' ordeal on what he called "the hot seat." When he saw me, he broke off abruptly. "Here's attorney Kunstler!" he boomed.

Pat Watters of the Southern Regional Council has described this episode so movingly in his pamphlet, *The American Middle Ground in St. Augustine,* that I prefer to use his words:

Kunstler . . . came forward, arms outstretched, grinning, and the Rev. Mr. Vivian moved down from the pulpit to meet him, and these two men, white and black, embraced each other in front of a church full of people who had not seen this sort of thing before, and in the silence of seeing it, a sweet, soprano voice rose and the others joined in, and they sang to it, this sight saying so much of the meaning and truth and simple hope there in the church.

Dr. King returned the following night.

"I want to commend you for the beauty and the dignity and the courage with which you carried out demonstrations last week," he told a mass meeting. "I know what you faced. And I understand that as you marched silently and with a deep commitment to nonviolence, you confronted the brutality of the Klan. But amid all of this you stood up. Soon the Klan will see that all of their violence will not stop us for we are on the way to Freedom Land and we don't mean to stop until we get there."

The truce ended on June 9 when Judge Simpson issued an order restraining the city from interfering with night marches. In a nineteen-page opinion, he declared that, as the Supreme Court had stated earlier, "the basic guarantees of our Constitution are warrants for the here and now and, unless there is an overwhelming compelling reason, they are to be promptly fulfilled."

The fundamental rights involved here: of speech, of assembly, and of petition are clearly such rights. Prior restraint against their exercise casts a heavy burden upon the Defendants to demonstrate "clear and present danger." This burden the Defendants failed to meet. To the contrary, the thrust of their proof is to the effect that the disturbances encountered were minor in nature, caused by a small number of youthful agitators or hecklers. True, they assert inconveniences to law enforcement officers in being required to patrol to preserve order, and the loss of sleep to do so. They told the Plaintiff and his class that they could no longer protect them, but their proof in court was convincingly to the contrary. The heavy presumption against the constitutionality of the type of prior restraint indulged in here is simply not met.

At all events, perhaps enough has been written to indicate the clear legal and constitutional basis for my conclusion that the orders promulgated to Plaintiff and his class by Defendants Stuart and Davis on Thursday, May 28, 1964, and Friday, May 29, 1964, were unlawful prior restraint of the exercise by Plaintiff and the class he represents of fundamental rights of freedom of speech, freedom of assembly, and of petition for redress of grievances, guaranteed by Amendment I and protected against infringement by State action by Amendment XIV to the Constitution of the United States. Preliminary Injunction will issue.

The case was over. A Southern judge, determined to follow the law as written, had, with one stroke of his pen, ended an era that had begun centuries before. If the Negroes of St. Augustine could march, they could demonstrate to their country that its oldest city shared the blight of racial segregation with many of its younger ones and that sheer antiquity could not render good that which was fundamentally evil.

"The heroes of St. Augustine," as Dr. King called them, finally had earned their victory.

I received news of Judge Simpson's order just as I had heard of the first arrests during Easter Week—late at night. But this time there was a substantial difference. When the AP reporter called me at midnight to tell me that we had won, I was suffused with the warm glow of a rebirth of faith in the American legal system. If Simpson, a North Floridian, could apply the law without fear or favor, then so might other judges in the deep South.

My hopes were justified. The following spring, Alabama federal Judge Frank M. Johnson, using much the same reasoning as Simpson, authorized the Selma-Montgomery March. In July of 1965, the Fifth Circuit ordered the officials of Jackson, Mississippi, not to interfere with Freedom Democratic Party demonstrations protesting the illegality of the state legislature. The law, it seems, was fast catching up with the movement.

The victory was my farewell to St. Augustine. The NAACP Legal Defense Fund, under a new agreement with Dr. King to handle all of SCLC's legal work, assumed the responsibility for further court action. One of the finest tributes I have ever received was an urgent wire from Dr. Hayling shortly after my departure, in which he said: I WISH YOU AND OTHERS ASSOCIATED WITH YOU TO CONTINUE YOUR LEGAL REPRESENTATION.

The day this telegram arrived, however, Mickey Schwerner, Andrew Goodman and James Chaney had just been murdered near Philadelphia, Mississippi.

CHAPTER **31**

The End

It was to take more than federal court orders to bring even momentary peace to St. Augustine. One day after Judge Simpson had issued his injunction, a howling mob of white racists broke through police lines to attack four hundred Negro demonstrators who had been exhorted by Dr. King to "march tonight as you've never marched before." It took a squad of state troopers aided by tear gas bombs to disperse the whites.

"Niggers have more freedom than we do," one red-eyed youth sobbed as a friend led him from the Plaza.

The next morning, a cache of sulphuric acid, chains, and clubs were uncovered beneath a wall along the usual Negro line of march. In a belated attempt to forestall trouble, the city quickly installed seven mercury vapor lights around the Plaza and removed all bricks from the flower gardens.

On June 12, J. B. Stoner, a pudgy Atlanta attorney who was the vice-presidential candidate of the National States Rights Party, an ultraright wing group centered in Birmingham, arrived in town. No sooner had he unpacked his bag than he was busy haranguing white racists at the Old Slave Market. "Tonight, we're going to find out whether white people have any rights!" he shouted. "The coons have been parading around St. Augustine for a long time!"

Neither King, whom he labeled a "long-time associate of Communists," nor the "Jew-stacked, Communist-loving Supreme Court" were going to stand in his way.

His tirade finished, he suddenly headed for the Negro section of town. "Follow me!" he shouted to his surprised audience. At his words, some two hundred white men waving Confederate flags marched after him.

As the police-escorted procession rounded Big Daddy's Blue Goose, a Negro tavern, a bystander shook his head sadly.

"They don't need all those cops down here," he said. "We aren't going to hurt anyone."

For the next week, Stoner, aided by Reverend Connie Lynch, a notorious anti-Semite from California, spent every night at the Slave Market addressing restless white crowds.* It was obvious to everyone in town that, unless somebody intervened at once, blood was going to flow in the city's quaint, old-world streets. In desperation, Judge Simpson urged Florida's Attorney General James W. Kynes to do something before it was too late.

"The state has the power to police a little town like St. Augustine," he told Kynes, in refusing his application to end night marches by Negroes. "I suggest rigid law enforcement, arrests, and real charges against the hoodlums who everybody down there is afraid to proceed against."

But, as one reporter put it, "nobody in officialdom was listening to federal judges, not even Southern-born ones." Every time the Negroes marched downtown, they were attacked by club-swinging and acid-hurling white mobs. Hours after Simpson's admonition, it took more than a hundred

* A year later, the two racists teamed up again in Bogalusa, Louisiana.

state troopers to protect the Negro demonstrators from serious injury.

On Thursday, June 18, the day before the Civil Rights bill passed the United States Senate, Fred Shuttlesworth and C. T. Vivian led seventy Negroes and whites to the dining room of the Monson Motor Lodge. The group, which included sixteen rabbis, was met at the door to the restaurant by James Brock, the motel's manager.

"This is private property," Brock explained, "and I will have to ask you to leave."

When the demonstrators refused to obey him, he began to push them away from the dining room entrance. As fast as he turned one back, another took his place. A crowd of white onlookers hooted their displeasure as the police took no action to arrest the integrationists.

While everyone's attention was riveted on the scene in front of the restaurant, five Negroes and two white guests of the motel who had changed into their bathing suits dove into the pool. As soon as Brock saw what was happening, he ran to a nearby storeroom, picked up two containers of muriatic acid, a cleaning agent, and emptied them into the pool. Despite the acid, the swimmers remained in the water until they were forced out by policemen.

The next day, Stoner and Lynch addressed five hundred whites in the Old Slave Market. Prophesying that the new civil rights legislation would "bring on a race war," they urged their followers to resist it. At that moment, several hundred Negro marchers celebrating the bill's passage approached the Plaza. Sheriff Davis promptly arrested leaders Andy Young and C. T. Vivian.

Fred Shuttlesworth immediately assumed command of the column.

"Keep walking!" he implored the demonstrators.

As the line headed for the old Spanish fort, two hundred

whites rushed after it. "Get the black apes!" one red-faced man screamed, stridently.

It took a small army of policemen and state troopers to keep the two groups apart.

For the next six days, Stoner and Lynch whipped up anti-Negro sentiment at the Old Slave Market. Early on the evening of June 25, the latter openly urged violence. "If it takes violence to preserve the Constitution," he ranted, "I say all right. I favor violence to preserve the white race any time, any place, anywhere. Now it may be some niggers are gonna get killed in the process, but when war's on, that's what happens."

The clergyman was still exhorting his audience when a silent Negro column entered the Plaza. Again led by Fred Shuttlesworth, the marchers began their nightly trek past the Slave Market. For one breathless moment, there was complete silence.

Then all hell broke loose.

Enraged whites, shouting obscenities, poured into King Street. When the police seized five hoodlums, the crowd screamed, "Turn them loose!" The officers released their captives at once and then stepped back as club-wielding whites ripped into the Negro ranks.

Reporter Larry Goodwyn watched the carnage in shocked disbelief.

"A teen-age Negro, his head bleeding, dashed through the crowd like a halfback, to disappear down the street toward home. A fat woman huddled over a young girl and a trooper ran up, looked around uncertainly, and finally bent down to inspect. The mob emitted an eerie cry as it crossed and recrossed the Plaza, attacking the dwindling remnants of Negro marchers. A small pile of black bodies lay in the street. In thirteen minutes it was all over. The injured numbered forty-five."

One Negro woman, her clothes torn from her body by screaming whites, was clawed and beaten by her attackers. A bleeding thirteen-year-old girl cowered in the bushes to avoid further injury. A reporter, who tried to protect her, was accosted by three white youths.

"Let that gorilla go!" they ordered.

"Run!" he told the girl.

As she scampered toward the safety of Cordoba Street, the reporter blocked her would-be pursuers with his body. For his pains, he was kicked in the stomach and trampled to the ground by the frustrated hoodlums.

Violence was not confined to the streets. Three days earlier, a band of white men had chased a group of Negro swimmers who had attempted to use one of the normally segregated Atlantic Ocean beaches. The whites, armed with clubs, had plunged into the surf and bludgeoned the Negroes out of the water.

For the next seventy-two hours, the beaches became a no-man's land. Negroes in bathing suits were savagely attacked by white men who, like jackals stalking wildebeests, would race across the sand whenever they spotted a lone swimmer. One victim, a Danish photographer, brought to five the number of newsmen who had been assaulted since the night marches began in late May.

It was not until June 25 that Governor Farris Bryant's high boiling point was finally reached. On that day, spurred by Judge Simpson, he ordered members of the Florida Highway Patrol to protect the demonstrators at the beach. For the first time, hit-and-run raiders trying to club Negro bathers were restrained by the police. One white youth was even clouted over the head and arrested by a trooper.

At long last, Florida had had enough. On Sunday, June 28, Bryant announced that he had named a four-man emergency biracial commission to "restore communications" between the white and Negro communities. Calling this step "a demonstration of good faith," King ordered all marches discontinued.

"Every thousand-mile journey begins with the first step," he said. "This is merely the first step in the long journey toward freedom and justice in St. Augustine, but it is a creative and important first step, for it at least opens the channels of communication."

Four days later, the President of the United States, with a plea to "close the springs of racial poison," signed the Civil Rights Act of 1964 into law.

Although a few St. Augustine merchants complied at once with the new statute and opened their doors to Negroes, it took additional court tests to implement it fully. The influence and power of Hoss Manucy did not end by one stroke of the Presidential pen, and many restaurateurs and motel operators hoped for the protection of a federal court order. Judge Simpson was quick to oblige them and, by autumn, it was possible to proclaim that surface integration had finally come to America's oldest city.

But it will take months and years for the scars etched by the summer of 1964 to disappear. Hoss Manucy and his vigilantes still walk the streets, and it would be the height of folly to assume that they have now exchanged bitterness for brotherhood. As one long-time resident put it, "They've built up a big head of steam and as long as they're not in jail, things in this town will be explosive."

The real meaning of St. Augustine must await the judgment of history. For the time being, we must accept the appraisals of those who watched the explosion of what the Florida Advisory Committee to the United States Civil Rights Commission described as "a segregated superbomb aimed at the heart of Florida's economy and political integrity." Of these, Pat Watters perhaps summed it up best when he wrote:

And if the dread, pale, and deathly spirit which prevailed for a time over St. Augustine ever should overwhelm America, the blame would not be on the ignorant and shabby and essentially pitiable people who follow the limping step of a professional hate-monger through dark and narrow streets. We would have to examine instead the institutions and society which produced them, and produced also the more numerous others who for many years were unable to act against human need and injustice, and were eventually incapable of acting for law, democracy, and human freedom itself.

For it was never clearer than in St. Augustine that the notion of a middle ground is a myth in the clash of human beliefs symbolized on the one hand by the Negro movement, and on the other hand by the thought and methods of racism. The people who claimed to be moderates were indeed paralyzed and impotent; the Negro stood on the true middle, American position. Not just Negro freedom or racial justice were threatened, but freedom and justice for all.

PART **IX**

CRACKS IN

THE WALL

CHAPTER 32

Mississippi Summer

Early on the morning of Monday, June 22, 1964, my telephone rang.

"Mr. Kunstler," a man's voice said, "my name is Nat Schwerner. You don't know me but my son Mickey asked me to call you if he ever needed a lawyer."

I had first met Mickey Schwerner in the middle of March when I had attended the organizing convention of the Council of Federated Organizations (COFO) Summer Project in Jackson. He and his petite wife, Rita, both CORE workers, ran the Community Center in Meridian. After the convention, we had flown back to New York together. During the flight, Mickey had given me a fascinating description of his life as a civil rights worker in Mississippi.

Two days before Nat's call, I had run into Mickey and Rita again at the orientation seminar held on the campus of Western College for Women in Oxford, Ohio, for the COFO Summer Project volunteers. I had gone to Oxford to say goodbye to my daughter Karin who was destined for Holly Springs, and to announce the first of several voter registration suits which Ben Smith, Arthur Kinoy and I had recommended to COFO as an adjunct to the Summer Project.

At a press conference called to explain the new suit, Mickey's astute analysis of Mississippi politics had proved invaluable. Afterward, he had walked me to my car. "If you're in Meridian this summer," he said as we parted, "please drop in on us."

"Mickey is missing," Nat told me. "He and two friends drove back to Mississippi on Saturday and they haven't been seen since they went to visit a burned church near Philadelphia yesterday afternoon. His mother and I are worried sick about him."

I promised that I would try to get some information for him. As soon as he hung up, I called COFO headquarters in Jackson. I spoke to Sherwin Kaplan, a young University of Chicago law student,* who told me that Mickey, a New York white volunteer named Andrew Goodman, and James Chaney, a local Negro youth, had not been heard from for more than twelve hours.

As soon as I heard the name Goodman, I recalled a couple Lotte and I had met at an orientation meeting held for parents of the New York volunteers at New York's Riverside Church a week or so earlier. One of the COFO staff workers had just finished explaining that it was highly possible that some of the students might be killed or injured during the coming summer.

At his words, a man sitting near me looked apprehensive. "You've had some experience in the South," he whispered to

---

* Kaplan was one of several hundred law students recruited for Southern service by the newly organized Law Students Civil Rights Research Council.

me. "Is this fellow just an alarmist or are these kids in any real danger?"

I tried to reassure him. "There's always a chance that someone will be hurt," I said, "but I think that everyone will come home safe and sound."

As we left the church that night, the man to whom I had been speaking walked over to us. "I wanted to thank you for your encouraging words," he said. "I'm Robert Goodman and this is my wife, Carolyn. Our son Andy is one of the volunteers."

For those who knew Mississippi, it was obvious that the three young men were dead. According to Neshoba County Sheriff Lawrence A. Rainey, they had been stopped for speeding on Sunday afternoon by Deputy Sheriff Cecil R. Price and imprisoned for some five hours until the local justice of the peace had set their fine. As soon as it was paid, they had left for Meridian.

The conclusion was inescapable that they had been held in jail long enough for a lynch mob to be assembled.*

Any doubts we might have had on this score were dispelled when the blue Ford station wagon in which the trio had been riding was found on Tuesday. The vehicle, which had been

---

* Early in 1965, the federal government, in indicting Sheriff Rainey and seventeen other white men for conspiring to violate the civil rights of Schwerner, Goodman and Chaney, took the same tack. "It was part of the plan and purpose of the conspiracy," the indictment read, "that Cecil Ray Price, while having Michael Henry Schwerner, James Earl Chaney and Andrew Goodman in his custody in the Neshoba County Jail, located in Philadelphia, Mississippi, would release them from custody at such time that he, Cecil Ray Price, Jimmy Arledge, Horace Doyle Barnette, Travis Maryn Barnette, Alton Wayne Roberts, Jimmy Snowden, James E. Jordan, Billy Wayne Posey, Jerry McGrew Sharpe and Jimmy Lee Townsend could and would intercept Michael Henry Schwerner, James Earl Chaney and Andrew Goodman upon their leaving the area of the Neshoba County Jail, and threaten, assault, shoot and kill them."

stripped of its hub caps, had been set on fire by whoever had driven it to the lonely back road where it was discovered. Despite the fact that the President had ordered the FBI and the Navy to scour the area for traces of the missing men, I did not think their bodies would ever be recovered.

By the last week in June, the Schwerners had abandoned all hope. "As far as I'm concerned," Nat said grimly, "you can now do what you want, legally. I know that Mickey is dead, and I want you to do whatever will help to prevent other such murders." Rita, who had come back to New York shortly after her husband's disappearance, shared Nat's views.

By this time, we were not quite sure what steps we ought to take. We did not find the answer until late in June when Arthur, Ben Smith, and I were driving to Jackson from Biloxi where we had argued a case involving the constitutionality of the antipicketing statute,* one of a package of special Mississippi laws passed to curtail the activities of the summer volunteers. Suddenly Arthur, who had been thumbing through a federal statute book, snorted.

"I've found just what we've been looking for!" he shouted.

Buried in the Civil Rights Act of 1866 was a section which provided for the appointment of special federal commissioners "so as to afford a speedy and convenient means for the arrest and examination of persons charged with a violation of this Act." Since we were sure that the three men had been killed to deter and intimidate the summer volunteers, why couldn't we ask the federal court to appoint commissioners to prevent similar violence?

That evening we explained to Bob Moses, the director of the Summer Project, what we had in mind. Moses, a light-skinned Negro in his late twenties who had taught school in

---

* On June 2, 1965, the United States Supreme Court reversed the lower court's refusal to enjoin the statute and ordered a reconsideration of its decision. The case is now pending.

New York before setting up shop in Mississippi, sat expressionless as we went over the little-used Reconstruction statute with him. After we had finished our presentation, he asked us to meet him at his apartment in a half hour.

When we arrived, he surprised us by agreeing at once to the proposed suit. This is typical of Bob. A deeply contemplative man, he arrives at decisions only after the most tortuous of soul searching. Once having made up his mind, however, he moves with decisive speed.

Moses is an extremely unusual human being. Like King, he radiates a mystique that quickly communicates itself to everyone around him.* But, whereas Martin is perpetually affable and quick to humor, Bob is moody and usually quite reserved. Despite their differences, both men have one quality in common: they inspire the ultimate in devotion from their followers.

Unfortunately, it is difficult to feel close to Bob. Only rarely have I been able to talk to him at any length and, even then, our conversation was confined to the business at hand. Although I have known him for more than three years, I have never succeeded in penetrating the wall of isolation with which he surrounds himself. This lack of essential communication has often exasperated me but, like so many others who share my frustration, I am quite prepared to acknowledge his uniqueness.

As soon as Arthur and I returned to New York, we began drafting the new lawsuit. It was to be brought in the name of COFO, several of its staff and volunteer workers, Rita Schwerner, and James Chaney's mother. The defendants were Rainey and Price, as representative of the law enforcement officers of the state's eighty-two counties, Highway Patrol Director Colonel T. B. Birdsong, the White Citizens

---

* Bob himself wants to avoid the development of such a mystique. This, in part, explains his recent selection of Parris, his middle name, as his last name.

Council, the Ku Klux Klan, and the Society for the Preservation of the White Race.

In addition to the appointment of commissioners, we asked for an injunction against further violence so that Bobby Kennedy could no longer take refuge in the lame excuse that he could do nothing without a federal court order.

In doing our research, we discovered that the Congressmen who had drafted the Civil Rights Act of 1866 knew exactly what they were doing. Acutely aware that Andrew Johnson was a Southerner with very limited capabilities, they were determined to safeguard the victory of the Civil War. If the President would not enforce the new law, they wanted federal judges to have the power to appoint people who would do so.

As was to be expected, Andrew Johnson vetoed the bill. "This extraordinary power," he said angrily, "is to be conferred upon agents irresponsible to the government and to the people, and in whose hand such authority might be a terrible engine of wrong, oppression, and fraud."

Senator Trumbull, the bill's floor manager, replied by pointing out that the proposed law had been copied from the Fugitive Slave Act for which Johnson, as a Tennessee Senator, had voted. "When you come to use the same machinery," Trumbull argued, "not for the purpose of reducing to bondage and keeping in slavery human beings, but for the purposes of liberating and protecting them, it is a very different thing."

Although Congress overrode the Presidential veto, the new statute, like so much of the Reconstruction legislation, was destined to be soon forgotten. The withdrawal of federal troops from the South that was part of the infamous deal that put Rutherford B. Hayes into the White House in 1877, spelled the end of national concern over the fate of the newly freed slaves. In rapid succession came the enactment of the

Jim Crow laws, their approval by the Supreme Court, and the reenslavement of the Negro that was destined to endure for five tormented generations.

The bright hopes that had been generated by the deaths of 650,000 young men were swiftly buried deeper than their bones.

On July 10, 1965, the day that J. Edgar Hoover came to Jackson to open a new FBI office, we filed the complaint in what had become known as *COFO v. Rainey*. Significantly, our local attorney was Leonard H. Rosenthal, a young white Mississippian who had agreed to help us with the suit. Hours after it became known that he was allied with us, his landlord ordered him to give up his tiny office.

Since we had asked for a temporary restraining order against violence in several Mississippi counties, a hearing was set before Judge Mize in Meridian on July 23. A week earlier, we had sent Michael B. Standard, an extremely capable New York lawyer, to Jackson to prepare for what we hoped would be a full-scale hearing. In short, he was to interview prospective witnesses about the existence of widespread violence and terror directed against Negroes and their white supporters.

Standard did his job well. When Rita Schwerner and I arrived in Jackson on July 21, he had amassed, with the help of Robert Weil, the COFO communications coordinator, almost one hundred affidavits testifying to scores of murders, bombings, burnings, and beatings throughout the state. In addition, he had a dozen witnesses ready to take the stand.

The next afternoon, we drove to Meridian. That evening, in Rita's tiny second-floor apartment, we assembled the requisite number of copies of the affidavits that Mike had collected. As we worked through the night, it seemed to me that it was particularly appropriate that we were where we were. I felt that Mickey Schwerner would have approved.

Shortly after midnight, Standard rented the last available

bed at the Lamar Hotel. Since Rita and Cornelia McDou-
gald, a Harvard law student who was helping us, had com-
mandeered the only bedroom in the Schwerner flat, I slept on
a cot near the front door. Before settling down, I looked
around for something to serve as a mattress. In one corner, I
found an olive-drab bedroll.

Wrapped in it were a pair of sneakers, some denim
trousers, a handful of shirts, and a sweater. As I started to
stack them on the floor, I suddenly was aware that Rita was
standing behind me. As my eyes met hers, I knew at once that
she was a million miles away.

"That's Andy Goodman's bedroll," she said softly. "He
must have left it here that last Sunday."

For a long moment, I groped for some response. Before I
could say anything, she had turned on her heels and walked
into the bedroom. I quickly stuffed all of Andy's clothing
back into the roll, tied it up, and returned it to where I had
found it.

Promptly at nine the next morning, we appeared in Mize's
courtroom. In addition to Rainey and Price, we had subpoenaed such hostile witnesses as the Neshoba County jailer
and his wife, the justice of the peace, and the two highway
patrolmen who had assisted in the arrest of the missing
workers. We also intended to put some of our own people on
the stand.

But no one was destined to testify that day. Mize, whose
skill at procrastination and delay had been so superbly
demonstrated during the *Meredith* case, promptly adjourned
the hearing for one week. He was doing this, he claimed, in
order to give us time to answer some defense motions which
had been handed to us as we entered the courtroom. Although we argued loud and long that we were ready to go
ahead with our case, he would not budge.

The new hearing was to be held in Hattiesburg. According

to Mize, he would first hear argument on the defendants' motions to dismiss our complaint. If he denied them, he would permit us to try to convince him with affidavits that he ought to restrain violence while the suit was pending. Only if he couldn't decide on this evidence would he listen to our live witnesses.

Just before Mize left the bench, Will Wells, the chief defense attorney, had a request to make. "In the event it does become necessary to put on testimony," he said, "I would like to be assured that counsel will have the three plaintiffs who swore to this complaint in court on the thirtieth so that if it becomes necessary to cross-examine them or call them as adverse witnesses, I will be able to do so."

Mize nodded. Our three plaintiffs would be "required" to be present in Hattiesburg on July 30.

After the hearing, we decided to hold a council of war in Mike Standard's room at the Lamar Hotel. As our integrated group entered the lobby, however, we were met by the manager, appropriately named Broadhead. "You people are not welcome at this hotel," he said curtly.

Our insistence that the new Civil Rights Act made it illegal for him to eject us failed to move him. "If you don't get out of this hotel," he said, "I'll call the police."

Miraculously, two Meridian policemen suddenly materialized from nowhere. I explained to them what had happened and stated that we would cause no trouble but that Standard, of course, could hardly be expected to pay for a room from which he had been unlawfully evicted. Although it was quite a struggle, racism finally won out over the profit motive and we walked out of the Lamar with a small but highly satisfying victory under our belts.

We had intended to return to Jackson that night. But we

changed our minds when a Lauderdale County deputy sheriff burst into Rita's apartment shortly after we had returned there to pick up our luggage. On the pretext that he had a message for one "William Smith," he took a good look at all of us.

His visit, plus the steady stream of police cars circling the block, were enough to convince us that it might be safer to wait until morning to navigate the eighty miles to Jackson. As soon as it was dusk, we drove out of town. Under assumed names, we checked into the first motel we could find and spent the night there.

Early the next morning we returned to Jackson.

As soon as the Hattiesburg hearing began, we knew that something was very wrong. Arthur, who had not been able to come to Meridian, was now at the counsel table. When Mize entered the courtroom, Len Rosenthal rose to his feet. "I would like to move at this time for the admission of Arthur Kinoy for the purpose of trying this case," he said. "I will defer ruling on that for a few moments," the judge countered.

Then he turned to me. "Did you bring the parties to the lawsuit as I directed to be done?" he asked sharply. "No," I replied, "I have them waiting in Jackson. It was my understanding that your Honor was going to determine whether to take testimony first, and if they were to go on the stand, they were on the defendants' case and not the plaintiffs' case."

Instead of proceeding with the hearing, Mize abruptly changed course. How many cases, he asked me, had I handled in Mississippi? Surprised as I was at the question, I managed to blurt out some sort of a reasonably accurate answer.

The judge's next remark was completely unexpected. Because of a letter he said he had received from the National Lawyers' Guild commending the Mississippi State Bar Association for issuing a resolution urging its members to accept civil rights cases, he was appointing two of the defendants' attorneys as a committee to investigate Arthur Kinoy and me to determine if we were "practicing law in violation of the laws of the State of Mississippi."

He then directed me to take the stand. As I started to comply, Will Wells hastily interrupted. He asked Mize to nonsuit us because we had willfully disobeyed the judge's orders.

To our utter amazement, the motion was immediately granted. In total disregard of the law, Mize dismissed our complaint because it was "a scatter load, the worst I have ever seen. Particularly, it should be dismissed because of a complete violation of a direct order fixing the time at nine o'clock this morning."

As the courtroom started to empty, Rainey, a burly prototype of every Southern sheriff I have ever seen, sauntered over to the counsel table. "I'd like my witness fee if you fellows don't mind," he drawled, insolently.

It took every bit of self-control I possessed to keep from screaming "Murderer!" at him. "I think you ought to pay the other side," I answered. "They saved you from having to take the stand and tell how those three boys were really killed!"

After filing a notice of appeal from Mize's ruling, Arthur and I returned to New York. Five days later, Lotte and I were having dinner at the Kinoys' apartment when the telephone rang. It was a reporter from the Associated Press who said that the FBI had just discovered three bodies under a dam site near Philadelphia.

The missing civil rights workers had been found.

When we heard that autopsies were to be conducted that night at University Hospital in Jackson, we decided to have a doctor of our own present. When the FBI indicated that it had no objection, we called the Medical Committee for Human Rights which had sent physicians to Mississippi to assist the Summer Project volunteers. It put us in touch with Dr.

Charles Goodrich in Jackson who promised to do what he could to attend the postmortems.

As soon as the bodies, encased in plastic zippered containers, arrived in Jackson, they were taken to the hospital. Unfortunately, the local authorities would not permit Dr. Goodrich to witness the autopsies, and we had to rely on the sketchy FBI report. All three men, we were told, had been shot to death with a .38-caliber pistol shortly after their release from the Neshoba County Jail.

The next day, we persuaded Dr. David M. Spain, the former Westchester County medical examiner who was vacationing at Martha's Vineyard, to fly to Jackson. After examining the body of James Chaney, he confirmed what our own investigation had indicated—that Chaney had been horribly beaten by his assailants. "The jaw was shattered, the left shoulder and upper arm were reduced to a pulp; the right forearm was broken completely across at several points, and the skull bones were broken and pushed in toward the brain."

Such injuries, he concluded, could only have been inflicted by an extremely severe beating with a blunt instrument or a chain. "In my extensive experience of twenty-five years as a pathologist and as a medical examiner, I have never witnessed bones so severely shattered, except in tremendously high speed accidents such as airplane crashes."

Dr. Spain did not examine Mickey's body until it had arrived in New York several days later. He found no evidence of any injury other than a bullet wound on the left side of the chest. "One must therefore assume," he said, "that the cause of death was due to a bullet wound entering the thorax anteriorly and penetrating a major vessel. There was no evidence of any other injury or bodily mutilation."

With Rita's concurrence, Lotte arranged for a memorial service at the Community Church. At 8 P.M. on August 9, more than two thousand people crowded into the red-brick

building to hear six speakers try to put into words the inex-
pressible tragedy of the death of young men. Two of Mickey's
college friends, CORE's Jim Farmer and Dave Dennis, John
Lewis of SNCC, and I were assigned this task.

From the moment of their disappearance, I was convinced
that the three civil rights workers had been killed in order to
stop the thousand COFO volunteers who were to follow
them. It was inconceivable to the murderers that American
parents would permit their children to walk into known
danger. A mass defection would have destroyed or seriously
crippled the Summer Project and, in the process, given the
closed society a much-needed breathing spell.

But, to the everlasting credit of the volunteers and their
families, there were no defections. Two days after Mickey,
Andy and James had disappeared, hundreds of frightened
but resolute college students were proceeding to their assigned projects throughout Mississippi. Young men and
women, determined to give their own lives meaning and
purpose, were proving to themselves and their country that
only if one is willing to die for his beliefs does he deserve to
live for them.

Before the summer came to an end, they would have established forty-seven Freedom Schools with some 2,500 pupils.
Through their efforts, thirteen community centers became
bustling headquarters for an enormous variety of useful and
cultural activities. Their voter-registration teams roamed the
state urging Negroes to register both for the regular election
and for that sponsored by the Freedom Democratic Party.

This was the measure of Mickey's death, we told the thousands who had come to memorialize him. The horrendous
gamble that had led to his execution on a Neshoba County
back road had failed and, if there was any glory in this world,
it had touched him and his two companions for one bright
and shining moment.

"It is true that a great tragedy has taken place," I concluded. "Three young men, guilty of no crime other than compassion, hope, and love, have been brutally and senselessly destroyed. But beyond the immediacy of our grief, every one of us feels, in one way or another, that we can look to tomorrow with brighter and clearer eyes, that we can face the morning sun with more faith and courage, that we are stronger and more resolute than ever before, because our three friends laid down their lives in the dark of a Mississippi night. We are not afraid because they were not afraid—we will walk hand in hand because they walked hand in hand—we will live together because they died together."

The appeal from Mize's ruling in *COFO v. Rainey* was argued before a three-judge panel in New Orleans on November 18. In our brief, we urged the court to protect the Negroes of Mississippi and their white supporters from the total breakdown of law and order in that state. "In desperation," we pleaded, "our clients have turned to the federal courts for the protection Congress has provided in such emergencies."

What we are confronted with here, of course, is the last-ditch effort of the hard-core racist element to accomplish what such legal devices as interposition, nullification, massive resistance, and other discredited methods have failed to do. They now increasingly place their reliance squarely on murder, mayhem, destruction, and terrorism to retain as much of the old order as is possible, for as long as is possible. In this frantic effort to head off the inevitable, they will stop at nothing as the three recent murders in Philadelphia so tragically illustrate.

This is a moment of intense crisis for the federal government. Each of its three branches has a responsibility for meeting it squarely and the judicial branch, no less than the executive and the legislative, must meet its constitutional obligations. Congress, after full and thorough investigation, has provided judicial remedies against the carnage that is today occurring in the streets, along the back roads, in the jails, and on the highways of Mississippi. In 42 U.S.C. 1983, the federal courts were given the equitable injunctive power—in 42 U.S.C. 1989, the right to appoint special commissioners. These statutory remedies are clearly available to the courts. The real question is whether they will be used.

The responsibility for the judicial branch is particularly solemn at this moment. It has become increasingly apparent that the traditional form of maintaining the highest standard of community mores—the normal enforcement of the criminal law —is not effective in one significant area of American life. The Negro seeking his civil rights and liberties and the fulfillment of his status as a citizen and a human being has become a virtual outlaw in Mississippi as well as in many other localities.

He can be shot down in broad daylight in the streets of his own town as was Herbert Lee in Liberty. He may be brutally beaten in jail by members of the police force, as was Mrs. Fannie Lou Hamer in Winona. He may have his place of business and home gutted by fire bombs as did Aaron Henry in Clarksdale. He may be lynched by mobs as were Mack Parker and Emmet Till. He may be massacred by hidden snipers as was Medgar Evers. He may be wantonly beaten to death as was James Chaney.

The catalogue of violence is as endless as the desperation of those who resist the enforcement of the Constitution. What provides the special character of crisis for the judicial branch of government at this moment in our national history is the harsh reality that the conventional institutions of criminal law enforcement are increasingly unable to provide the deterrent to this widespread behavior which these institutions normally are designed to provide.

The recent outcome of the trial of Klan members for the wanton murder of Colonel Lemuel Penn in the Georgia courts can only intensify the rapidly accelerating fear throughout the deep South that reliance upon the conventional channels of state criminal law enforcement for the deterrence of the conspiracy of violence is futile and empty.*

The danger which this poses to our entire system of government is enormous. The crisis for a democratic society occurs when confidence is lost in a system of structured law. The federal courts in the deepest sense of the word have now the ultimate responsibility in demonstrating that law and legal forms and institutions are still available to meet the impending threat to constitutional rights and to the lives of those who bravely assert those rights.

If the confidence of the Negro citizens of Mississippi in the structure of law is to be retained, if the faith of the American people in their judicial institutions is to remain strong, the federal courts must now exercise their equity powers to do what the state courts are unwilling and/or unable to do—namely, to utilize the criminal law as a deterrent to violence and brutalization directed against the Negroes of Mississippi in their efforts to assert their American constitutional rights.

This action on the part of this Court would be in the highest tradition of equity jurisprudence. Traditionally, equity would act when there was no remedy at law or where the remedy provided was inadequate. At this moment, there is *no* remedy at law in Mississippi through the normal enforcement of the criminal law to deter individuals and clandestine organizations who are openly flouting the laws of the United States. *Federal equity must provide this remedy.*

As important as this relief is to the preservation of constitutional principles and for the safeguarding of the lives of the Negroes of Mississippi, it is even more important for the preservation of a system of government grounded on the ordered administration of law. Nothing less than confidence in the American

---

* Barely four months later, an all-white jury in Hayneville, Alabama, refused to believe an eyewitness to the murder of Mrs. Viola Liuzzo during the Selma-to-Montgomery march. On September 30, 1965, in the same court, part-time deputy sheriff Thomas L. Coleman was acquitted of the shotgun slaying of an Episcopal seminary student.

system of law is at stake. If the federal courts close their doors and refuse the relief requested here, where can Americans turn?

In his summation, Kinoy, in as eloquent an argument as I have ever heard, urged the court, if it did nothing else, to issue an order forbidding violence until the appeal had been decided. "Even if it has no effect on the perpetrators of violence," he said, "it will tell the Negroes of Mississippi and the people of America, 'Do not despair, do not despair of the American system of government. There *is* rule of law, there *is* a judicial tribunal that will answer your pleas for justice.'"

One month later, the court replied. Although it refused to issue an antiviolence order, Judge Mize's dismissal was unanimously overruled, and the case was reinstated.* "We think it must be inferred from the record that counsel for the plaintiffs misunderstood the district court's order for the appearance of the verifying plaintiffs and that their absence was not willful or in bad faith. This being so, it follows that the drastic sanction of dismissal is an abuse of discretion."

Judge Mize was also soundly criticized for failing to give us a hearing. "The dismissal of the complaint for failure to state a claim," the court ruled, "was without a hearing and without an opportunity to be heard. The right of a litigant to be heard is one of the fundamental rights of due process of law. A denial of the right requires a reversal."

In a curious aside, the court suggested that if any further violence had occurred since July, the complaint might be amended to include it. It also recommended that at the appropriate time Mize "might advise the United States Attorney of the pendency of the cause so that the United States might, if it sees fit, apply for leave to intervene or to appear as *amicus curiae*."

The lessons of the summer had apparently been learned on many levels.

---

* Because of Mize's death, it is now on Judge Cox's trial calendar.

CHAPTER 33

The Challenge

While the Summer Project did not succeed in registering very many Negro voters, it was far from being a failure.
Among its other accomplishments, it established the Mississippi Freedom Democratic Party (FDP) as a meaningful and
potentially powerful political entity. With COFO volunteers
supplying much of the manpower, FDP managed to organize
the necessary precinct meetings and county and state conven-
tions to select delegates to the Democratic National Convention in Atlantic City.

Everyone who watched the convention on television will
remember FDP's valiant fight to garner all of the Mississippi
seats. Since it was the only group of Democrats in the state
loyal to the party's national platform and open to all regardless of race or color, FDP insisted that it was entitled to such
an allocation. Its rejection of the convention's offer of two
token seats was both moral and logical.

As soon as the convention had ended, FDP decided to
make a determined effort to place candidates on the ballot for
the November elections. In early September, independent

nominating petitions were filed with the State Board of Elections pursuant to Section 3260 of the Mississippi Code, asking that the names of four Negroes be added to the list of candidates. Signed by the required number of qualified voters, the petitions nominated Dr. Aaron Henry for United States Senator and Mrs. Fannie Lou Hamer, Mrs. Annie Devine, and Mrs. Victoria Gray for Congresswomen.

Heber Ladner, the Board's secretary and a power in state politics, refused to accept the petitions. Although Section 3260 did not require it, he insisted on the certification of each signature by the appropriate circuit clerks. If this could be done by October 2, he said, he would file the papers.

The supporters of the four Negroes found it impossible to comply with Ladner's ruling. The experience of Clinton Douglas Smith in Forrest County was typical.

1. On 29 September 1964, I went to the Forrest County Circuit Clerk's office and asked to see the registrar, Theron C. Lynd. Lynd came to the counter and I told him that I had been advised by the Secretary of State to bring these petitions to the Circuit Clerk to have them certified. (Sixty-six signatures on a petition for Mr. Aaron E. Henry, and sixty-eight for Mrs. Victoria Gray.) The Circuit Clerk told me that I would have to have the petitioners' signatures arranged by precinct before he could certify them.

2. At approximately 3:50 P.M. on the same date, George Harper and I went back to the Circuit Clerk's office with the petitions arranged in precinct order. The clerk agreed to certify the signatures. After giving the clerk the petitions, I then asked him for a receipt. Lynd told me that he could not give me a receipt. He gave them back to me and told me to bring them back the next day. I picked up the petitions and left his office.

3. On 30 September 1964 at approximately 10 A.M. George Harper and I returned to Lynd's office and gave the petitions to him. Lynd asked me when I would like to have them returned

and I told him Thursday (1 October 64) afternoon. He agreed and we left.

4. On 1 October 1964, with Sanford R. Leigh, I returned to Lynd's office to pick up the petitions I had left with Lynd on 30 September. Lynd handed them to me. Upon examination I found that there were only 12 signatures certified. I returned to Lynd's office and asked Lynd whether these were all of the 68 signatures which represented "qualified electors." Lynd replied that "under the laws of Mississippi, these are the only signatures which can be construed as 'qualified electors.' I am not saying that all the rest of the signatures are not registered voters, but some of them have not paid their poll taxes."

5. When I protested that the election was of a federal nature and that the laws of the state, because of the candidates' seeking federal office, did not apply, he told me that he was judging the signatures according to Mississippi law, and that federal laws had nothing to do with these signatures.

6. After thanking Lynd for nothing, I took the petitions and left the office.

Because they were prevented from having their names placed on the official ballot, Mrs. Hamer, Mrs. Gray, and Mrs. Devine ran in a Freedom Election held by FDP from October 30 to November 2. During this four-day period, anyone possessing the qualifications required by Mississippi law was permitted to vote without discrimination as to race or color. As was to be expected, each woman received an overwhelming majority of the votes cast.

The FDP candidates are remarkable in every sense of the word. All native Mississippians, they are as different from each other as they are, collectively, representative of the Negro citizens of their state. Mrs. Hamer, a short, heavy-set resident of Ruleville in Senator Eastland's Sunflower County, is the FDP vice-chairman and was one of its delegates at the Atlantic City Convention. After eighteen years as a time-keeper on a local plantation, she was fired in 1962 for trying to register.

Although profoundly despondent over the failure of America to live up to its promises as far as Negroes are concerned, Mrs. Hamer is not without hope. Despite the loss of her job, and a brutal beating supervised by the police of Winona, Mississippi, in the middle of 1963, she has carried FDP's message to every corner of the country. "Go Tell It on the Mountain," her favorite song, has become for her a way of life.

Mrs. Devine, who calls Canton home, is as astute as she is retiring. A slim, gray-haired woman, she is the FDP Secretary and, like Mrs. Hamer, was a delegate to the Democratic National Convention. Warm and sympathetic, she is a thoroughly delightful person.

Victoria Jackson Gray, of Hattiesburg, always looks as if she had just stepped out of a Saks Fifth Avenue window. A young and beautiful woman with stylish, upswept hair and a proud carriage, she is, in addition to being a member of the FDP Executive Committee, the state supervisor of the SCLC citizenship education program. In the 1964 primary campaign she was an unsuccessful candidate for a seat in the United States Senate.

All three women have much in common. Fully committed to the proposition that only through political organization can the Negroes of Mississippi really break the chains that bind them, they have abiding faith in FDP as the vehicle with which to achieve such a goal. They have sacrificed much of their private lives for the good of the party and have placed themselves completely at its disposal.

"If those three boys could die for me," Mrs. Hamer often says, "then I must do what I can for my brothers and my sisters."

Shortly after the regular election on November 3, Arthur, Ben Smith, and I were asked by Lawrence Guyot, the FDP Chairman, to become its lawyers. Guyot, a tall, heavy-set man in his middle twenties, was particularly interested in challenging the right of the five Mississippi Congressmen to sit in the House of Representatives. "Since most of our state's Negroes can't vote," he reasoned, "the elections can't be valid."

Legally, he was quite correct. Article I, Section 2, of the federal Constitution provides that "the House of Representatives shall be composed of Members chosen every second year by the People of the several states." Since a little more than five percent of the state's Negroes could vote, it was obvious that the word "People," in the eyes of Mississippi officialdom, meant only whites.

Moreover, when Mississippi was readmitted to representation in Congress in 1870, it agreed "never to deprive any citizen or class of citizens of the right to vote" who were entitled to suffrage by its constitution. According to that document, every sane adult resident without a criminal record could become a qualified elector.

From 1870 on, Mississippi Negroes registered in such great numbers that they soon outnumbered white voters. For a time, violence and outright corruption were the methods used to keep white control of most of the state's elective offices. But in 1890 it was decided to put disfranchisement on a more "legal" basis.

A year earlier, United States Senator James Z. George had thrown his considerable weight behind the calling of a constitutional convention to curb Negro suffrage. "Our chief duty when we meet in Convention," he told the state legislature, "is to devise such measures, consistent with the Constitution of the United States, as will enable us to maintain a home government, under the control of the white people of the State."

The election of John M. Stone, a staunch George supporter, as governor in the fall of 1889 resulted in the scheduling of a constitutional convention for the following August. "The controlling factor in increasing the desire for a new Constitution was one creditable to the citizenship of the state," one observer commented. "Thoughtful men saw quite distinctly that the way elections were being carried corrupted the morals of the people and brought into disrepute the purity of the ballot box. Bad as the domination of a Negro majority of voters had proved itself to be, the then prevalent way of preventing it led to serious evils and rendered efforts to escape the consequences of both imperative."

When the convention was called to order on August 12, there were 189,884 registered Negro voters in the state as compared to 118,890 whites. In his opening address, Judge S. S. Calhoon, the President of the Convention, reminded the delegates that "this ballot system must be so arranged as to effect one object. We find the two races now together—the rule of one has always meant economic and moral ruin; we find another whose rule has always meant prosperity and happiness to all races."

By the time the convention ended, the legal groundwork for disfranchising the Negro had been laid. The establishment of a poll tax and the requirement that all prospective registrants be able to read or understand any section of the new constitution resulted in an immediate decimation of black voters. Within two years, only 8,615 remained on the rolls.

In Judge Calhoon's words, the convention had been a complete success for the state's white population. "That race alone," he said in his concluding address, "can now safely exercise the function of ruling with moderation and justice, and accomplish the great purpose for which governments are established."

But even with the exclusion of the Negro from the ballot,

many Mississippians were willing to go even further to insure white political supremacy. In 1903, Governor James K. Vardman recommended that Negroes not be permitted to attend school to make sure that they did not qualify to vote.

"The Negro should never have been trusted with the ballot," he said. "He is congenitally unqualified to exercise the most responsible duty of citizenship. We must repeal the Fifteenth and modify the Fourteenth Amendment. Then we shall be able, in all voter legislation, to recognize the Negro's racial peculiarities and make laws to fit them."

Between 1890 and 1962, Mississippi kept a persistent finger in the dike. Legislature after legislature ground out new laws designed to keep Negroes from voting. Such devices as making good moral character, as interpreted by local registrars, a condition of registering, publicizing the names of prospective voters, and requiring that the registration form be completed without a single error, no matter how immaterial, succeeded in keeping the Negro voting population at the five percent level.

In 1963, the federal government brought suit to declare all of these restrictive statutes unconstitutional. "The history of racial discrimination in Mississippi," its complaint read, "the legislative setting in which the statutes were enacted, the lack of any reasonable or objective standards for the registration of voters, and the arbitrary character of these requirements which bear no reasonable relationship to any legitimate state interest render them invalid and in violation of the Constitution of the United States."

It seemed to us that with this graphic background, we had all the evidence we needed to prove our point. What was required was some way in which to use it to unseat the Mississippi Congressmen. Fortunately, with the aid of some Harvard law students we found what we were looking for in Title 2 of the United States Code. It provided a way in which to challenge elections to the House of Representatives.

According to this rather antique statute, thirty days after the certification of an election, a notice of challenge could be filed with the Clerk of the House. At the same time, a copy had to be served on the legislator whose seat was challenged. These steps set into motion a chain of events that would eventually result in a vote on the House floor.

Since a challenge based on the systematic exclusion of almost half the electorate had never been made before, we had our work cut out for us. Although FDP had run candidates in only three Congressional districts, it decided to challenge the entire state delegation. It took three weeks of experimentation by Morty Stavis, Arthur Kinoy, and me to produce five notices that satisfied us.

On December 4, the day that the FBI announced the arrests of nineteen men accused of the murders of the three civil rights workers in Neshoba County, I met Mrs. Hamer, Mrs. Devine, and Mrs. Gray in Washington. Together, we went to the office of Ralph R. Roberts, the Clerk of the House, and filed the notices of contest. In Mississippi, Ben Smith was busy seeing to it that the five Congressmen were served at their homes.

The challenge had started.

The next step was to find a Congressman who would be willing to stand up on January 4, the first day of the Eighty-Ninth Congress, and introduce a resolution that would prevent the Mississippi members from being seated until the challenges had finally been decided by their colleagues. We found our man in William Fitts Ryan, a Manhattanite beginning his third term.

Because of the Johnson landslide, a great many new Democrats had been elected to the Eighty-Ninth Congress. Shortly after the challenges had been filed, the Administration invited these freshmen lawmakers to Washington for a one-day briefing session. Ryan felt that this would be an opportune moment to bring the Mississippi situation to their attention.

On December 8, Arthur and I met Ryan at the Sheraton Park Hotel where the briefing session was being held. Because the Administration was hardly overjoyed at the prospect of the FDP challenges, it did everything it could to prevent the new Congressmen from contacting us. By stretching out the afternoon period until it was almost time for a White House reception, Speaker John McCormack successfully torpedoed a 4 P.M. meeting Ryan had set up. ·

Undaunted, the New Yorker rescheduled his meeting for late that evening. Through the efforts of Bill Higgs, who was serving as FDP Washington counsel, notices of the new time were mimeographed and distributed to the Congressmen as they boarded the buses for the White House. Now we could only sit and wait.

We were pleasantly surprised when some dozen new members showed up after the President's reception. They included Patsy Mink of Hawaii, Joe Resnick of New York, Phil Burton of California and John Conyers of Michigan. After they had been briefed on what FDP was trying to do, they promised to support the challenge and to urge other Congressmen to do the same.

Despite this encouraging start, however, we did not believe that we had widespread House support. Mike Thelwell and Jan Goodman, who staffed FDP's Washington office, contacted as many Congressmen as they could during the next thirty days, but no one dared to hope that we would count on a substantial number to back up Ryan on opening day. By Saturday, January 2, we were prepared to be satisfied if we had twenty-five in our camp.

The House was called to order at noon on January 4. After McCormack had been elected Speaker and sworn in, he addressed the crowded chamber. "According to precedent," he said, "the Chair is now ready to swear in all Members of the House. The Members will rise."

At this moment, Ryan stood up. "Mr. Speaker," he began, "on my responsibility as a member-elect of the Eighty-Ninth Congress, I object to the oath being administered to the gentlemen from Mississippi, Mr. Abernethy, Mr. Whitten, Mr. Williams, Mr. Walker, and Mr. Colmer. I base this upon facts and statements which I consider to be reliable. I also make this objection on behalf of a significant number of colleagues who are standing with me."

To our astonishment, some fifty Congressmen, including some of the House's most influential members, rose.

The Speaker, who had been informed in advance of Ryan's contemplated action, ruled at once. "Under the precedents," he said, "the Chair will ask the gentlemen who have been challenged not to rise to take the oath with the other Members for the present at least. The other Members will rise and I will now administer the oath of office to them."

As soon as the House had been sworn, Carl Albert of Oklahoma, the Majority Leader, offered a resolution. We listened attentively as it was read aloud by the Clerk.

"Resolved, that the Speaker is hereby authorized and directed to administer the oath of office to the gentlemen from Mississippi, Mr. Thomas G. Abernethy, Mr. Jamie L. Whitten, Mr. John Bell Williams, Mr. William M. Colmer, and Mr. Prentiss Walker."

When the resolution had been read, Albert amplified it. "Mr. Speaker, the members-elect whose names are referred to in the resolution are here with certificates of election in due form on file with the Clerk of the House of Representatives just as all other Members of the House," he said. "Any question involving the validity of the regularity of their election is one which should be dealt with under the laws governing contested elections. I therefore urge the adoption of the resolution."

James Roosevelt leaped to his feet. The Californian wanted

to know whether, if the House voted down Albert's resolution it would be proper for Ryan to introduce another one "providing that the five representatives-elect from Mississippi not be sworn at this time." McCormack promptly agreed that it would.

Edith Green then rose. She asked if twenty percent of the members could demand a recorded vote. When McCormack replied that they could, she insisted that the House be polled. By a show of hands, it was clear that Mrs. Green had won her point.

As the Clerk began to call the Congressmen's names, it was soon obvious that we were going to get a much larger vote than we had ever dreamed possible. J. P Coleman, a former Mississippi governor who had been retained to represent the four challenged Democrats,* looked visibly worried as the nays began to pile up. It was only toward the end that he broke out in a broad smile.

The yeas had won, 276 to 149.

When the vote had been recorded, McCormack, who looked almost as relieved as Coleman, asked the Mississippi delegation to come forward and be sworn. The first stage of the challenge was over.

Almost five hundred Mississippi Negroes had come to Washington for opening day. During the vote, they stood in a silent vigil across the street from the Capitol. Despite the fact that George Lincoln Rockwell, the leader of the American Nazi Party, attempted to provoke them by parading back and forth in front of their line, they waited quietly for the result of the House action.

After the vote, Arthur and I informed the people on the vigil what had happened. While we were talking to them,

* Prentiss Walker, the lone Republican, who had been elected as a protest against federal intervention in Neshoba County after the disappearance of the three civil rights workers, was represented by B. B. McClendon.

Coleman, a big, bluff man, walked over to where we were standing with Mrs. Hamer, Mrs. Devine, and Mrs. Gray. "I want to serve you with the answers of the four Congressmen I represent," he said. With that, he handed each woman a very formal-looking legal document.

After he had left, we took a hurried look at the answers. In the main, each of Coleman's clients denied that he knew anything at all about voter discrimination in Mississippi. But if it did exist, they insisted that they had nothing to do with creating or perpetuating it.

What was of more interest to us was the envelope in which the response to Mrs. Hamer's notice of contest was contained. On its rear side were a series of hatch marks penciled by Coleman as he had made his unofficial count of the vote on Albert's resolution.

It was quite obvious that the ex-governor, at least, was taking the challenges very seriously indeed.

Before the House turned to other business, Roosevelt reminded its members that they had not seen the last of the challenge. In a powerful and moving speech, he brought the moral issue home to everyone listening to him. His words bear repeating:

Mr. Speaker, the occasions are rare that a member of this House must take upon himself the high and heavy duty of rising to say that he must speak upon his honor as a member. We have seen such an occasion today. And now all of us face together, as the United States House of Representatives, the high and heavy duty that some of our members had to face as individuals earlier today. This House must speak upon its honor to the people of the United States.

We are beyond politics in the ordinary sense; we are beyond the contentions of party and program that ordinarily concern us. We must speak upon politics in the very highest sense: we must speak upon the way a free people governs itself, we must speak upon the meaning of the words and the spirit of our Constitution, we must speak upon what to an American is the most terrible of political facts—that some Americans are not freemen. . . .

I said that we must today not merely as individuals but as a House, speak upon our honor to the people of the United States. We must not only speak, we must act upon our honor. This House is honorable because from the origins of our Republic, it has been the people's forum. It is the only branch of our federal government whose members have always been chosen by the people themselves, never by appointment or by succession or by electors or by state legislators. This House is honorable because it flows from the wellsprings of democracy and the open society—from the people's vote. If those wellsprings are poisoned, this House is poisoned. We dare not let men pretend to a seat in this honorable House who have been chosen by a closed vote in a closed society. If we do, we betray this House and the people of the United States and the Constitution they wrote for us.

Such men are standing before us today, pretending to seats among us. They say their constituents will have no representation if we do not seat them. But their constituents will not have representation if we do seat them. We must say to them that . . . they cannot win "elections" from a system based on murder and then claim the right to govern free men. We must tell these men to go back to their homes and to run in free elections where all their constituents can vote. We will be glad to seat men who win these elections; we will welcome to our midst Congressmen who have really been chosen by the people of Mississippi; but we must say to the people of all the States that until such men arrive here from Mississippi, we will not besmirch ourselves or the Constitution or the American people by seating persons who merely pretend to have been freely elected to our midst. When we say this, and not until then, we shall have spoken and acted upon our honor as the House of Representatives.

Under Title 2, we had forty days from January 4 to take any testimony we wanted in or out of Mississippi. We spent the first half of this period recruiting lawyers and court reporters to help in this respect. Ben Smith and I held briefing sessions in California and Chicago respectively, while Arthur and Morty Stavis did the same for Eastern volunteers at New York's Broadway Congregational Church.

The response was magnificent. By the time the first depositions were scheduled, more than 130 lawyers and a sufficient number of court reporters had signed up for Mississippi service. Throughout the state, friendly witnesses were standing by to testify to the fact that Negroes simply could not vote at any level. Subpoenas had been prepared and served on such personages as ex-Governor Ross R. Barnett, Attorney General Joe T. Patterson, Secretary of State Heber Ladner, and Erle Johnston, Jr., Director of the State Sovereignty Commission.

With lawyers flocking into Jackson from all over the country, Stavis undertook the responsibility of opening our "challenge law office." He and Ed Stern of San Francisco, who had been instrumental in persuading many California attorneys to come to Mississippi, functioned as managing attorneys of a law firm whose personnel changed almost weekly. Working with Roberta Galler, who was in charge of the FDP office, they saw to it that prospective witnesses were interviewed, subpoenas were served, and places in which to hold our hearings were obtained.

We anticipated a great deal of trouble in getting notaries to act as hearing officers. Mississippi has very few Negro notaries, and they are concentrated in the more populous urban centers. Coleman, however, who had been thoroughly frightened by the size of our vote on January 4, was determined to give Congress the right impression. He volunteered to supply all the notaries we needed in the outlying counties.

The testimony of the state officials was taken at the beginning of February. We had scheduled these hearings in a Negro church, but Coleman would have none of this. "I can't have our state officers going into a Negro building," he said. "If I can get rooms in the Federal Building, would this be acceptable to you?"

Several weeks earlier, we had asked Judge Cox for space in this building, but our request had been curtly denied. Coleman apparently had more influence with Cox than we did, and the Civil Service examination room was immediately made available. Because we felt that it was highly appropriate that the testimony of the state officials be taken on federal property, we accepted Coleman's offer.

I arrived in Jackson late in the evening of January 28. On the flight down, the man sitting next to me spent the entire trip reading a sheaf of mimeographed papers. As he pored over them, I suddenly realized that what was absorbing his interest was a copy of our notice of contest. Congressman Whitten, it seems, had reproduced the one served on him and distributed it to his constituents. A covering letter stated that the challenge was extremely serious and that he expected the people back home to rally to his support.

The FDP office was a beehive of activity when I entered it. Lawyers, court reporters, and office workers completely filled the four tiny rooms on the second floor of 507½ North Farish Street. The overflow was accommodated in the National Lawyers Guild quarters across the hall.

As I watched the hustle and bustle, I was conscious for the first time of the enormous magnetism of the challenge. People from all over the United States, shocked by the calculated exclusion of Negroes from the political life of Mississippi, had banded together to do what they could to bring about a better day. To the lawyer from Detroit, the court reporter from San Francisco, the secretary from Manhattan, the enemy was as visible as he was now unexpectedly vulnerable.

I recognized many of the people in the office. There was Peggy Lilienthal, the daughter-in-law of the first chairman of the Tennessee Valley Authority, who had left her novelist husband and four children in Martha's Vineyard to spend a month in Jackson. A year earlier, we had defended Peggy when she had been arrested in Williamston, North Carolina, for demonstrating against segregation in that city.

Ed Stern and Cynthia Washington, a SNCC worker on loan to FDP, were studying a deposition schedule that filled an entire wall. Ephraim Cross, a retired professor of romance languages from New York, had just returned from interviewing witnesses in Hinds County. Nancy Montgomery, one of San Francisco's best court reporters, was busy checking her stenotype machine.

Shortly after I arrived, a group of eight lawyers from Los Angeles burst into the office. In a matter of minutes, they were being briefed by Stavis in the back room. Before they left for their billets in the homes of FDP supporters, they each had an assignment for the next day. Some would be sent into the field to check on witnesses. Others, who were scheduled to conduct depositions, would study the reports of lawyers who had preceded them. The rest would make sure that everything was ready for tomorrow's hearings.

I felt intensely proud to be a part of what we had begun to call Deposition Caravan. A small segment of the legal profession had at last come to grips with the central issue of our times—the political emasculation of the Southern Negro. Selma was soon to dramatize the denial of the right to vote, but the Mississippi challenge had furnished a powerful antidote. In the long run, it would prove irresistible.

The Jackson hearings were impressive. For the three days they lasted, the Civil Service examination room was crowded with FDP supporters who were treated to the unusual sight of many of the state's highest officials on the witness stand. Moreover, four of the Mississippi Congressmen, who had apparently been advised by Coleman that they could do their cause more good in Mississippi than in Washington, attended most of the sessions.

The tone was established at the outset when thirty young Negroes filed silently into the room to watch the proceedings. As soon as he saw them, Coleman rose and declared that he had not known that the hearings were to be held for the entertainment of a local audience. "So I'm going to take it upon myself to lock the door," he said. "These people have no interest in this."

Stavis was on his feet in an instant. "Just a moment, Mr. Coleman," he barked. "This is a group of people vitally interested in the proceedings, and they are quietly standing and listening. As long as these proceedings remain orderly, we will insist that the door remains open. We will not tolerate the exclusion of any citizen of Mississippi."

Coleman capitulated at once. "Let's move on," he sighed as he sank back into his chair.

We learned a lot from the testimony of the state's witnesses. Attorney General Patterson, for example, admitted that in the five dozen voting suits filed against county voting registrars by the federal government, he had sprung to the defense of the attacked officials without investigating their guilt or innocence. Director Johnson of the Sovereignty Commission conceded that he had dispensed hundreds of thousands of dollars from the state treasury to help the White Citizens Council maintain racial segregation. One of his investigators revealed that it was part of his job to spy on Negroes trying to register.

We must have drawn blood because, shortly after the Jackson hearings, no less a figure than Senator Eastland accused FDP of fomenting a Communist-inspired Negro revolution in his state. In particular, he attacked the many lawyers who had participated in the taking of the depositions. If they were not outright Communists, he asserted in a Senate speech, they certainly had represented a great many suspicious people in the past.

The real reason for maligning the lawyers was clear to everyone. The moment we read his words in the *Congressional Record* we knew that he was running as scared as his fellow Mississippians in the House of Representatives. If they were unseated, he who owed his own position to the same unconstitutional election procedures was surely next.

Before our forty days ended, more than four hundred Negroes throughout the state had testified that it was virtually impossible for members of their race to register. Many were frightened away from the courthouse by the threat of economic reprisal or violence. Those who were brave enough to try to register found that they couldn't qualify because the tests were administered unfairly. Still others were kept standing in line so long that they were forced to return home before being able to fill out the registration forms.

Joe Stone, who testified in Starkville, perhaps best articulated the plight of the Mississippi Negro:

I don't think that the Negro will ever register and vote freely until they do something about the power structure—the white power structure here. They have a Negro in a position where he can't afford to take a chance on going down and registering to vote, because they know that the white man can turn him off his job or he can prevent him from getting another job or they can beat him up or they can bomb his home and they don't do anything about it. They have two different sets of laws down here. One of the Negro, and one of the white. They don't convict whites for doing anything to Negroes. Therefore, they are free. They want to vote, they tell you they are willing to go, but they say they can't take the chance. They say you don't have to live here. "I have to live here, all my life" or "I have been living here all my life." These people just don't want to take the chance.

They know what the white people would do to Negroes in Mississippi.

While our stenographers were busy typing the transcripts, the Congressmen's forty days passed without a single deposition being taken. Coleman explained this by stating that since he didn't believe that the contestants had the right to institute the challenges, he had advised his clients to remain silent. In effect, he was not contesting the validity of our claims—merely our right to assert them.

Mississippi's real answer to the challenge was far more subtle than anguished denials. Governor Johnson set the stage when, just before the Jackson hearings, he urged his more volatile constituents to avoid violence "for the next six months at least." Mississippi was determined to save its Congressmen by building a new image. We might have made mistakes in the past, Johnson told a national television audience in March, but we're asking you "to get off our backs and on our side."

The only trouble with this logic was that nothing had really changed in Mississippi. To prove this we took rebuttal depositions late in March. Two weeks later, a federal judge in the northern part of the state found that the Sunflower County registrar had been depriving Negroes of the right to vote for years. His order suspending some of the registration provisions of the Mississippi Constitution so that Negroes could "catch up" was the best answer to the state's "new look."

Shortly after this decision, Rita Schwerner drove through Mississippi with transcripts of the depositions. It was her job to get them signed by the notaries who had presided at the hearings. Because the attorneys for the five Congressmen had instructed the white notaries to read each deposition word for word, it was to take more than a month before these documents finally reached Washington.

On June 2, a meeting was held at the office of House Clerk Ralph R. Roberts to determine the positions of the respective parties as to which transcripts were to be printed. Although we insisted that Congress should have the benefit of the entire record, Governor Coleman and B. B. McClendon, counsel for the five Congressmen, strenuously objected to the printing of any depositions. The sole ground upon which they relied was their insistence that our clients didn't have the legal right to institute the challenges.

At the conclusion of this day-long conference, Roberts stated that he would decide the issue in forty-eight hours. On June 4, he advised us that he would print all but a handful of the depositions and suggested that we send someone to his office to help prepare them for the presses. Three days later, Rita and Bill Higgs conferred there with representatives of the Government Printing Office.

When some ten days passed without any further action by Roberts, Stavis called him. To his utter amazement, he learned that the Clerk had now decided not to print a word of the depositions. The reason—he had received a letter from McClendon on June 8 informing him that we had not complied with certain technical requirements of Title 2, such as having the depositions signed by the various witnesses.

During the depositions in Mississippi, both Coleman and McClendon had said that they would not insist on strict compliance with the 1851 statute. On February 10, Coleman stated that "we have agreed to waive signatures of deponents. . . ." A few days later, McClendon stipulated that "the signature of the witnesses will not be required, only the oath and signature of the court reporter and the presiding officer."

Now the two attorneys, obviously nonplussed by the

Clerk's decision to print the entire record, repudiated their own agreements. "Of course," McClendon wrote to Roberts, "Governor Coleman and I realize that any stipulations and agreements which we made with attorneys for the opposite parties would not be binding upon you in your official capacity as clerk of the House of Representatives on the performance of your duties set forth by law, unless you, too, joined in any such stipulatons and agreements."*

Roberts, who was keenly aware that the challenges did not have White House approval, seized upon the McClendon letter as gospel. Without notifying us, he rescinded his instructions to the Government Printing Office. It looked as if the challenges which had weathered so many storms were going to perish in what Drew Pearson has called "the most amazing series of backstage wire-pulling and delays in any recent Congress."

But Roberts did not anticipate the furor caused by his refusal to carry out his promise to us. During the next two weeks, he was inundated by irate telephone calls, letters and personal visits from people around the country concerned with fair play. A group of outraged Congressmen even suggested that his transigence might well cost him his job.

In early July, he reversed his stand once more and ordered the depositions printed. At the end of the month, he forwarded three 1000-page volumes to Speaker McCormack for transmission to the Subcommittee on Elections. Almost eight months after they had been instituted, the challenges were officially before the representatives of the people of the United States who, as Roosevelt said on January 4, then "must speak upon what to an American is the most terrible of political facts—that some Americans are not freemen."

---

* A short time later, Coleman, despite vigorous opposition by civil rights groups, was confirmed as a member of the United States Court of Appeals for the Fifth Circuit.

While we were waiting for the Clerk to make up his mind, we prepared and filed a 220-page brief which conclusively proved that Negroes had been systematically disenfranchised in Mississippi for seventy-five years. A joint effort by Kinoy, Stavis and myself, it could not have been written as fast as it was without the devoted efforts of William Crain, Sherwin Kaplan, James Kittsley, Nancy Stearns and Harriet Van Tassel, five law students who had been assigned to us for the summer by the Law Students Civil Rights Research Council.

As we worked on the brief, we realized that we had a lawyer's dream case. Almost everyone in the United States conceded that Negroes could not vote in Mississippi. President Johnson's message to Congress of March 15, 1965, in which he asked for a new voting bill, pointed out that "the Fifteenth Amendment of our Constitution is today being systematically and willfully circumvented in certain State and local jurisdictions of our Nation." Two months later, the United States Commission on Civil Rights, an independent, bipartisan agency, reported to Johnson that "Negro citizens of Mississippi have been denied and are being denied the right to vote in violation of our Constitution."

The same charge had been contained in scores of lawsuits brought by the Department of Justice to end discrimination against prospective Negro voters. In one of these suits entitled, appropriately enough, *United States* v. *Mississippi*, the Supreme Court summarized the issue as follows:

> The complaint charged that the State of Mississippi and its officials for the past three quarters of a century have been writing and adopting constitutional provisions, statutes, rules and regulations, and have been engaging in discriminatory practices, all designed to keep the number of white voters at the highest possible figure and the number of colored voters at the lowest. It is alleged

that the common purpose running through the State's legal and administrative history during that time has been to adopt whatever expedient seemed necessary to establish white supremacy in a completely segregated society.

If all of these authorities were not enough, Mississippi itself had conceded that its two most restrictive registration provisions were unlawful. "It is my considered judgment," Governor Johnson said on June 7, 1965, "that we should remove from our statutes these qualification requirements which have heretofore been determined by the United States Supreme Court to be unconstitutional." Convinced that this was the only way to keep federal voting examiners out of the state, the legislature promptly eliminated the offending requirements.*

But the most eloquent argument we could muster were the words of John R. Lynch, the last Negro Congressman from Mississippi, who, in 1882, successfully challenged his white opponent. In a stirring speech on the floor of the House, Mr. Lynch put to his colleagues the fundamental nature of the impact of Negro disfranchisement upon the structure of American society.

The impartial historian will record the fact that the colored people of the South have contended for their rights with a bravery and a gallantry that is worthy of the highest commendation. Being, unfortunately, in dependent circumstances, with the preponderance of the wealth and intelligence against them in some localities, yet they have bravely refused to surrender their honest convictions, even upon the altar of their personal necessities.

* On August 17, 1965, Mississippians approved a referendum reflecting the legislature's action. In urging his constituents to support the referendum, Governor Johnson assured them that its lowered qualification requirements would make it possible for "400,000 white voters [to] be added to the rolls in a state-wide white registration campaign."

They have said to those upon whom they depended: You may deprive me for the time being of the opportunity of making an honest living; you may take the bread out of the mouths of my hungry and dependent family; you may close the school house door in the face of my children; yea, more, you may take that which no man can give, my life, but my manhood, my principles you cannot have. Even when the flag of our country was trailing in the dust of treason and rebellion; when the constitution was ignored, and the lawfully chosen and legally constituted authorities of the Government were disregarded and disobeyed; although the bondman's yoke of oppression was then upon their necks, yet they were then true and loyal to their government, and faithful to the flag of their country.

They were faithful and true to you then; they are no less so to-day. And yet they ask no special favors as a class; they ask no special protection as a race. They feel that they purchased their inheritance when upon the battlefields of their country they watered the tree of liberty with the precious blood that flowed from their loyal veins. They ask no favors; they demand what they deserve and must have, an equal chance in the race of life. They feel that they are part and parcel of you, bone of your bone, flesh of your flesh. Your institutions are their institutions, and your Government is their Government. You cannot consent to the elimination of the colored man from the body-politic, especially through questionable and fraudulent methods, without consenting to your own downfall and to your own destruction.

The condition of the colored people of this country to-day is a living contradiction of the prophecies of those who have predicted that the two races could not live upon the same continent together upon terms of political equality. In spite of these predictions we are here to-day, clothed with the same rights, the same privileges, and the same immunities, with complete political assimilation; loyal to the same Government, true to the same flag; yielding obedience to the same laws revering the same institutions actuated by the same patriotic impulses, imbued with the same noble ambition; entertaining the same hopes, seeking the gratification and satisfaction of the same aspirations; identified with the same interests, speaking the same language; professing the same religion, worshiping the same God. The colored man asks you in this particular instance to give effect to his ballot, not for his sake alone, but for yours as well. He asks you to recognize the fact that he has the right to assist you in defending, protecting, and upholding our Government and perpetuating our institutions. You must, then, as I am sure you will, condemn the crimes against our institutions, against law, against justice, and against public morals that were committed in this case.

The Mississippi Congressmen never answered our brief. Instead, on August 24 they filed a motion to dismiss the challenges on the technical—and legally insupportable—grounds that since our clients had not been on the ballot in November, they did not have the right to institute them. Speaker McCormack promptly referred the motion to the Election Subcommittee.

We expected short shrift from this nine-man committee which is dominated by Southerners. But we were in for a surprise. Although Chairman Robert T. Ashmore (S.C.) tried to steam-roller his colleagues into endorsing the motion without a hearing, three Republicans and two Democrats insisted that we at least be given an opportunity to present our case.

Reluctantly, Ashmore scheduled a closed hearing for Monday, September 13. The day before, five hundred delegates to the Freedom Democratic Party's annual state convention, which, because of the subcommittee's action, had been shifted to Washington, began to stream into the Capitol.

At 8:30 A.M. on the thirteenth, Kinoy, Stavis, Higgs, Smith, and I, accompanied by the contestants, entered the Capitol. As we walked through the labyrinthine building we were surprised to see policemen and barricades everywhere. At the entrance to the third-floor hearing room we were stopped by a uniformed sergeant and asked to identify ourselves. Only after he had checked off our names on a typewritten list were we permitted to enter the room.

I don't believe that there has ever been a more heavily guarded Congressional hearing. We learned later that Ashmore had ordered these elaborate security precautions because he feared that FDP delegates might wish to witness the proceedings.

Although the rules of both the House of Representatives and the subcommittee itself did not authorize closed hearings, the South Carolinian had turned down our request to throw open the doors to the public and the press. Because of his decision, the Negro people of Mississippi, who had risked so much to bring the challenges, were not permitted to witness their climax.

The hearing took the better part of two days. In addition to attacking the FDP lawyers, the five Mississippi Congressmen repeated their dreary argument that if the contestants had the right to unseat them, then nobody's seat was safe. "If these people can force us out of Washington," one of them warned the subcommittee's members, "every Congressman from the Potomac to El Paso can expect the same."

When Mrs. Gray, Mrs. Devine, Mrs. Hamer, Reverend Allan Johnson, and Mrs. Augusta Wheadon, each representing one of the five Congressional districts, addressed the subcommittee, we could only regret that all America was not there to hear them. In deeply emotional and moving terms they reminded their listeners that to dismiss the challenges would be to endorse the violence, the intimidation, and the illegality which had made it impossible for the Negroes of Mississippi to vote since the end of reconstruction.

"We look to you," Mrs. Wheadon said, "to save our souls as well as your own."

But the die had been cast by other hands. Late Tuesday a resolution urging the dismissal of the challenges was hastily reported to the floor by the Committee on House Administration.* It was placed on the House calendar for Friday, September 17.

With the help of Dr. King, Jim Farmer, John Lewis, and Dr. Robert W. Spike of the National Council of Churches, FDP frantically appealed to Congressmen to vote against the resolution. John V. Lindsay, who was busy campaigning for the mayoralty of New York, sent telegrams to one hundred of his Republican colleagues in the House urging them to oppose dismissal. Miraculously enough, money was raised by challenge supporters to place anti-resolution ads in both the New York *Times* and the Washington *Post.*

A telegram from Dr. King to William Fitts Ryan best expressed the opposition to dismissal. "In these days of strife and bitterness," King wired, "one must support the just moral claims of the Mississippi Freedom Democratic Party. They have not rioted. They have destroyed neither person nor property in their pursuit of justice. They have, instead, sought to diligently apply the statutes of our Constitution. To deny them a full and adequate hearing by dismissing their challenge without full debate of the merits of the case is to deny the very moral fiber of our democratic way of life."

On Thursday, the Speaker, much to our surprise, sent telegrams to Mrs. Hamer, Mrs. Devine, and Mrs. Gray, inviting them to be on the floor when the vote was taken the next morning. Under House rules contestants have the right to be present when their challenges are being debated, but we had not expected to have this opportunity. For the first time since 1882, Mississippi Negroes would be sitting on the floor of the House of Representatives.

---

* The parent body of the Election Subcommittee. The minority report accompanying the resolution castigated the majority position as "so violative of precepts of morality and . . . such an assault upon the dignity and standing of the House of Representatives that it imperils the stature of this House in the minds of the American people."

The House met at noon on Friday. As it was called to order, hundreds of FDP delegates and their supporters stood in front of the Capitol in a silent vigil that had begun the day before. The galleries, normally empty on the last day of the legislative week, were filled to capacity. Throughout the chamber there was an unmistakable air of expectancy that a significant page in American history was about to be written.

After Representatives Ryan, Edwards and Burton had escorted Mrs. Hamer, Mrs. Devine, and Mrs. Gray onto the floor, debate began on the dismissal resolution. For almost three hours Congressmen who favored or opposed the resolution had their say. Party loyalties forgotten, Republicans and Democrats lined up on both sides of the issue.

In all, some forty Representatives joined the debate. Many of the speeches in support of the challenges were extremely moving and deserved a far better fate than their destined burial in the pages of the *Congressional Record*. In particular, those of Hawkins, Roosevelt, Edwards, Gubser and Burton of California, Ryan and Lindsay of New York, Conyers of Michigan, Curtis of Missouri, Helstoski of New Jersey, and Dawson of Illinois merited this standard.

Finally Minority Leader Gerald Ford called for a vote on the resolution. As the Clerk intoned each name, it looked for one shining moment as if the motion to dismiss the challenges might be defeated, but we soon realized that we simply did not have enough support to win. The final vote was 240 yeas to 155 nays.

The long fight was over.

In Mississippi, another fall has arrived. The magnolia trees that dot the landscape have long since lost their white fragrant blossoms, while the phenomenal summer growth of the kudzu vines imported to prevent highway washouts has begun to abate. In the Delta cotton fields, small bands of Negroes are scavenging for the few remaining bolls that were missed by the mechanical pickers that have made their jobs obsolete.

Along its western border, the river that gives the state its name is slowing its pace toward the Gulf of Mexico; and the Vicksburg battlefields, the stately Natchez homes and the vacation spots on the Gulf Coast are bidding farewell to their usual influx of summer tourists. The University of Mississippi is beginning its 118th year of operations with high hopes that its football team will again rank as one of the nation's best.

The patterns of Mississippi life are repeating themselves as they have for generations past. But this year there is a difference that is as real as a pecan tree and as fundamental as life itself. In every corner of the state, the black people who have built its roads, picked its cotton, tended its babies, washed its laundry, cooked its meals and done its odd jobs for more than three centuries are now demanding full admittance to a society of free men.

Inspired by a new voting bill, they are patiently standing in long lines before courthouses across the state. Fully aware that only the presence of federal examiners in every county will insure the registration of all Negro applicants, they are willing to show their own good faith in the democratic process by coming downtown once more. They know that violence against them and their supporters is again on the increase throughout the state, but they who have surmounted so much are convinced that "we shall overcome."

Even if they failed to unseat their illegally elected Congressmen, they have proved that an oppressed people can, by dint of the justice of their cause, make their voices felt in the halls of government. Without burning a building, firing a shot or looting a store, the Negroes of Mississippi have witnessed to their belief that their just grievances can be remedied through the orderly processes of the law. No country can ask more of its citizens.

For those who wish to see, the walls that surround the closed society are beginning to crack. The fissures may be small but they can be seen by those whose eyes are open. In the end the force that brings them down will be that exerted by a black finger on a voting machine lever or a black hand on a paper ballot. And when they topple at last, the victory shall belong to besieged and besieger alike—for, as Gandhi once said, by suppressing others, we suppress ourselves.

CHAPTER 34

The Road Ahead

On March 17, 1965, St. Patrick's Day, I sat around a conference table in the Grand Jury Room of the County Courthouse in Montgomery, Alabama. The day before, mounted possemen, led by Sheriff MacSims Butler in a sombrero, had charged into a group of Negro and white college students who were demonstrating in front of the state capitol. As a result, eight students were hospitalized.

Following so closely on the heels of the frightful assault by state troopers at the foot of the Edmond Pettus Bridge in Selma, the incident caused great indignation throughout the country. Because of this adverse reaction, the Montgomery County authorities decided to meet at once with Negro representatives. Their objective was to produce a joint statement that would allay national anger and prevent Montgomery from becoming another Selma.

Seated at the table were Martin Luther King, Ralph Abernathy, and Jim Forman. Across from them were Sheriff Butler and Circuit Solicitor Dave Crosland. Fred Gray, a Montgomery attorney represented SCLC while I was there

on SNCC's behalf. The others in the room included two of
the injured students, delegates from local Negro organizations, and a federal conciliator.

The negotiations, which had started in midafternoon, concluded at 11 P.M. The resulting statement included the first
public apology ever made by a Southern sheriff to members of
the civil rights movement. "In our meeting," the one-page
document began, "the Sheriff of Montgomery County, Mr.
M. S. Butler, expressed regret that the force used to disperse
the demonstrators yesterday resulted in the injury of several
persons."

As the discussions wore on, my mind went back to the
summer of 1961 when, not only would such a concession have
been unthinkable, but no Southern official would even have
met with militant Negroes. The movement had come a long
way since a few hundred intrepid souls had dared to ride
integrated buses through the segregated Southland. I was
glad that I had had a small role in that progression.

But much more had changed than the acceleration rate. As
I watched King and Forman bargaining with the officialdom
of Montgomery County, I realized that they represented two
sharply divergent views. In essence, King saw his role as the
architect of dramatic confrontations with local white power
structures, the purpose of which was to rouse the national
conscience. Forman, on the other hand, sought the emergence of indigenous Negro leadership and the development
of political organization in local communities.

The difference between the two approaches is much more
than a matter of mere tactics or strategy. It marks a fundamental dichotomy in objective that goes to the heart of the
Southern dilemma. King's formula has been remarkably successful in focusing national attention on every aspect of
Negro oppression. But too often it has left in its wake

enervated and bitter communities with nothing but a moment's glory to show for their monumental efforts.

In the beginning, I looked upon each new campaign as an end in itself. Whether it was Albany or Danville or Birmingham or St. Augustine, it was all the same. Demonstration would follow demonstration in ever increasing intensity until hundreds of men, women, and children filled the jails. Then it would be the responsibility of the movement to see to it that everybody was bailed out so that the process could be repeated again and again.

As the operation gained momentum, the whole world, it seemed, would flock to the scene. Every mass meeting was eagerly filmed by television cameramen from all the major networks. Newspaper reporters, out-of-town clergymen, Northern students, and civil rights devotees poured into town on every plane, train, and bus. With so many willing bodies swelling the ranks of the local Negroes, it was possible to mount larger and larger demonstrations.

Then, quite suddenly, it was all over. The cameramen packed up their equipment, and the reporters headed for their next assignment. The out-of-towners returned to their pulpits, their classrooms, or their jobs, and the vibrant mass meetings rapidly dwindled to sporadic gatherings in half-filled churches. The thunder and the lightning had passed and things were very much as they had always been.

As the SCLC staff began organizing another town whose name would shortly be headline news across the world, the old community was busy pulling itself together. But in most cases, absent the SCLC leadership quotient and the King *charisma,* the beachhead which had been won at so much cost could not be consolidated and often vanished entirely. A paper triumph soon yielded to the reality of inertia.

I do not mean in the least to suggest that King's victories have been empty ones or that he and his aides are more interested in headlines than accomplishment. Obviously, the reverse is quite true. But I do want to emphasize that if the civil rights movement is to achieve lasting results, it must develop and maintain solid grass roots leadership. More has to be left behind than the memories of protest marches and stirring oratory.

In other words, the SNCC, and to some extent the CORE, concept of painstaking community development with emphasis on the growth of local leadership is the wave of the future. Long after every outward vestige of segregation has disappeared, the Southern Negro, like his brothers in the North, will still be seeking equal education, job opportunity, and housing. The achievement of these long-range objectives demands extensive and continuous planning by those most intimately affected by them.

In the last analysis, the old order will change in direct ratio to the intensity and the perseverance of the demands of its successor. A militant Negro community, adequately versed in the intricacies of independent political organization, fully aware of its available resources and their most fruitful utilization, and capable of producing able and conscientious leaders will eventually insure equality in the deepest sense of the word.

Concededly, this is an oversimplification. Nothing short of a massive and sustained national effort can ever hope to eradicate the racism which, unhappily, is our American heritage. The spectre of Selma—as well as that of such northern ghettos as the Watts district of Los Angeles and New York's Harlem—will yield only to such an approach. But as has been proved so often during the last decade, the Negro must provide the impetus and the direction. If he waits for the white community to point the way, he will wait forever.

I cannot close this book without acknowledging my heartfelt personal debt to the civil rights movement. The adventure that began for me in a Los Angeles motel four short years ago has turned into the lesson of my life. In the process, I have discovered that there is considerably more to the practice of law than learning precedents or interpreting statutes. The Freedom Riders had taught me that I was a human being first and a lawyer second. The three civil rights workers who laid down their lives in Neshoba County have given that distinction consummate importance.

By all odds, the practice of law in the deep South should have been infinitely depressing. Lawyers look to the courts with a respect born of centuries of the common law, and it came as a bitter surprise to me that the judicial system below the Mason-Dixon line is, in the main, wholly unable to be impartial in cases involving Negroes or their white supporters. Prisoners of a deep-rooted caste structure, Southern judges and juries are not free, where race is an issue, to apply the law without fear or favor. The result is an almost total perversion of the administration of justice.

Judge Sidney Mize, who died on April 26, 1965, hours before the Supreme Court reversed the 1961 convictions of the Freedom Riders, was a classic example of such perversion. During a recess in the *Dewey Greene* case, he invited me into his chambers. There, in a rare moment of complete candor, he revealed his total unfitness to sit in judgment in racial cases. "As long as I'm on the bench," he said, "I'll do everything in my power to keep white and black apart."

Yet despite the initial hopelessness of almost every case in which I was involved, I found that, far from becoming morose, I was both moved and exhilarated. The judge who valued his membership in the White Citizens Council more than he did his oath of office, the frankly prejudiced jurors, the openly hostile court clerks and attendants, none of these really counted because they were only temporary barriers on a broad highway that led inevitably to the triumph of equality.

To survive as a person, one had only to look beyond them to the road ahead.

It took me some time to attain this spiritual resilience. I can still remember the shock I felt in August of 1961 when Henry Thomas was convicted of breaching the peace when he rode an integrated bus into Jackson. Almost four years later, I have come to realize that victories are not always triumphs and that a state of mind can mean infinitely more than a jury verdict. This inner awareness is perhaps the measure of the metamorphosis that has taken place in me, both as a lawyer and a man.

But my experience in the South has done more than implant in me some philosophical shock absorbers. It has taught me that to be a surrogate of a profound social movement, one has to be a member of it also. In other words, the lawyer, no more and no less than the voter-registration canvasser or the Freedom School teacher, possesses skills that must be put to use in pursuit of the mutual goal.

Once the lawyer has acclimated himself to the demands and dimensions of his movement responsibilities, he sees a horizon wholly different from that which delineates his normal professional duties in New York, Chicago or San Francisco. He is activated, not by the promise of money or prestige, but by the sharing of a common cause with those he represents.

Quite obviously his motivation is far more complex than that. For one thing the practice of civil rights law in the deep South, with all its attendant hardships and problems, is undeniably exhilarating. The combination of a meaningful field of law, stimulating clients and momentous cases has its own great personal rewards. But he first must grasp— and accept—the true nature of his involvement.

This recognition does not come overnight. I can still recall my earnest recommendation to Jack Young during the Freedom Riders trials that we not address our clients at a mass meeting. "A lawyer must remain aloof," I had told him. "If we become emotionally involved in our clients' problems, we will not be able to be dispassionate courtroom advocates."

Now I know that no member of a great social movement, be he lawyer or layman, can remain untouched by the forces that impel it. When Clarence Darrow left his lucrative position as general counsel of the Chicago & Northwestern Railroad to defend Eugene V. Debs and his penniless American Railway Union, his resignation was testimony that attorneys owe a deeper obligation to humanity than they do to their individual careers.

Fortunately, many lawyers have now learned this lesson. The South in the 1960's has been the catalyst of a growing professional awareness that the law does not exist in a vacuum but is grounded in life. The hundreds and thousands of people, young and old, black and white, who have offered their bodies as witnesses to the attainability of a just society have finally shamed the American bar into standing beside them.

For generations, lawyers have looked aside while Southern Negroes have been systematically dehumanized. All in the name of the law, black men have been driven away from the polls, segregated out of the mainstream of their communities, and forced back into a slavery every bit as intense as that which had theoretically been lifted from them a hundred years earlier. Yet the legal profession, for all its high-sounding principles, uttered not one word of collective protest.

That lawyers should have ignored the plight of the Negro is the bitterest of paradoxes, for the bar has a special obligation to create and preserve the equality on which our entire system of jurisprudence is expressly founded. It is no accident that the motto "Equal Justice Under Law," in one form or another, is engraved on courthouse friezes across the land.

President Kennedy was deeply conscious that American

lawyers, in and out of the South, had failed to live up to the solemn responsibilities of their profession. In June of 1963, he summoned several hundred attorneys to the White House to discuss the bar's role in the Southern struggle. The result was a committee whose avowed purpose was "to try to ease racial tensions and provide national and local leadership." A few weeks later, the American Bar Association formed a similar committee.

But these well-intentioned committees are hardly the answer to the failure of Southern lawyers to live up to the Canons of Professional Ethics to which all members of the bar subscribe. "No fear of judicial disfavor or public unpopularity," Canon 15 declares, "should restrain him [the lawyer] from the full discharge of his duty." Such fears, and they are real ones, tend to strip Canon 15 of all substance below the Mason-Dixon line.

In 1953, the American Bar Association, hoping to stiffen the spines of lawyers who are asked to defend unpopular clients, passed the following resolution: "The American Bar Association reaffirms the principles that the rights of defendants to the benefit of assistance of counsel and the duty of the bar to provide such aid even to the most unpopular defendants involves public acceptance of the correlative right of the lawyer to represent and defend, in accordance with the standards of the legal profession, any client without being penalized by having imputed to him his client's reputation, views, or character."

In recommending the adoption of this resolution, the Association's Special Committee on Individual Rights as Affected by National Security stated:

Counsel of outstanding reputations, well known for their anti-Communist views, in several recent cases involving Communists or persons accused of being Communists, which they took out of a sense of public duty, have been subjected to severe personal vilification and abuse. Many persons showed by their changed attitude toward these lawyers that they assumed that such representation meant that the lawyer is to be regarded as sharing the views of the client. Leading counsel, acting by court assignment, at great personal sacrifice, representing a Nazi during the war, was spat at in the courtroom. A leading lawyer has been attacked editorially for undertaking to represent an alleged racketeer in a trial involving grave constitutional questions. Important legal business has been taken elsewhere rather than going to reputable counsel who were preferred but who had represented defendants accused of being Communists. These episodes could no doubt be multiplied. Their existence is a serious cloud on the proper discharge of the lawyer's duty; the bar must throw its weight against such things. We are hopeful that the resolutions we propose may be a beginning in a reversal of these bad trends.

The only Southern white lawyers who are able to escape community retaliation when they appear in cases involving racial issues are those who do not raise the very constitutional defenses that may make ultimate victory for their clients possible. According to Canon 15, every client "is entitled to the benefit of any and every remedy and defense that is authorized by the law of the land."

The Fifth Circuit recently found it necessary to hold that defendants in racial cases do not waive their constitutional defenses merely because their white attorneys neglected or refused to raise them at trial. In its opinion, the court pointed out that, as judges who supervised the administration of justice in the states of the deep South, they were required to take notice of the fact that intense community pressures deterred local white lawyers from raising constitutional defenses in state courts.

The Montgomery, Alabama, *Advertiser-Journal*, commenting on the decision, observed candidly that "white lawyers in the South, because of social and economic pressures," simply do not raise "controversial" constitutional questions in cases with "racial overtones."

Despite President Kennedy's urgent appeal, very few state and city bar associations have bestirred themselves on this issue, and those that do express some concern have, with few exceptions, taken no action to improve matters. It is lamentable that, of all people, lawyers should remain silent on an issue that is so corrosive of the very principle upon which their profession is grounded.

The unfortunate vacuum created by the failure of local counsel to respond to the appeal of Canon 15, has been only partially filled by the journeymen lawyers whose motto well might be "Have writ, will travel." Ever since Samuel I. Leibowitz traveled South to defend the Scottsboro boys some thirty years go, out-of-state counsel have made regular appearances in Dixie courtrooms.

Whether they are independent practitioners or members of such organizations as the National Lawyers Guild, the NAACP Legal Defense Fund, or the newly created Lawyers Constitutional Defense Committee and the Lawyers Committee for Civil Rights Under Law, they are keeping alive the illustrious traditions that motivated a sick and ailing Andrew Hamilton in 1734 to journey from Philadelphia to New York to take up the cudgels for John Peter Zenger when the printer's local attorneys had been disbarred by an autocratic and corrupt provincial governor.

The availability of such lawyers, no matter how devoted their efforts, cannot disguise the fact that even a reasonable approximation of equal justice under law is impossible under these conditions. It is the duty of the bar, both nationally and on the local level, to reaffirm its own tradition that no person shall ever be denied adequate counsel. But that solution—

simple as it is—cannot be attained under present circumstances.

Not only have social and economic pressures prevented local lawyers from representing racial defendants, but a concerted attempt has been made to cut off the supply of non-resident counsel or nullify their efforts. In August of 1961, Judge Russel B. Moore, III, refused to permit more than four out-of-state attorneys to represent hundreds of Freedom Riders in Jackson. He was taking this tack, he explained, because a local bar association had complained to him that there was something insidious in permitting "foreigners" to invade his court.

Two years later in Danville, Judge Aiken refused to let out-of-state counsel practice before him unless they produced their certificates of admission to the bar. When Ann Cooper, a Boston lawyer, complied with this unusual request, the judge ordered her to prove to his satisfaction that her home state of Massachusetts permitted Virginia lawyers to practice there. It was three days before Miss Cooper could represent Negro demonstrators in Aiken's court.

In Mississippi, federal judges in the southern part of the state have been vigorously enforcing a local court rule that makes it mandatory for a local lawyer to sign all filed papers— a requirement that apparently conflicts with the Federal Rules of Civil Procedure. Since only three Negro attorneys are available in the entire state, it often happens that they are representing clients many miles from the state capital. This makes it impossible for out-of-of-state attorneys who are allied with them in civil rights cases to file immediate motions in Jackson and, in effect, denies them the right to counsel at crucial stages in their cases.

In the Spring of 1964, the Fifth Circuit was required to resort to the extraordinary writ of mandamus to remind Mississippi's Judge Cox that his court could not "close its doors" to litigants represented by lawyers from other states when local counsel was unavailable.

Until the American bar recognizes its own solemn responsibilities, the stopgap solution must continue to be found in the development of procedures to enable out-of-state counsel to offer their services in the defense of constitutional rights. In the nineteenth century, judges, because of their scarcity, were forced to travel from town to town in order to make justice readily available. In this era, the circuit riders are on the opposite side of the bar.

Like their clients, they, too, look toward the road ahead.

INDEX